A Guide to Military Criminal Law

A Guide
to
Military
Criminal
Law

Michael J. Davidson

Naval Institute Press • Annapolis, Maryland

Library of Congress Cataloging-in-Publication Data

Davidson, Michael J.
    A guide to military criminal law / Michael J. Davidson.
        p.   cm.
    Includes bibliographical references.
    ISBN 1-55750-155-6 (alk. paper)
     1. Military offenses—United States.   2. Military discipline—United States.
3. Courts-martial and courts of inquiry—United States.   I. Title.
KF7609.D29   1999
343.73′0143—dc21   98-46460

Printed in the United States of America on acid-free paper ∞
06 05 04 03 02 01 00 99 9 8 7 6 5 4 3 2
First printing

To Nancy

The sword of justice has no scabbard.

—Joseph de Maistre

Contents

Preface

The United States Supreme Court once remarked that "the military is, by necessity, a specialized society separate from civilian society . . . [and] has, again by necessity, developed laws and traditions of its own during its long history."[1] Unlike any other institution in this country, the military is charged with safeguarding the nation's vital interests and ensuring our national survival. In response to its unique mission, the military has developed its own culture, value system, and mores. Concepts of duty, honor, and country, often considered archaic elsewhere, enjoy continued vitality in the uniformed ranks.

To satisfy the quintessential demands of obedience and discipline, servicemembers must relinquish rights normally taken for granted and assume additional duties and burdens not found in the civilian community. Servicemembers' freedom of speech is greatly curtailed once they don a uniform. Argument and insolent language may undermine a leader's authority and ability to command, ultimately jeopardizing lives and the success of a unit's mission. Expressive conduct considered merely rude in the civilian sector may form the basis of criminal charge in the armed forces.

To meet the unique demands that the nation places on it, the military has developed its own criminal justice system. This system strives to ensure both discipline and justice. Critical charging decisions are made by the military defendant's (called the "accused") own commanders rather than disinterested third parties, and members of the local military community determine the accused's ultimate fate.

The military's system of justice has existed since the beginning of our nation and many of America's most famous and infamous citizens have had some involvement with it. Nearly a decade before his demise at the Battle of the Little Big Horn, George Armstrong Custer was convicted of disobeying orders and sentenced to forfeit all rank and pay for one year.[2] During World War II, baseball great Jackie Robinson was acquitted of disrespect charges at a Camp Hood, Texas, court-martial stemming from his refusal to sit in the back of a bus.[3] During the same time frame, future Watergate special prosecutor Leon Jaworski court-martialed German prisoners of war as an army judge advocate.[4] As a young lawyer, Supreme Court Justice Thurgood Marshall fought to overturn the court-martial convictions of Korean War–era black soldiers.[5]

Like the military itself, the military justice system has often been the subject of intense scrutiny and criticism. During the Vietnam War era, books critical of the military justice system, such as Robert Sherrill's *Military Justice Is to Justice as Military Music Is to Music* and Robert Rivkin's *G.I. Rights and Army Justice,*[6] reflected widespread concern about the fairness, and perhaps even the legality, of military law. In 1969, the Supreme Court lambasted the military justice system existing at the time, highlighting the military's problems with excessive command influence, opining that a court-martial was "not yet an independent instrument of justice," and referencing "sobering accounts of the impact of so-called military justice on civil rights of members of the Armed Forces."[7] The Vietnam War–era scrutiny was neither unusual nor entirely unwarranted.

After every major war, Congress—usually at the prodding of veterans groups—has examined the system, modified it, and attempted to improve it. Since Vietnam, the military justice system has adopted many of the procedural protections found in the civilian sector and emplaced additional protective measures to reduce the occurrence of the military justice system's traditional Achilles' heel—unlawful command influence. While far from perfect, the current military justice system now stands on an equal, if not superior, footing with any system of justice in the nation.

Famed criminal defense attorney F. Lee Bailey, who obtained an acquittal of Capt. Ernest Medina—Lt. William Calley's company commander—following the massacre at My Lai,[8] once remarked, "If I had an innocent client, I would want that person to be tried in a military court." Bailey continued: "Unlike many other systems, the military justice system is not a ballet full of due process, but rather is one in which the accused receives a full and fair trial of the facts."[9]

The rights of the accused are many and scrupulously observed. Long before the Supreme Court required that defendants be informed of their *Miranda* rights, the military mandated that servicemembers suspected of a crime be informed of their Article 31 rights. In the civilian sector the grand jury is considered a tool of the prosecutor, where the defendant may neither appear nor present evidence. In the military's analogous proceeding, the Article 32 hearing, the accused may appear, cross-examine the government's witnesses, and present witnesses and evidence. Unlike the civilian defendant, a servicemember accused of a crime is entitled to a military lawyer free of charge, at both trial and on appeal, regardless of income level.

Today, the civilian legal community struggles with how to better tailor the jury system to the interests of justice. Should there be a "professional" pool of jurors? Should they be allowed to take notes during the trial and then bring those notes into the deliberation room? How interactive should the jury be? Can they ask questions or should they depend solely upon the adversarial skills of the competing lawyers? Is the typical jury intelligent enough to understand complicated cases?

The military jury (called a "panel") is generally a well-educated body of professional, seasoned soldiers, sailors, marines, or airmen. They are chosen for service on a panel based upon such criteria as "age, education, training, experience, length of service, and judicial temperament." Rule for Courts-Martial (RCM) 502(a)(1). Serving in multiple cases for an extended period of time, panel members possess many of the trappings of a professional jury. Further, because they are chosen from the accused's military community and are members of the same profession, panel members are in a very real sense a jury of the accused's peers. Designed to be proactive, panel members—who enjoy an equal voice and vote, regardless of rank— typically take notes during the court-martial and may question witnesses by submitting questions to the military judge.

However, while fair, the military justice system is, by necessity, swift and efficient. Charged with maintaining discipline, it is designed to quickly bring cases to trial. Accordingly, the system does not permit indecisive juries. A two-thirds vote is required for conviction. If two-thirds of the panel votes guilty, the accused is convicted; anything less results in an acquittal. There are no "hung juries" in the military.

This book is not written for uniformed lawyers and is not intended to be a comprehensive legal treatise on military law. It is designed to serve as a guide for those men and women of all branches of the armed forces who would like to know something about our criminal justice system, and to familiarize the new recruit, cadet, midshipman, or officer with his or her legal rights and responsibilities under military law. This work is also offered as a ready reference source for the NCO or commander charged with dispensing justice at the unit level, and as such, ample citations to the Manual for Courts-Martial (MCM) will appear throughout. Finally, this book is written for the American public who charge the military with the well-being of their sons and daughters and have more than a passing interest in how they will be treated.

Acknowledgments

I would like to acknowledge the many years of quality training and experience received from the U.S. Army's Judge Advocate General's Corps and its school in Charlottesville, Virginia. Further, I would like to thank the following military lawyers who were kind enough to take time out of their busy schedules to review various sections of this book: Cdr. Robert E. Korroch, USCG; Lt. Col. (Ret.) Douglas P. DeMoss, USA; Cdr. Mark E. Newcomb, USN; Lt. Col. Jill M. Grant, USA; Maj. Dwight Sullivan, USMCR and a managing attorney with the American Civil Liberties Union; and Maj. Thomas F. Doyon, USAF.

Additionally, I would like to acknowledge the military service of MSGT (Ret.) Burton V. Davidson and GYSGT (Ret.) Franklin Davidson, two career marines who served their country during an unpopular war without thanks or regret; and former lieutenant Harry H. Daugherty, USN, for his service during the Korean War.

All opinions contained in this work are my own and do not reflect the position of the Departments of Defense and Army, or any other government agency.

Abbreviations

CFR	Code of Federal Regulations
C.M.A.	United States Court of Military Appeals (currently the United States Court of Appeals for the Armed Forces)
C.M.A.	Court-Martial Reports
JAG	Judge Advocate General's Corps
MCM	Manual for Courts-Martial
M.J.	Military Justice Reporter
MJM	U.S. Coast Guard Military Justice Manual
RCM	Rule for Courts-Martial
NJP	Nonjudicial Punishment
POW	Prisoner of War
UCMJ	Uniform Code of Military Justice
U.S.C.	United States Code

A Guide to Military Criminal Law

1

Jurisdiction

"Jurisdiction" refers to the authority or power of a court to decide an issue before it. To constitute a legal proceeding, the court must possess jurisdiction over both the subject matter and the person whose rights would be affected by the court's decision. To illustrate, a military court-martial has jurisdiction over all offenses punishable by the Uniform Code of Military Justice (UCMJ) (subject matter) and over all active duty members of the military (person). However, a military court-martial would have no authority to determine whether a dependent spouse violated the UCMJ because the spouse is not subject to the code. Similarly, a military court would not be authorized to determine whether an active duty service-member violated the criminal laws of Mexico because the court has no jurisdiction over Mexican laws.

The military justice system derives its authority from Article I, Section 8, of the United States Constitution, which provides that Congress shall have the power to "make Rules for the Government and Regulation of the land and naval Forces." Pursuant to its constitutional authority, Congress enacted the UCMJ, which is contained in Title 10 of the United States Code (U.S.C.). Articles 2 and 3 are the UCMJ's jurisdiction provisions.

Legal proceedings within the military justice system require more than jurisdiction over person and subject matter. A military court must be properly composed (have the correct people present) and properly convened (assembled), and the criminal charges must be properly referred (ordered to trial). If any of these requirements are unsatisfied, a military court has no legal authority to determine the innocence or guilt of a servicemember.

Jurisdiction over the Subject Matter

A military court is a court of limited authority; it is concerned exclusively with violations of the UCMJ. However, within those parameters, the military justice system enjoys broad criminal jurisdiction over military offenses.

Previously, before a military court could exercise its authority, the offense had to be "service-connected." In 1987, the U.S. Supreme Court jettisoned this standard in the case of *Solorio v. United States*.[1] In *Solorio*, the accused, who had sexually abused two young girls in his off-post home while stationed in Alaska,[2] had initially been successful in having the charges dismissed because of an insufficient connection between the misconduct and his status as a coastguardsman.

The Supreme Court upheld the authority of the Coast Guard to court-martial Solorio for his off-post misconduct, determining that jurisdiction over an offense is dependent solely upon the person's status as a member of the armed forces: the offense need not be service connected.[3] Accordingly, a military court has jurisdiction over *any* UCMJ offense, regardless of the status of the victim or the location of the crime.

Jurisdiction over the Person

Individuals Subject to the UCMJ

Article 2 lists twelve categories of persons who may be prosecuted for violations of the UCMJ. Subject to various limitations, the military possesses jurisdiction over all regular component servicemembers, including cadets and midshipmen, reservists, retirees, military inmates, prisoners of war, and certain civilians accompanying a military force. Noticeably absent from this list is the president of the United States. Although he serves as the commander-in-chief, the president is not subject to military law.

Cadets and Midshipmen

Cadets and midshipmen at the Military and Naval Academies, respectively, have always been considered part of the military.[4] They are a unique form of officer falling somewhere between a commissioned officer and an enlisted person.[5] Legal authorities have referred to them as "*inchoate* officers."[6]

As members of the military, cadets and midshipmen have been subject to military law.[7] In 1954, in response to the establishment of the U.S. Air Force Academy (USAFA), Congress provided that USAFA cadets would be subject to the same laws as West Point cadets.[8] Currently, Article 2(a)(2) provides for jurisdiction over all "cadets, aviation cadets, and midshipmen," which is defined to include cadets at the Military, Coast Guard, and Air Force Academies and midshipmen at the Naval Academy or "any other midshipman on active duty in the naval service." Art. 1(6) and (7). ROTC cadets are not subject to military jurisdiction.[9]

Cadets and midshipmen have been court-martialed for a variety of offenses. Court-martial convictions have occurred for such misconduct as taking indecent liberties with a minor;[10] wrongful appropriation and absent without leave (AWOL);[11] and "causing certain midshipmen of the fourth class to stand on their heads, to hang from a locker [and] to do a physical exercise known as the 'sixteenth.'"[12] In *United States v. Sassaman*,[13] a cadet first class (senior) at the Air Force Academy was dismissed from the service, forfeited pay, and was confined for eight months after being convicted of disobeying orders, writing bad checks, and stealing from a fellow cadet. Because the UCMJ treats cadets and midshipmen as officers, they must be dismissed rather than discharged.[14]

Reservists

Articles 2(a)(1) and (3) provide the basis for military jurisdiction over reservists. Reservists are subject to the UCMJ when ordered to active duty, ordered to active duty for training, or participating in inactive-duty training. Members of the Army National Guard and Air National Guard are subject to military jurisdiction only when in a federal, as opposed to state, status. Art. 2(a)(3).

For reservists called to active duty for training, jurisdiction exists only over those crimes committed at a time when the accused was subject to military law. For example, in *United States v. Chodara*,[15] an army reservist was convicted for cocaine use, discovered as a result of a urinalysis initiated within thirty-six hours of the accused's reporting for duty. Because the prosecution could not prove that the accused used the cocaine while on active duty, the Army Court of Military Appeals reversed the conviction.[16] However, if reservists do commit violations of the UCMJ while on active duty, jurisdiction is not lost by virtue of the fact that they have been released from their active duty or inactive-duty training status. Art. 3(d).

Retirees

Military retirees are subject to military criminal jurisdiction and may be recalled to active duty for trial by court-martial. Should it so desire, the military may even prosecute a retiree in his or her retired status, as long as the retiree is reimbursed for actual costs associated with the endeavor.[17]

The misconduct need not have occurred while the accused was on active duty; retirees may be court-martialed for criminal activity occurring while retired.[18] In *Hooper v. United States,*[19] the U.S. Court of Claims upheld the authority of the navy to court-martial a retiree, in his retired status, for misconduct committed seven years after his retirement. A court-martial convicted Hooper for various homosexual acts that took place in his private home.[20]

The statutory authority for military jurisdiction is found in Article 2(a)(4) of the UCMJ, which provides that "retired members of a regular component of the armed forces who are entitled to pay" are subject to the code. The rationale for military jurisdiction is premised on the retiree's status as a member of the armed forces and the potential for the retiree's involuntary return to active duty in time of war or national emergency.[21]

Each of the services has a different criteria for determining the appropriateness of court-martialing retirees. As a matter of policy, the army, which possesses the most restrictive requirements, will not court-martial a retiree "unless extraordinary circumstances are present."[22] The air force requires that the "conduct clearly links them with the military or is adverse to a significant military interest in the United States."[23] In the U.S. Navy and Marine Corps, recall authorization must be obtained from the secretary of the navy.[24] Similarly, in the Coast Guard no case involving a retiree may be referred to court-martial without the prior approval of the commandant.[25]

Not surprisingly, the military rarely exercises its authority to court-martial a retiree. Many in the military view a retiree's pension as a sacrosanct entitlement that may be placed in jeopardy under only the most compelling circumstances. A recent published case illustrates the circumstances under which the military is willing to exercise jurisdiction over a retiree. In *Sands v. Colby,*[26] a retired army sergeant major, working in Saudi Arabia as an army civilian employee, was tried by court-martial for murdering his wife in their government quarters. Because the Saudi government was not inclined to prosecute, if the military had not stepped in, the retiree literally would have gotten away with murder.

Court-martialing a retiree is particularly appropriate when extremely serious misconduct occurred while the servicemember was on active duty or when the misconduct is of such a nature as to call into question the retiree's fitness to serve as a member of the armed forces in the event of recall to active duty in times of war or national emergency. Concededly, the decision to place a retiree's hard-earned pension in jeopardy should not be made lightly, but a retirement certificate was never intended to serve as a get-out-of-jail-free card. As a federal district court judge in California posited, "Where a retired officer has manifested his unfitness for a return to full time military service, and has failed to maintain proper qualifications in conformity with military ethics and standards, it is not unreasonable to assume that the [military] may choose to terminate his status."[27]

Inmates

Article 2(a)(7) provides for jurisdiction over "persons in custody of the armed forces serving a sentence imposed by a court-martial." Service-members confined in an armed forces confinement facility do not lose their military status upon expiration of their enlistment. Military inmates lose their military status only after a discharge is executed and they are released from confinement.[28]

Prisoners of War

Article 82 of the Geneva Convention Relative to the Treatment of Prisoners of War subjects a POW to the same laws, regulations, and orders as those followed by servicemembers of the capturing nation.[29] During World War II, 48 special and 119 general courts-martial were convened against 326 Axis prisoners of war (277 German and 49 Italian) held in the United States.[30] Axis defendants were provided with both attorneys and interpreters; fellow POWs were allowed to serve as assistant defense counsel.[31] The results of these proceedings ranged from outright acquittal to imposition of the death penalty.[32]

In 1943 a German soldier suspected of cooperating with American military authorities was beaten to death in an Oklahoma POW camp. Prosecuted by Lt. Col. Leon Jaworski of the army, who would later achieve fame as a special prosecutor during Watergate, five German soldiers were tried, sentenced to death, and eventually hanged for the murder.[33]

The current domestic authority to exercise military jurisdiction over enemy POWs is contained in Article 2(a)(9). Accordingly, the United States may court-martial POWs under the UCMJ, subject to any restrictions imposed by the Geneva Convention.

Timing and Status

Coming In

Until a person is officially in the armed forces, the military has no authority to prosecute under the UCMJ. It is thus worthy of some discussion to determine when, and if, that magical moment exists.

An agreement to join the military is insufficient for military jurisdiction; there must be an actual event, such as an enlistment, that changes the person's status from citizen to servicemember.[34] Article 2(a)(1) provides that military jurisdiction attaches over "volunteers from the time of their muster or acceptance into the armed forces; [and] inductees from the time of their actual induction into the armed forces." For a voluntary enlistee, the magic moment occurs "upon the taking of the oath of enlistment." Art. 2(b).[35] For an inductee (draftee), military jurisdiction attaches upon being "actually inducted" into the armed forces, that is, completing the induction ceremony,[36] even if the inductee refuses to take the oath of enlistment.[37] If jurisdiction is disputed or the induction is defective, the courts will determine the existence of military status on a case-by-case basis.[38] Officers become subject to military jurisdiction upon accepting a commission by executing the oath of office and entry onto active duty pursuant to military orders.[39]

Defective enlistments may void the servicemember's status as a member of the armed forces, thus precluding court-martial jurisdiction. In *United States v. Catlow*,[40] an army private, charged with being AWOL for twenty-one months, challenged the authority of the military court to hear the case, arguing that his enlistment was invalid. The evidence established that Catlow had been arrested and presented with the option of five years in a juvenile detention facility or three years in the army; not surprisingly, Catlow chose the army.[41] In violation of army regulations, the recruiter signed Catlow out of jail and processed him for enlistment.[42] Upon entering the army, Catlow engaged in a continuous pattern of misbehavior.

The United States Court of Military Appeals (C.M.A.) determined that Catlow's "enlistment was void at its inception" and dismissed the charges for lack of jurisdiction.[43] The court reasoned that Catlow was coerced into enlisting, continuously protested against remaining in the army, and did nothing to suggest that he desired to remain on active duty.[44]

Not all defective enlistments will preclude military jurisdiction. Under the legal doctrine of "constructive enlistment," codified at Article 2(b) and (c), an individual who understands the significance of enlisting in the military, voluntarily enters the service, satisfies minimal mental competence and age requirements at some point after entering the military, receives military pay or allowances, and performs military duties is subject to court-martial jurisdiction despite improprieties in the enlistment process.

Getting Out

Generally, the military's legal authority ceases once a servicemember has been discharged or otherwise released from the military. However, for purposes of terminating military jurisdiction over a servicemember leaving active duty, it is truly "not over until its over." Article 2(a)(1) specifically provides for jurisdiction over servicemembers of the regular components of the armed forces who are "awaiting discharge after expiration of their terms of enlistment." Military jurisdiction continues over servicemembers held beyond their separation dates, even when the military's delay in issuing the discharge is deemed unreasonable.[45]

The U.S. Court of Appeals for the Armed Forces (CAAF) has determined that three requirements must be satisfied before a servicemember is legally discharged from the military. Those requirements are: "(1) 'delivery of a valid discharge certificate'; (2) 'a final accounting of pay'; and (3) undergoing 'the clearing process required under appropriate service regulations to separate' a servicemember 'from military service.'"[46]

The military courts strictly construe these requirements in favor of retaining jurisdiction. Indeed, in *United States v. Pou,*[47] an air force court held that an airman who had been officially declared dead was not discharged. In *United States v. Batchelder,*[48] the accused sailor's orders provided for discharge as of midnight. At 4:30 P.M., agents apprehended Batchelder as he was packing his personal belongings prior to departing the base. At that time, he had received his certificate of discharge, completed his unit's check-out process, and made a final accounting of his pay.[49] Nevertheless, the CAAF determined that jurisdiction still existed, stating, "There is absolutely nothing in this case to suggest that the accused's orders were effective a single instant prior to the time specified. Until midnight, the accused was merely a person in possession of orders not yet operative."[50]

When a discharge is obtained by fraud, the military may court-martial the former servicemember for fraudulent separation in violation of Articles 83-4. Art. 3(b). If—and only if—the accused is convicted of fraudulently obtaining a discharge, then the military acquires jurisdiction to prosecute the accused for misconduct occurring prior to the fraudulent discharge. Art. 3(b); RCM 202(a), Discussion, ¶ (2)(B)(iii)(d).[51] The military courts have yet to determine if jurisdiction exists over crimes committed between the time of the fraudulent discharge and return to military control, but it appears likely that the fraudulently obtained discharge will be viewed as being without any legal effect and military jurisdiction should continue until the time of a valid discharge.[52]

Generally, a valid discharge terminates jurisdiction over a servicemember for offenses committed during that period of service, even if the person immediately reenters military service.[53] However, the military retains jurisdiction over the prior misconduct if there is no actual break in service. Accordingly, servicemembers who reenlist prior to the end of their term of service and receive a discharge solely to reenlist are subject to trial by court-martial.[54]

Court Properly Composed

For a court-martial to be properly composed all the right players must be present. The military judge, attorneys, and panel members must be properly qualified and, in the case of panel members, present in sufficient numbers and rank. Article 26(b) requires that the military judge be a commissioned officer, a member of the bar of a state or federal court, and certified as qualified to be a military judge.

Detailed military trial and defense counsel must be graduates of an accredited law school or members of a state or federal bar and certified as competent to perform trial duties. Art. 27(b). Any commissioned officer may serve as a prosecutor in a special court-martial or an assistant prosecutor or defense counsel in a general court-martial. RCM 502(d)(2).

Any active duty servicemember is eligible to serve on a court-martial panel. However, a warrant officer may not serve in the trial of a commissioned officer and an enlisted member may not serve if the accused is in the same unit. Art. 25(b) and (c)(1). Normally, the panel members cannot be junior to the accused in rank or grade and cannot be involved in the case as a government witness, accuser, investigating officer, or counsel. Art. 25(d)(1) and (2). The convening authority—usually a high-ranking commander—details members for court-martial duty. RCM 503(a)(1).

A military judge may neither determine the accused's guilt nor sentence unless the accused waives the right to a panel and specifically requests trial by judge alone. Art. 16(1)(B) and (2)(C). The request for a judge alone trial may be made either in writing or orally in open court. Art. 16(1)(B). Likewise, an enlisted accused may be tried by a court-martial that includes enlisted panel members only if the accused specifically requests an enlisted panel. Art. 25(c)(1).

Members of a court-martial panel must be lawfully appointed, otherwise the trial may be viewed as a nullity, particularly when the number of properly appointed panel members is below the statutorily required amount.[55] Further, the convening authority must select the panel members based on the Article 25(d)(2)'s selection criteria of "age, education, training, experience, length of service, and judicial temperament."[56]

Court Properly Convened

Articles 22–24 dictate who may properly "convene" or assemble a court-martial. With few exceptions, only a commanding officer (known as the "convening authority") may order the court-martial to be assembled, and this power may not be delegated. RCM 504(b)(4). The authority to convene a court-martial is determined by its type: general, special, or summary. The greater the level of court-martial, the higher the level of commander required to convene it.

To illustrate, the commander of an army, air division, or fleet may convene any type of court-martial, including the highest level, a general court-martial. A vessel commander may convene a special or summary court-martial, but not a general court-martial. Finally, the commanding officer of a detached company may convene a summary court-martial, but not a special or general court-martial. Art. 22-24.

Under certain circumstances commanders may lose their convening authority. An accuser — the person who signs the charge sheet or directs that it be signed — is disqualified from assembling a general or special court-martial and a commander junior in rank to the accused may not act as a convening authority unless that commander is the accused's commanding officer. RCM 504. Additionally, the power to convene a court may be withdrawn by a higher level authority. RCM 504.

Charges Properly Referred

Referral means "the order of a convening authority that charges against an accused will be tried by a specified court-martial." RCM 601(a). The form of the order is not critical; it may be informal or formal, oral or written.[57]

The government may make minor amendments to charges and specifications unilaterally before arraignment, or with the permission of the military judge after arraignment. RCM 603. A major change may not be made if the accused objects. RCM 603(d). Even absent an objection, a charge or specification is not properly referred if substantially amended without the convening authority's permission.[58] Minor administrative errors will not defeat military jurisdiction.[59]

Lower-level convening authorities may not exceed their power when referring a case. In *United States v. Sykes*,[60] the rape conviction of a sailor was reversed — over the *sailor's* objection[61] — because the charge was improperly referred to a special court-martial. Because rape is a crime punishable by death, the charge could only be referred to a special court-martial with the consent of the general courts-martial convening authority, which did not occur. RCM 201(f)(2)(A) and (C)(ii). Accordingly, the special court-martial had no jurisdiction over the rape charge.[62]

2

Pretrial Confinement and Restraint

Few servicemembers pending court-martial actually end up in the brig or stockade. The majority remain with their units performing normal military duties. However, circumstances arise when the accused's freedom must be curtailed to some degree. Usually these restrictions are imposed when the command views the accused as a flight risk or a danger to others, but only the minimum amount of restrictions necessary to guarantee the accused's presence at trial or to ensure the safety of others should be used. This chapter discusses the various types of restrictions on a servicemember's freedom and their effect, if any, on postconviction sentences.

Apprehension

"Apprehension" is the military term for arrest. Art. 7(b), UCMJ. Any person subject to the UCMJ may by apprehended by military law enforcement officials, both active duty and civilian; officers, petty and noncommissioned officers (NCO); and civilian officers when taking a deserter into custody. RCM 302. The Manual for Courts-Martial cautions against the apprehension of a commissioned officer by a petty or noncommissioned officer, unless they are performing law enforcement duties, have been directed to seize the officer by another officer, or when necessary to prevent the officer from escaping or disgracing the military. RCM 302(b)(2), Discussion.

Not all servicemembers who have committed a crime must be taken into custody. Generally, a servicemember may be apprehended only when there are reasonable grounds (probable cause) to believe that a UCMJ

11

offense has been or is being committed and the servicemember to be seized committed the offense. Art. 7(b); RCM 302(c). Officers and NCOs are authorized to take into custody all servicemembers involved in "quarrels, frays, or disorders, wherever they occur." RCM 302(c).

To illustrate, the naval officer who walks into a bar to find sailors from several ships involved in a barroom brawl, may order all participating sailors into custody and secure them until their immediate commanders are notified and reassume control. Additionally, if necessary, the officer may use a reasonable amount of force to effect apprehension. RCM 302(d)(3). Any sailor who physically opposes the effort to take him or her into custody may be charged with a separate violation of Article 95 for resisting apprehension. However, there must be active resistance to an apprehension; merely arguing about the propriety of taking the sailor into custody or fleeing the scene in an effort to elude the arresting authority does not violate this UCMJ provision.[1] MCM, Part V, ¶ 19c(c).

In *United States v. Carver,* a petty officer serving as the duty master-at-arms was investigating a barracks theft, which involved questioning the accused.[2] Tired of the questions, Carver left the area despite an order to the contrary and stated to the pursuing petty officer, "Jack, don't touch me. If you do, I will f——k you up."[3] Upholding Carver's conviction for communicating a threat, among other offenses, the U.S. Navy–Marine Corps Court of Criminal Appeals explained that the petty officer while in the execution of his duties was authorized to temporarily detain Carver and have him identify himself as part of the investigation, apprehend Carver when he refused the order to remain, and exercise whatever force was reasonably necessary to effect that apprehension.[4] The court also noted that even if the petty officer lacked probable cause to apprehend the accused, that legal shortcoming did not permit the accused's use of physical force to resist apprehension and would not serve as a defense to charges of disrespect and assault, unless the petty officer's conduct was so far outside the scope of his lawful authority that he was deemed to have legally abandoned his status as the duty master-at-arms.[5]

Generally there are no restrictions on where a servicemember may be apprehended. Also, neither a warrant nor command authorization is required to take a servicemember into custody when located in a public area.[6] A "private dwelling" or home serves as the major exception to this rule. Rule for Courts-Martial 302(e) provides that unless the servicemember consents or certain emergency (exigent) circumstances exist, an apprehension may not take place in a private dwelling absent a civilian arrest warrant or authorization by the appropriate military authority. A civilian arrest warrant, based on probable cause, must be obtained to apprehend a servicemember in a private dwelling that is not owned or controlled by the military. An arrest in military quarters may be authorized by the controlling military command, a military judge, or a military magistrate.

A private dwelling is analogous to a civilian home. It includes "single family houses, duplexes, and apartments" on and off post, regardless if rented, leased, or owned. RCM 302(e)(2). The term also includes off-post residences located overseas.[7] Excluded from the warrant/authorization requirement are military barracks—whether open bay or the modern dormitory style,[8] "vessels, aircraft, vehicles, tents, bunkers, field encampments, and similar places." RCM 302(e)(2).

Once a servicemember is apprehended, military authorities are authorized to search the individual as a "search incident to apprehension." Unlike the probable cause required to conduct a search, which may grow stale, the probable cause required to apprehend is largely unaffected by the passage of time. Probable cause to search is concerned with the likelihood that a thing—evidence—will be present at the time of search. In contrast, probable cause to apprehend is only concerned about whether the person to be seized committed a crime, regardless of when the crime was committed. So long as the apprehension itself is legal, military authorities need no additional justification to conduct a search of that person and his/her immediate surroundings.

Types of Pretrial Restraint

The Manual for Courts-Martial recognizes four forms of restraint: (1) conditions on liberty, (2) restriction in lieu of arrest, (3) arrest, and (4) pretrial confinement. The first three are considered "moral" restraints because no one is actually imposing a physical impediment to the servicemember's freedom of movement. The servicemember is restricted by virtue of an order from a military superior. The fourth form of restraint is a physical one, where the servicemember is actually confined. Prior to ordering pretrial restraint, the applicable authority must first determine that a reasonable factual basis exists to believe that (1) a UCMJ offense has been committed, (2) the servicemember committed it, and (3) the type and severity of restraint to be imposed is required under the particular circumstances. RCM 304(c).

The authority to order pretrial restraint is limited by the type of restraint and the status of the servicemember. An officer may be placed in pretrial restraint only by his or her commanding officer, whereas an enlisted person may be ordered into pretrial restraint by any commissioned officer. RCM 304(b). This authority may not be delegated for the restraint of officers, but it can be delegated for enlisted persons. RCM 304(b)(3). A commanding officer may delegate pretrial restraint authority, over a servicemember under his or her command or authority, to a warrant, petty, or noncommissioned officer.

Regardless of the form used, pretrial restraints may not be used as punishment because the servicemember has neither been convicted of a crime nor received a sentence. The MCM specifically forbids the imposition of punitive duty hours, training, or labor, and the use of uniforms normally reserved for postconviction prisoners. RCM 304(f). However, as with any prisoner, an accused in pretrial confinement may be disciplined under Article 13 for violating any rules imposed on the prisoners by the confinement facility. Art. 13, UCMJ; RCM 304(f).

Condition on Liberty

The least restrictive form of restraint, a condition on liberty, is an order "directing a person to do or refrain from doing specified acts." RCM 304(a)(1). Although a permissible restriction to impose on an accused awaiting trial by court-martial, its use is not dependent upon the preferral of charges. Conditions on liberty are also considered administrative tools for the commander to correct a servicemember's behavior and may be used even when the command had no intention of subjecting the wayward servicemember to criminal charges.

Conditions on liberty include such things as an order to sign in with the charge of quarters (CQ) periodically when off duty so that the unit can monitor the servicemember's continued presence, to stay away from a particular bar where the servicemember originally got in trouble, and to stay away from the servicemember's spouse after an incident of spousal abuse. RCM 304, Discussion. Because living off post is considered a privilege, revocation of pass privileges and requiring the servicemember to sleep in the barracks after a domestic dispute is a common and permissible form of condition on liberty. Similarly, servicemembers who abuse their driving privileges may be restricted from driving their automobiles on the post or installation for a reasonable period of time.

Restriction in Lieu of Arrest

This type of restraint involves an order to remain within certain specified limits. RCM 304(a)(2). For example, a commander may order the accused restricted to the brigade area, place of work, gymnasium, post exchange, and place of worship.

The order may be oral or in writing and should not interfere with the accused's ability to carry out military duties. However, if the restrictions are too stringent, the accused may be entitled to a reduction in sentence after a court-martial conviction to reflect the unwarranted restrictions on liberty.

Arrest

Like restriction in lieu of arrest, the accused is ordered to remain within a certain specified area, but the area is usually smaller and the accused normally is prohibited from performing certain military duties. As an illustration, the MCM states that a servicemember under arrest should not serve in a command or supervisory position, stand guard, or bear arms, but may be required to participate in routine training and perform normal barracks- and room-cleaning duties. RCM 304(a)(3). The arrest status immediately terminates when the servicemember under arrest is ordered to perform duties inconsistent with his status by an authorized military superior. RCM 304(a)(3).

Confinement

Confinement occurs when a member of the armed forces is actually locked up pending trial by court-martial, suffering physical rather than a moral restraint. RCM 304(a)(4). Pretrial confinement is permissible only if a reasonable belief exists that the servicemember to be confined committed an offense under the UCMJ and confinement, rather than a lesser form of restraint, is necessary. RCM 305(d). Necessity may be established when the accused is either a flight risk or is likely to engage in further criminal misconduct of a serious nature, such as intimidating witnesses or threatening the safety of others.[9] RCM 305(h)(2)(B). Confinement should not be ordered merely because the charged offense is a serious one.

The manual also permits confinement of those who present a serious threat "to the effectiveness, morale, discipline, readiness, or safety of the command." RCM 305(h)(2)(B). The Analysis to the manual describes this person as the "quitter" who has such an adverse effect on unit morale and discipline that he or she "is not merely an irritant to the commander, but is rather an infection in the unit." MCM, Appendix 21, at A21-18.

In *United States v. Heard*, the U.S. Court of Military Appeals declared unlawful the pretrial confinement of an airman who was a "pain in the neck" to the unit leadership because he refused to attend formations or perform his normal duties, but who was neither a flight risk nor a danger to others.[10] However, in *United States v. Rosato*, the U.S. Air Force Court of Military Review agreed that pretrial confinement was appropriate for an airman in a student squadron who was repeatedly disruptive and disrespectful while in the presence of other easily impressionable airmen who had only been in the military for a few months and who had informed his first sergeant that he had no intention of changing his behavior.[11]

When placed into pretrial confinement, the accused is entitled to various rights. The government must inform the accused of (1) the nature of the offense, (2) the right to remain silent, (3) the right to an attorney, and (4) the procedures for reviewing the appropriateness of the accused's confinement. RCM 305(e). If the accused requests a military attorney, one will be made available within seventy-two hours or by the time of the initial pretrial confinement hearing, whichever occurs first. RCM 305(f).

If the accused's commander did not order the confinement, the circumstances of the accused's confinement must be brought to the commanding officer's attention within twenty-four hours. RCM 305(h). The commander is authorized to order the accused's release from confinement. RCM 305(g). The manual permits the commander another seventy-two hours to determine whether continued confinement is appropriate and seven days for a "neutral and detached officer"—usually a military magistrate in the army—to independently review the existence of probable cause and the necessity for confinement. RCM 305(h)(2)(A) and 305(i). This officer may also order release from confinement. RCM 305(i)(5). However, this time line was significantly shortened by recent case developments.

In *United States v. Rexroat*, the highest military court determined that review by a neutral and detached officer would be presumed late if not conducted within forty-eight hours of confinement, but the court allowed the government to rebut the presumption by establishing that military exigencies precluded timely review.[12] This forty-eight-hour requirement may be satisfied by the commander's initial probable cause determination (RCM 305[d]) or subsequent review (RCM 305[h]) if the commander is in fact "neutral and detached," meaning that the commander cannot be directly involved in a "prosecutorial or law enforcement role in the case."[13] In *United States v. McLeod,* a probable cause review of McLeod's company commander's pretrial confinement decision by the accused's brigade commander and staff judge advocate satisfied the *Rexroat* mandate.[14] Significantly, the forty-eight-hour probable cause review requirement only applies in cases of pretrial confinement; it does not extend to other forms of pretrial restraint regardless of severity.[15]

The reviewing officer examines all related documentation ordering confinement or justifying its continuation and may consider any written submissions provided by the government or the defense. RCM 305(i)(3)(A). With the exception of certain rules regarding privileged or confidential communications, the military rules of evidence—the formal rules addressing the introduction of evidence at a court-martial—do not apply to the pretrial confinement review. RCM 305(i)(3)(B).

The servicemember in confinement, his or her attorney, and the government may appear before the reviewing officer and argue for or against the appropriateness of continued confinement. The reviewing officer must determine by a preponderance of the evidence (more likely than not) that the accused committed a UCMJ offense and that continued confinement is required. The reviewing officer's decision must be memorialized in writing, with supporting documents attached, and be provided to the accused or government attorney if requested. RCM 305(i)(6).

Either side may request the reviewing officer to reconsider the confinement decision based upon new evidence. RCM 305 (i)(7). Additionally, once the charges are referred to court-martial, the military judge may review the confinement decision and order release if appropriate. However, a military judge may order release from pretrial confinement only when (1) the reviewing officer abused his or her discretionary authority and the evidence before the judge does not justify continued confinement, (2) new information not seen by the reviewing officer compels the accused's release, or (3) a proper probable cause review was not completed and the evidence before the judge does not support continued confinement. RCM 305(j)(1).

Sentence Credit

If the accused is convicted and sentenced to be incarcerated, periods of pretrial confinement may be subtracted from the length of that sentence. There are four types of administrative sentence credits that an accused may receive.

The first type of sentence credit is known as *Allen* credit, named after the case bearing the same name. In *United States v. Allen,* the Department of Justice's system for computing sentence credit was applied to the military, giving an accused day-for-day credit to be applied to his actual sentence for any time spent in pretrial confinement.[16] Further, an accused will receive credit for periods held by civilian authorities *solely* for military offenses; the services are split as to whether an accused may receive sentencing credit for periods held by state authorities when such custody is not requested by the military.[17]

The second type of administrative sentence credit is known as *Mason* credit, which is named after the case of *United States v. Mason*[18] and applies to severe forms of restriction that are considered to be the functional equivalent of pretrial confinement. In a particularly egregious case in which *Mason* credit was given, the accused was confined, under guard, in an unsanitary basement storage room of his artillery battery, where he was not permitted to exercise, speak, or read.[19]

In addition to *Mason* or *Allen* credit, an accused may receive additional credit for various violations of the procedures contained in RCM 305. If the accused has not been sentenced to confinement or was in pretrial confinement for a period longer than the adjudged sentence, the court may apply the credit to other aspects of the sentence such as fines and forfeitures. RCM 305(k). In *United States v. McCants,* the accused received an extra fifty-five days of sentence credit to reflect every day the military magistrate was late in providing McCant's defense counsel with a copy of the pretrial confinement memorandum.[20]

Finally, the military judge enjoys almost unlimited discretion to reduce a sentence in response to illegal pretrial restraints violative of Article 13, UCMJ, and is usually permitted to sanction actions taken under the guise of pretrial restraint whose real purpose or intention is to punish. Sentence reductions have been granted when a first sergeant publicly humiliated an accused in front of a unit formation, and when an NCO accused was reassigned to perform menial tasks intended as a form of punishment even though the particular tasks were not degrading.[21]

Following an airman's conviction but prior to sentencing, the military judge denied a government request to place the accused in confinement, but the airman's commander elected to countermand the judge's decision and ordered the confinement. In *United States v. Mahoney,* the judge at trial gave the accused an additional ten days sentencing credit for the brief period of illegal confinement.[22] Subsequently, the chief judge of that circuit appointed himself to the case to conduct a post-trial investigation into the illegal confinement order, eventually ordering eighteen months' credit to punish the commander's "cavalier disregard for due process and the rule of law."[23]

Under the appropriate circumstances an accused can receive one or all of these sentencing credits. For example, a soldier is placed in pretrial confinement for ten days without receiving a probable cause review. At this point, the soldier is entitled to both *Allen* and RCM 305 credit. If the reviewing officer releases the accused, but the unit places him in restriction tantamount to confinement and then publicly humiliates him by making him wear a large "P" (for prisoner) on his uniform, the accused will also receive *Mason* and Article 13 sentencing credit.

3

Rights Warnings

Most people possess at least a passing familiarity with *Miranda* rights from television and the movies and could probably recite them from memory. You have the right to remain silent. Anything that you say can and will be used against you in a court of law. You have the right to an attorney; if you cannot afford one, an attorney will be appointed for you.

The rights referred to in the warning are the Fifth Amendment right against self-incrimination and the Supreme Court–created right to counsel during custodial interrogations.[1] The Fifth Amendment right is contained in the Bill of Rights, which is part of the United States Constitution. In the grand hierarchy of laws, the Constitution ranks as number one and cannot be ignored or overruled by the UCMJ or any military directive or regulation. Coupled with the Fourth Amendment's restrictions on search and seizures and the Sixth Amendment's right to counsel, these constitutional rights serve as the basis for a servicemember's greatest sources of protection when involved with the military justice system.

Fifth and Sixth Amendment Rights

The Fifth Amendment right against self-incrimination provides that no person "shall be compelled in any criminal case to be a witness against himself." Accordingly, the government cannot force a person who elects to remain silent to give a statement, respond to questions, or testify at any trial or hearing. Generally, once a person invokes the right to remain silent or requests an attorney all questioning must immediately stop, precluding the police from badgering a person into waiving their rights. Military Rule of Evidence (MRE) 305(f). However, a request for counsel must be clear and unambiguous; if not, the investigators are not required to stop the interview.[2]

If the servicemember is not in custody, after waiting a reasonable period of time, military investigators may return, readvise that person of his or her rights, and determine if the person is still unwilling to talk.[3] Conversely, if the servicemember has remained in continuous custody after asking for an attorney, the government cannot return and attempt to reinitiate the interview unless the servicemember's attorney is present.[4] However, someone who elects to remain silent or to seek an attorney can give up these rights by reinitiating the interview.

Significantly, the fact that a person elects to remain silent may not be used against him or her at trial. In *United States v. Riley,* a sailor's convictions for indecent acts and forcible sodomy with his daughter were set aside (thrown out) because an agent of the Naval Criminal Investigative Service, testifying at Riley's court-martial, made three references to the accused's invocation of his right to remain silent during an interview.[5]

However, the right against self-incrimination is limited to "evidence of a testimonial or communicative nature." MRE 301(a). This right is designed primarily to protect a person's thought processes and preclude the forced creation of incriminating evidence. MRE 301(a), Drafter's Analysis. Accordingly, no Fifth Amendment protection exists for such things as samples of handwriting or a fingerprint, exhibiting a body part or physical characteristic, or producing government records.[6]

The Sixth Amendment states in relevant part: "In all criminal prosecutions, the accused shall enjoy the right . . . to have the Assistance of Counsel for his defence." Unlike the right to counsel in *Miranda* which begins once the suspect is taken into custody, the Sixth Amendment's right to counsel does not attach until "the initiation of adversary criminal proceedings."[7] In the military, the Sixth Amendment right to counsel usually is triggered by the preferral of charges. MRE 305(d), Drafter's Analysis.

This right to counsel becomes significant when the accused is not interrogated, and thus not entitled to a rights warning, but is nevertheless subjected to a critical stage of the criminal process—one in which the presence of an attorney would be helpful. This scenario occurs when the accused is required to participate in a lineup which may be arranged in such a manner as to subtly suggest to the identifying witness that the accused is the culprit. An attorney, for example, can object to the accused being placed in the center of the lineup, with other participants slightly turned toward the middle — and the accused — so that the identifying witness is naturally focused on the accused.

Rights Warnings

In the armed forces, the military's version of *Miranda* rights is contained within Article 31, UCMJ. These rights are broader than those found in the civilian system and predate the *Miranda* warning requirement by more than fifteen years. In fact, in *Miranda v. Arizona,* when mandating that law enforcement officials advise persons in custody of their rights, the U.S. Supreme Court justified its decision, in part, by pointing out that the military possessed a similar rights warning requirement.[8]

In the area of rights warning requirements, servicemembers get the best of both worlds. Not only does Article 31's protections apply, but also the Supreme Court's mandate from *Miranda*. Only a year after the Court's ruling, in *United States v. Tempia,* the U.S. Court of Military Appeals determined that servicemembers were also entitled to *Miranda* rights.[9] Although similar, the two rights warning requirements possess a number of important differences in scope and applicability.

Article 31

During the majority of American military history, no requirement existed to advise servicemembers of their legal rights. Albeit ever so slowly, progress was made in this area. The army began to "suggest" that its judge advocates (lawyers) advise accused of their right to an attorney beginning in 1917, of their right against self-incrimination in 1920, and finally mandated rights warnings to those formally accused of a crime in 1948.[10] In 1950 Congress enacted the Uniform Code of Military Justice, which contained a significantly expanded rights warning requirement.

When enacting Article 31, Congress sought a procedural mechanism to protect a servicemember's constitutional right against self-incrimination when confronted by the subtle pressure inherent in superior-subordinate relationships within the military. It was believed that subordinates, if questioned by a military superior, would feel compelled to respond, even to the point of admitting to a crime they had not committed.[11] As one court explained: "Because of the effect of superior rank or official position upon one subject to military law, the mere asking of a question under certain circumstances is the equivalent of a command. A person subjected to these pressures may rightly be regarded as deprived of his freedom to answer or to remain silent."[12]

Article 31 is divided into four sections. The first section reflects the constitutional right against self-incrimination and provides that servicemembers may not be forced to either incriminate themselves or be made to answer any question that "may tend" to incriminate themselves. The third section merely prohibits a servicemember from compelling another to provide irrelevant and degrading statements or evidence at any military tribunal. Article 31(c) may be invoked during an Article 32 investigation to limit degrading questions asked of a rape victim concerning her past sexual history. MRE 303, Drafter's Analysis.

The fourth section provides a remedy to the wronged accused, prohibiting the use at a court-martial of any evidence obtained "through the use of coercion, unlawful influence, or unlawful inducement" or obtained in violation of Article 31. However, some authority exists in the federal courts that statements violative of Article 31 may still be used in administrative discharge proceedings.[13]

The second section contains the military's rights warning requirement. Article 31(b) provides that no person subject to the UCMJ "may interrogate, or request any statement from an accused or a person suspected of an offense without first informing him of the nature of the accusation and advising him that he does not have to make any statement regarding the offense of which he is accused or suspected and that any statement made by him may be used as evidence against him in a trial by court-martial."

Article 31 identifies two classes of servicemembers who must receive a military rights warning: (1) an accused and (2) a suspect. Once charges are formally preferred against a servicemember that person becomes an "accused." The term is similar to the civilian equivalent, "defendant." A servicemember becomes a "suspect" at the point that the government questioner believes, or should have believed given the circumstances, that the servicemember committed a crime.[14] In other words, at the point the servicemember is "suspected" of having committed an offense.

Although the literal language of Article 31 indicates that only a person subject to the UCMJ must give rights warnings, the scope of Article 31 is much broader. Under certain circumstances, civilians may be required to inform military suspects of their Article 31 rights. The military's rules of evidence define a person subject to the UCMJ to include knowing agents of military personnel. MRE 305(b)(1). Courts have fleshed out this evidentiary rule. For purposes of Article 31, civilian law enforcement officials are considered to be agents or instruments of the military when (1) the cooperation between military and civilian investigators is so strong that the two are deemed to have merged, and (2) "when the civilian investigator acts 'in furtherance of any investigation, or in any sense as an instrument of the military.'"[15] Under the appropriate circumstances a military court may require Article 31 rights from an Army and Air Force Exchange Service (AAFES) store detective,[16] state law enforcement officials working with installation-level investigators on a joint antidrug operation, or FBI agents working with a military attorney detailed as a Special Assistant United States Attorney.

However, military law also excludes various groups from the rights warning requirement, as long as they are not acting in concert with American military personnel. The military rules of evidence specifically exempt foreign police. MRE 305(h)(2). In *United States v. Lonetree,* U.S. civilian intelligence agents were not required to warn a marine embassy guard of his rights when questioning him about his involvement with Soviet intelligence agents.[17] Also excluded from the rights warning requirement are undercover agents; health care workers engaged in interviews for medical or psychiatric-related purposes; and civilian agents of the Defense Investigative Service, who conduct personnel security investigations for security clearances but are not considered law enforcement officials.[18]

Even persons subject to the UCMJ need not provide a rights warning in all circumstances. Article 31 rights are mandated only in "situations, in which, because of military rank, duty, or other similar relationship, there might be subtle pressure on a suspect to respond to an inquiry."[19] Consequently, for Article 31 to be applicable, the following two-part test must be satisfied: (1) the questioner must be acting in an official law enforcement or disciplinary capacity rather than acting under some form of personal motivation, and (2) the questionee must perceive the inquiry as something more than a casual conversation.[20]

In *United States v. Duga,* for instance, two air force security police were chatting at the base gate when one (airman Byer) asked Duga about rumors that the accused had been questioned concerning the theft of various government property.[21] Surprisingly, Duga volunteered to his fellow policeman that he had stolen the property and that he needed to hide his van because more stolen goods were located in it. Not surprisingly, Duga was subsequently convicted of larceny. Brushing aside Duga's argument that he should have received a rights warning at the base gate, the court determined that Byer acted solely out of personal curiosity and that the conversation was a casual one between two friends.[22]

Additionally, Article 31(b) requires that the suspect or accused be informed of the "nature of the accusation." This does not appear to be a particularly exacting standard. Anything in the general ballpark seems to be enough to satisfy the law. Military courts have ruled that informing a suspect of an investigation into "an overpayment" was sufficient for larceny (theft), a "traffic accident" was enough for negligent homicide, and "sexual assault" placed the servicemember on notice that he was suspected of raping his sister.[23]

Military law requires that a rights warning be provided before the questioner "may interrogate, or request any statement." The rules of evidence define interrogation as "any formal or informal questioning in which an incriminating response either is sought or is a reasonable consequence of such questioning." MRE 305(b)(2). Accordingly, the term is broader than merely asking a specific question; it includes other conduct likely to provoke the questionee into talking about the crime. MRE 305(b)(2), Drafter's Analysis.

As an interrogation technique, instead of directly questioning a suspect, law enforcement officials may talk to each other about some aspect of the offense or investigation, or simply lecture the suspect, deliberately attempting to provoke the suspect into responding. The most famous illustration of this technique occurred in *Brewer v. Williams,* in which the Supreme Court considered as "tantamount to interrogation" police comments to a deeply religious defendant about the need to provide his victim with a proper Christian burial, deliberately enticing the defendant into identifying the location of the victim's body.[24] Similarly, in *United States v. Byers,* the court found improper the actions of an agent of the air force's Office of Special Investigations, who for twenty to forty minutes lectured an airman suspected of using drugs about the certainty of the suspects's guilt and the importance of cooperating with the government prior to reading him his Article 31 rights.[25]

Conversely, an interrogation does not include genuinely spontaneous statements — those made without being asked a question — or a request for the suspect to consent to a search.[26] Further, an exception to the military rights warning requirement exists when questioning a witness at a "judicial proceeding," which includes a court-martial and, as long as the witness is not a suspect, at an Article 32 hearing.[27]

Miranda Rights

Miranda was not a crusading lawyer who managed to convince the Supreme Court to require that custodial interviews be prefaced by a rights warning. In fact, Ernesto Miranda had been convicted in Phoenix of kidnapping and rape.[28] Miranda was merely one of four cases consolidated to be brought before the Supreme Court. Coincidentally, representing the state of New York in one of those cases was Telford Taylor, formerly the chief American prosecutor of German war criminals at Nuremberg following World War II.

In *Miranda,* the Supreme Court was concerned about the coercive effect of custodial interrogation: "swept from familiar surroundings into police custody, surrounded by antagonistic forces, and subjected to the techniques of persuasion."[29] As a counterweight against the inherently compelling pressures of police interrogation, the Court believed that procedural safeguards were required to protect the defendant's constitutional rights against self-incrimination and to an attorney. Accordingly, the Supreme Court mandated that "prior to any questioning, the person must be warned that he has a right to remain silent, that any statement he does make may be used as evidence against him, and that he has a right to the presence of an attorney, either retained or appointed."[30] The police were required to stop questioning any defendant who requested an attorney or elected to remain silent. The defendant could give up these rights—once warned—but any such waiver had to be "made voluntarily, knowingly and intelligently."[31]

For members of the armed forces, the protections afforded by the Supreme Court's *Miranda* decision provide an additional safeguard, filling the gaps in those areas not specifically covered by Article 31. For example, a military court will not require civilian police, who are not agents or instruments of the military, to provide Article 31 rights to a servicemember suspected of an offense. The civilian police officer is not subject to the UCMJ. However, once that servicemember is taken into custody, the requirement for *Miranda* rights is triggered. Evidence obtained by civilian police in violation of *Miranda* may be excluded at a court-martial.

In *United States v. Miller,* a California police officer investigating an assault complaint against Lieutenant Miller requested that the soldier come to the police station for an interview, which Miller did.[32] Later, at his court-martial, Miller attempted to have his statement to the civilian police officer, in which the accused admitted hitting the victim, excluded from evidence, claiming that he was in custody during the interview and that the police officer failed to give Miller his *Miranda* rights warning. If Miller were in *civilian* custody and had not received a rights warning prior to being questioned, then Miller's statement would have been refused as evidence at his *military* trial.

Unfortunately for Miller, the court ruled that he was not in custody and permitted his pretrial statement to be admitted into evidence at his court-martial.[33] Looking at all the circumstances, a person is in custody if there has been a formal arrest or apprehension or such a restraint on the person's freedom of movement that a reasonable person would have believed he or she was not able to stop the interrogation and depart.[34] Miller voluntarily came to the police station and could have left at any time. Thus, *Miranda* rights were not required.

Comparing the Two

Both rights warning requirements are designed to ensure that persons who are questioned in the criminal context are at least made aware of their constitutional rights before responding. Further, both Article 31 and *Miranda* reflect concerns about the effect certain pressures will have on those subject to governmental questioning. However, while many similarities between the military and civilian warnings exist, the two are far from identical. The following chart, offered by the U.S. Court of Appeals for the Armed Forces (47 M.J. 135 [1997]), summarizes the differences between *Miranda* and Article 31 rights:

	Art. 31(b)	*Miranda*
Who must warn	person subject to code	law enforcement officer
Who must be warned	accused or suspect	person subject to custodial interrogation
When warning required	questioning or interrogating	custodial interrogation
Content of warning	1. nature of offense 2. right to silence 3. consequences	2. right to silence 3. consequences 4. right to counsel

In one regard, the military's rights warning requirement is narrower than *Miranda*. Article 31 contains no requirement to inform servicemembers of their right to consult an attorney. However, Article 31 grants rights not seen in the civilian arena in three significant instances. First, *Miranda* rights are not required until the person to be questioned is in "custody." Article 31 applies not only to custodial interrogations but also to any official questioning of a servicemember suspected of having committed an offense, even though not in custody. Second, *Miranda* rights are required from law enforcement officials. Article 31 rights must be provided by anyone subject to the UCMJ and by civilian authorities working for, or closely with, military officials. Third, unlike Article 31, *Miranda* does not require that the defendant be told of the nature of the offense.

Because there are differences between the two rights warning requirements, civilian courts have been required to determine the effect of a violation of Article 31, but not *Miranda,* when a servicemember is prosecuted in a civilian court. Every state and federal court to address the issue has ruled that Article 31's exclusionary rule does not apply outside the military courthouse, so long as the accused's constitutional rights are not violated.[35] Accordingly, a statement taken in violation of Article 31, which cannot be used in a court-martial, may be used in any federal or state criminal trial.

At first glance, such a state of the law seems to give a green light for military investigators to deliberately violate Article 31 knowing that they can turn over the accused, and any illegally obtained evidence, to the state or federal systems for prosecution. Fortunately, at least three *potential* safeguards are in place to prevent such misconduct.

First, at least one court addressing this issue was apparently aware of the potential for abuse. In *United States v. Newell,* the U.S. Court of Appeals for the Ninth Circuit determined that Article 31's protections did not apply to federal criminal proceedings but left open the possibility that a federal court could exclude evidence violative of Article 31 when such action was necessary to deter "non-compliance by military investigators with military procedure."[36] However, no published case to date has done so.

Second, the UCMJ provides a criminal sanction for the deliberate failure to provide Article 31 rights when they are required. Article 98(2) provides that any member of the armed forces who "knowingly and intentionally fails to enforce or comply with any provision of this chapter regulating the proceedings before, during, or after trial of an accused; shall be punished as a court-martial may direct." Unfortunately, this safeguard may only be a theoretical one; not a single reported case containing an Article 98 violation exists.

Third, ethical rules governing the conduct of military attorneys may provide the most realistic protection of the Article 31 warning requirement. Judge advocates are frequently involved with, and influence the conduct of, military investigations. Lawyers advise commanders and investigators, review evidence, and suggest additional investigative efforts. Army Rule of Professional Conduct Rule 4.4 (Respect for Rights of Third Persons), which is identical to the navy/marine and air force rules, provides: "In representing a client, a lawyer shall not . . . use methods of obtaining evidence that violate the legal rights of such a person."[37] A violation of this, or any other, ethical rule carries serious professional ramifications for a military lawyer.

While participating in a military operation overseas, an army judge advocate deliberately failed to read Article 31 rights to six soldiers, who were suspected of illegally taking several vehicles while acting under the orders of a lieutenant.[38] Operational necessity required the return of the vehicles and the command indicated that it had no intention of prosecuting the soldiers, but was instead investigating the lieutenant. Finding a violation of Rule 4.4, the Judge Advocate General's Corps (JAG) officer's superior, the major command's staff judge advocate, issued his subordinate a memorandum of counseling. In its review of this case, the army's Office of the Judge Advocate General's Standards of Conduct Office posited: "Article 31 . . . is not merely a rule of evidence. It imposes an affirmative duty toward all persons suspected of offenses. A questioner must advise a suspect of his or her rights under Article 31 before he or she may begin questioning, even if the suspect's answers are not solicited with a view toward incriminating the suspect."[39]

4

Search and Seizure

The basis of search and seizure law is the Fourth Amendment to the U.S. Constitution, which states, "The right of the people to be secure in their persons, houses, papers and effects, against unreasonable searches and seizures, shall not be violated, and no Warrants shall issue, but upon probable cause, supported by Oath or affirmation, and particularly describing the place to be searched, and the persons or things to be seized."

Courts have determined that the Fourth Amendment applies to both members of the armed forces[1] and civilians on military installations.[2] As a general rule, evidence obtained in violation of the Fourth Amendment, either directly or indirectly, is not permitted to be used at trial,[3] a preclusion known as the "exclusionary rule." Significantly, the law has carved out several instances when the protections of the Fourth Amendment do not apply. Many of these exceptions mirror the law found in the civilian system, but, as discussed below, the unique demands of military society have produced its own body of law in this area.

Fourth Amendment Protection and Application

By its terms, the Fourth Amendment only protects against "unreasonable" searches by agents of the government. A search is not unreasonable if the accused has no reasonable expectation of privacy in the thing or area to be searched. For example, no expectation of privacy exists in garbage left on the curb. Also, because of the unique demands of military life, the reasonable expectation of privacy found in the armed forces is often less than that found in the civilian sector. Generally, servicemembers have no reasonable expectation of privacy in the common area of a barracks, a military vehicle, or in government property unless it has been issued for personal use. Military Rule of Evidence (MRE) 314(d). Even in areas where an expectation of privacy is reasonable, such as a barracks room, in the military that expectation of privacy may be a diminished one.

Evidence obtained by a private citizen—someone not acting on behalf of the command or law enforcement officials—does not violate the Fourth Amendment and will not be excluded at trial. The Fourth Amendment only protects against government searches, not private ones. In *United States v. Reister,* a marine lieutenant invited his enlisted girlfriend to live in his apartment while he was on leave, giving her a key and unrestricted access to the dwelling.[4] Unfortunately for Reister, his girlfriend decided to meander through his things and found the accused's logbook of sexual conquests, prompting her to give the book to naval investigators and to consent to a search of the accused's apartment. In response to a defense challenge to the search and seizure of the accused's property as evidence, the court determined that Reister's girlfriend could lawfully consent to a search of his apartment and that any search she made was a private one, not triggering constitutional protections.[5]

Suppose a sailor drives into Mexico from San Diego and the Mexican police search his or her automobile without justification and discover stolen military equipment. The Mexican police then offer the seized property to American Naval authorities. Can the navy use that property as evidence against the sailor in a subsequent court-martial, even though the search was conducted without a warrant or probable cause? You bet! As a general rule, the Fourth Amendment does not apply to the actions of foreign law enforcement officials.

The nonapplicability of the Fourth Amendment to foreign officials is not without exceptions. A foreign search is considered illegal if the accused is subjected to "gross and brutal maltreatment." MRE 311(c)(3). Additionally, when American military officials conduct, instigate, or actively participate in the search with foreign officials, American law will apply. MRE 311(c). However, to trigger the Fourth Amendment protection, American participation must amount to more than mere presence at the search location, acting as an interpreter or escort, or taking actions designed to safeguard property or the accused's physical safety.[6]

Search Warrants

The Fourth Amendment sets forth the general rule that before the government can search places and things in which a reasonable expectation of privacy exists, such as a private residence or personal computer, a warrant based on probable cause must first be obtained. In the federal system, a search warrant is usually obtained from a federal magistrate after a law enforcement agent provides a sworn statement and/or testimony. Military agents are required to obtain a civilian search warrant to search off-post quarters in the United States.

In the military, search authorizations, rather than warrants, are issued by military magistrates and military judges, and — unique to the armed forces — by commanders. The authorization to search may be granted orally or in writing, and may be given after reviewing written statements and evidence or simply after being briefed over the telephone. MRE 315(b)(1), (f)(2).

Interestingly, the Services vary in terms of their preferred source for obtaining a search authorization. For example, the navy and marines rely almost exclusively on commander-issued authorizations, whereas the Coast Guard officially prefers the use of military judges.[7] The air force, as a matter of practice, favors magistrate-issued authorizations.

Military law follows an "area of control" approach to commander-authorized searches. Basically, the military's rules of evidence state that commanders can authorize a search (1) of a person in their unit and (2) of any person or thing located within their area of control. MRE 315(d)(1). This search authority extends not only to servicemembers but also to civilians. MRE 315(c)(3). Accordingly, a company commander may authorize a search of an automobile found in the company parking lot or the wall locker of a unit member. A ship's captain can authorize a search of anyone on board his/her vessel. A base commander can authorize the search of a civilian employee of the hospital.

Only impartial, or "neutral and detached," commanders may authorize a search, which eliminates any commander who "participates as a law enforcement official or is personally and actively involved in the process of gathering evidence."[8] Accordingly, a commander who actively participates in a search or investigation, or is a witness or victim of that crime, should not grant search authorization because the military judge may invalidate the search and refuse to admit into evidence anything seized as a result.

Commanders who are not impartial or who are uncertain that their search authorization authority extends to a particular person or place should seek search authorization from a military magistrate or a higher level authority, such as their immediate commander or the base commander.

Search authorizations may only be granted after a finding of "probable cause," and then the authorization should be limited to the specific room or area where the item will likely be located. This means that the authorizing official must have a reasonable belief that stolen property or evidence of a crime is more likely than not located at a specific location or upon a particular person at the time the authorization is granted or by the time the search is to be carried out. Accordingly, before commanders authorize searches they should inquire into the basis of the investigating agent's knowledge, seeking detailed information. How reliable is the agent's informant or witness? Did that person actually see the crime/evidence or merely hear about it through the rumor mill? Does other evidence exist to support that witness? Did the witness agree to provide a sworn statement? Is the information "stale," is it too old to reasonably support a determination that the evidence is currently present at the place to be searched? Commanders cannot merely rely on an agent's assurances of probable cause; commanders must independently determine that, based on all the circumstances, a reliable and believable factual basis for the search exists.

When reviewing the legality of search authorizations, military courts give favorable consideration to a commander's consultation with a military lawyer prior to authorizing a search.[9] Additionally, the commander's probable cause determination requires a greater amount of corroborating details or evidence when the source of the information is an informant working with law enforcement, who may be criminally involved or motivated to lie in order to obtain some benefit from law enforcement officials. A victim or concerned citizen — particularly a servicemember who can be prosecuted for providing false information — is generally treated as a highly reliable source of information.[10]

As a slight aside, one should be aware that the probable cause necessary to apprehend (or arrest) a servicemember differs slightly from that required to conduct a search. Rule for Courts-Martial (RCM) 302(c) provides that probable cause exists when there is a reasonable belief that an offense was committed by the person to be apprehended. To apprehend, government agents do not need to link the suspect to any particular place. Also, the timeliness of the factual information supporting a probable cause determination for an apprehension is not as important as it is for searches. For a search, the authorizing official is trying to determine the likelihood that the item to be seized is present at a particular location, as opposed to having been moved, destroyed, or concealed. Accordingly, the timeliness of the information is important. For an apprehension, it really does not matter if the crime was committed last week or last year, so long as there is reasonable information to believe that a crime has in fact taken place and the servicemember to be apprehended committed it. Further, once probable cause to apprehend exists, it remains valid unless evidence of innocence comes to light.[11]

Occasionally, despite the government's best efforts, a search authorization may be defective in some way. Military Rule of Evidence 311(b) offers three exceptions to the general rule that evidence obtained as a result of an unlawful search may not be used against an accused at a court-martial. First, if the accused elects to testify at trial, the prosecution may use the unlawfully obtained evidence to contradict or "impeach" the accused's testimony. Second, the "inevitable discovery" rule permits the prosecution to admit the evidence at trial if it can establish that the evidence would have been found anyway even if no search were conducted.

Finally, Rule 311(b)(3) codifies the "good faith" exception. This exception to the exclusionary rule allows the admission of the unlawfully obtained evidence if: (a) the evidence was obtained as a result of a search warrant or authorization, (b) even if probable cause did not exist, the authorizing official possessed a "substantial basis" for believing that it did exist, and (c) the agents or officials who sought and executed the search warrant/authorization acted in good faith and reasonably relied on that search authority.

In *United States v. Lopez,* the good faith exception was applied to a commander who authorized a search although the supporting information was "stale," having been obtained five weeks earlier.[12] However, the court offered several instances when the exception will not apply: when (1) the commander is not neutral and detached, but acts out of revenge or vindictiveness; (2) the government officials intentionally provide the authorizing official with false information or act with a "reckless disregard for the truth"; and (3) the authorization or warrant is obviously unsupported by probable cause or so deficient in its description of what is to be searched and seized that no competent law enforcement official could say with a straight face that the authorization was relied upon as being valid.[13]

Warrantless Searches

In a number of circumstances, searches may be conducted without the benefit of a search warrant or authorization, and despite the absence of probable cause. First, anyone can voluntarily consent to a search of themselves or their property, or property under their control; and evidence obtained as a result will be admitted at a court-martial. MRE 314(e). For example, a servicemember can consent to a search of his/her bodily fluids by providing a blood or urine sample. Under certain circumstances, a third party who possesses some control over the property or premises of another may consent to a search of that person's property. Usually, a spouse can consent to a search of a servicemember's automobile or private residence. In the *Reister* case discussed earlier, the court determined that the accused's girlfriend, who was house-sitting for the accused while he was on leave, possessed the requisite authority to consent to a search of the accused's apartment.

To be valid the consent must truly be voluntary and that consent may be withdrawn at any time. A commander cannot order or threaten a subordinate to agree to a search. In *United States v. White,* a female airman's consent to a urinalysis was determined to be invalid when the accused's commander told her to voluntarily provide a urine sample or he would order her to do so.[14] Significantly, even if the servicemember is suspected of having committed a crime, Article 31 rights warnings are not required prior to obtaining consent to search.[15]

If a law enforcement agent or other governmental official is lawfully present and sees evidence or contraband "in plain view," that evidence may be seized without first obtaining a warrant. To illustrate, a military policeman who is invited into a private residence to gather information about a soldier's vandalized car and sees marijuana growing in the kitchen may immediately seize the marijuana. In *United States v. Curry,* military police, without authorization or probable cause, entered the barracks room of a marine who had attempted suicide, seizing an apparent suicide note that actually contained a murder confession.[16] Because the military police were lawfully present in an effort to save the accused's life, they could lawfully seize the incriminating letters that were sitting out in the open.

Another exception to the search authorization requirement is the "search incident to arrest," which permits the arresting officer or agent to search the individual for weapons and for evidence or contraband. In the military an arrest is referred to as an "apprehension." This exception is designed to protect the arresting officer and prevent the destruction of evidence.

In *United States v. Wallace,* an army CID agent, who apprehended a suspected drug dealer, lawfully searched the accused's wallet as a search incident to apprehension.[17] There exists no requirement that the apprehending officer have a reasonable belief that the suspect actually possessed a weapon or was likely to destroy evidence; however, the search is limited to the suspect's immediate area of control and cannot be conducted too long after the apprehension.[18]

"Exigent circumstances" provide another exception to the search authorization requirement. This situation occurs when probable cause exists but there is not enough time to obtain a search authorization because the evidence is likely to be destroyed, concealed, consumed, or moved out of the area. This exception also extends to an "operable vehicle." MRE 315(g)(3). The scope of a probable cause search of a vehicle extends to every part of the vehicle, including any containers that may conceal the evidence or contraband.[19]

In *United States v. Claypole,* a Coast Guard deserter living under the name of William H. Bonney (aka Billy The Kid) was apprehended at Williams AFB, Arizona, by military agents who also seized Claypole's car keys.[20] Without obtaining search authorization, the agents searched the accused's car for weapons and identification documentation, which would serve as evidence of desertion. In addition to finding probable cause for the search, the Coast Guard appellate court ruled that the car was not rendered inoperable merely because Claypole's keys were seized. Having no way of knowing who else might have an additional set of keys, the agents were not required to leave the car unattended and risk someone taking it while obtaining search authorization, and posting a guard on the car would have constituted a warrantless seizure.[21]

Commanders may authorize, without probable cause, searches of vehicles and persons entering and exiting overseas military installations, aircraft in foreign countries or in international airspace, and U.S. vessels in foreign or international waters. MRE 314(c). In *United States v. Watson,* the Air Force Court of Military Review upheld the legality of a search of an airman's box containing marijuana, which was nailed and glued shut, located on a military chartered aircraft that had landed at Kadena Airbase, Japan.[22] Airports are considered points of entry. Military courts have extended the rule, upholding such searches upon entry onto Naval ships and military installations within the United States, so long as those personnel executing the examination exercised no discretion as to the time and place of the search, the method of selecting those to be searched, and the procedure to follow if something is found.[23] However, some discretion may be exercised as to the extent of the search.[24]

Finally, military law authorizes "emergency" searches without authorization or probable cause if undertaken for valid medical purposes, to assist someone in need of immediate medical aid, or to save someone from death or personal injury. MRE 312(f), 314(i). Military courts have upheld the admission at court-martial of the results of urine samples taken by catheter by a physician from a combative and disoriented sailor admitted to the hospital; and the search of a barracks room after police, who suspected a suicide attempt, noticed a motionless man lying with palms upward, who failed to respond to knocks on his door.[25]

Inventories and Administrative Inspections

Occasionally a servicemember deserts, is jailed, or is listed as missing-in-action, and the unit must secure and account for that person's property. Similarly, a military policeman apprehends a drunk driver and secures the driver's vehicle and any personal effects contained within it. Contraband or other evidence of a crime discovered during that accounting process may be admitted into evidence at a court-martial as long as the primary purpose of the property inspection is administrative and not designed as a means of collecting evidence for disciplinary purposes. MRE 313(c). The "inventory" exception to the Fourth Amendment permits the examination of personal property lawfully in the government's possession, for the purposes of ensuring that it is harmless, to safeguard valuables, or to protect the government against false claims for loss or damage.[26]

An inspection is an examination whose principal purpose is to ensure a unit's "security, military fitness, or good order and discipline." MRE 313(b). Its primary function is to ensure military readiness and is considered to be an inherent function of command and essential to the existence of an effective military force. MRE 313(b), Drafter's Analysis. Military inspections have survived legal challenges under either of two legal arguments: (1) an inspection is legally permissible because it is not considered a "search," or (2) if it is a search then it is a reasonable one not violative of the Fourth

Amendment. As the Court of Military Appeals once noted, an inspection "is a reasonable intrusion which a serviceperson must expect in a military society."[27] Inspections may be conducted to check such things as a unit's state of readiness, sanitation, or personnel accountability, and to locate illegal weapons and drugs.

Health and welfare inspections and the military's random urinalysis testing program fall under this administrative inspection umbrella. During a health and welfare inspection, the commander preschedules an inspection of all or part of the unit. At the prearranged time, members of the chain of command inspect servicemembers' equipment, living area, and personal storage areas, such as wall and footlockers. Similarly, as part of a random urinalysis inspection, the commander preschedules a collection of urine samples from all or part of the unit.

The legality of inspections is tested pursuant to the subterfuge rule, which is codified in Military Rule of Evidence 313(b). The rule lays out a two-pronged test: (1) the primary purpose inquiry and (2) the subterfuge rule. First, if an inspection's primary purpose is to obtain evidence for use in any disciplinary proceeding, then that examination is not an "inspection" and the usual Fourth Amendment protections apply. Second, if *one* of the purposes of an inspection is to "locate weapons or contraband" and one of three scenarios exists, then the inspection is presumed to be a subterfuge for a search, requiring the prosecution to prove by a high standard of proof that the suspect search really was a lawful inspection. The three factual scenarios are: (1) an unscheduled examination immediately followed the report of a crime in the unit, (2) specific servicemembers and/or their things were examined, or (3) during a group inspection particular individuals were subjected to a substantially more rigorous examination.

In *United States v. Campbell,* a company first sergeant heard a rumor that soldiers within his unit were using drugs so he chose several soldiers, who were known to associate with a soldier who had previously tested positive, to submit urine samples for testing.[28] The first sergeant informed the commander of the drug-use rumors and persuaded the officer to order the tests, although no random urinalysis had been scheduled. The military's highest court threw out Campbell's positive urinalysis results and reversed his conviction for cocaine use, holding that the urinalysis was not a valid inspection.[29]

However, the continued vitality of the subterfuge rule as a bulwark against circumvention of Fourth Amendment protections suffered a serious blow in *United States v. Taylor.*[30] Staff Sergeant Taylor worked in the S-1 (Adjutant) section of a marine regiment and was assigned to that regiment's headquarters company. The regimental substance abuse control officer (SACO) received two tips—one anonymous—that Taylor may be using drugs and informed the regimental S-1, a marine captain. The S-1 contacted the headquarters company commander and volunteered the S-1 section for a prescheduled, random urinalysis without informing the company commander about the reports of Taylor's drug use. Because no one had ever volunteered a section before, the company commander contacted the SACO, who assured him that there was nothing going on in the S-1 section about which the commander needed to know. After the commander ordered the urinalysis, the SACO informed the S-1 that another report of Taylor's drug use had been received, prompting the S-1 to order Taylor, who was home on bed rest after dental surgery, to report to work, where he was required to provide a urine specimen.[31]

Despite this egregious set of facts, the U.S. Court of Military Appeals upheld Taylor's conviction for wrongful use of marijuana, determining that the urinalysis was not a subterfuge search. The court focused narrowly on the knowledge of the company commander, who ordered the urinalysis, rather than on the knowledge of the S-1 and SACO, who effectively arranged for Taylor to be tested after receiving reports of his drug use. The court's decision opens the door to manipulation of the urinalysis program and avoidance of the constitutional protections of the Fourth Amendment merely by keeping the commander in the dark as to why particular sections of a unit have been selected for urinalysis.

5

Nonjudicial Punishment

Nonjudicial punishment (NJP) refers to disciplinary punishment imposed under Article 15, UCMJ, for minor offenses. Although the services have operated under the same article since the enactment of the Uniform Code of Military Justice in 1951, the NJP procedure is known by different names in the various services and each branch of the armed forces employs slightly different procedures. In the U.S. Navy and Coast Guard NJP is referred to as "Captain's Mast," the Marine Corps calls it "Office Hours," and the U.S. Army and Air Force simply refer to it as "Article 15." The old brown-boot army referred to the procedure as "Company Punishment."

Significantly, the procedure is neither a form of court-martial nor a criminal proceeding, hence the name "nonjudicial." Because punishment awarded under Article 15 is considered administrative rather than a criminal conviction, many of the rights associated with the criminal process are either limited or eliminated entirely.

Article 104 of the Articles of War served as the army and air force's predecessor to the current version of Article 15. The Articles of War also applied to marines detached to the army pursuant to presidential order.[1] Article 104 stated that "the commanding officer of any detachment, company, or higher command may, for minor offenses not denied by the accused, impose disciplinary punishments upon persons of his command without the intervention of a court-martial."[2] Similar to the current version, Article 104 authorized the soldier to reject the procedure and demand a court-martial; provided a mechanism for appeal; authorized the commanding officer, his successor, or a military superior to reduce the punishment; and noted that this disciplinary procedure did not preclude a subsequent court-martial for the same offense.[3] Punishment was limited to "admonition, reprimand, withholding of privileges, extra fatigue, and restriction to certain specified limits, but shall not include forfeiture of pay or confinement under guard."[4]

The term "Captain's Mast" originated from the naval practice in which a ship's commanding officer would impose discipline upon members of his crew at the widest part of the ship, which was usually near the mainmast of the main or quarterdeck.[5] The greater space "before the mast" facilitated assembling the ship's crew. Until the UCMJ, the navy and marines derived their NJP authority from Article 24 of the Articles for the Government of the Navy.[6] Article 24 applied to the Coast Guard in times of war, otherwise the Coast Guard's NJP authority was found in the Disciplinary Laws of the Coast Guard.[7]

Pursuant to Article 24 an officer could be reprimanded, suspended from duty, arrested, or confined for up to ten days. Enlisted sailors and marines could lose shore liberty, perform extra duties, be reduced in rating, confined with or without irons for up to ten days, placed on bread and water for up to five days, or placed in solitary confinement for up to seven days.[8] Peacetime Coast Guard commanders possessed similar punishment authority.[9] Naval personnel had no right to refuse NJP largely because the ship's captain was also a court-martial convening authority. Demanding a court-martial in lieu of NJP would have only brought the servicemember before the same officer in a different forum with increased punishment potential.[10] Even after the enactment of the UCMJ, the navy and Coast Guard continued to deny their personnel the right to reject NJP, regardless of whether they were attached to or embarked in a vessel, until 1962 when Congress amended Article 15 to provide a statutory right to demand a court-martial.[11]

Historically, Captain's Mast was not an infrequent event, apparently even for officers. While serving on the USS *Cincinnati*, Ensign (later Fleet Admiral) Ernest King was placed "under hatches" (restricted to quarters) on four separate occasions by the ship's commanding officer for offenses ranging from returning late from liberty ashore to insubordinate and disrespectful conduct toward superior officers, with appropriate entries made in his fitness reports.[12] In contrast, similar administrative punishment appearing in an officer's service record in today's downsizing military would effectively terminate that officer's career.

Currently, Article 15, UCMJ, provides the legal authority for commanding officers to impose punishment on members of their command for minor offenses. The process is designed as a corrective measure and to provide the commander with a disciplinary tool with more teeth than the nonpunitive administrative measures available (letter of reprimand, withdrawal of pass privileges, extra military instruction, etc.), without resorting to the more formal court-martial process. Because each service implements Article 15 differently, variations occurring between the services will be highlighted and explored throughout this chapter.

Procedural Overview

Generally, upon receiving a report of misconduct the commander makes, or causes to be made, an inquiry into the alleged offense. Usually this inquiry is an informal one and merely determines whether an offense has been committed and whether the suspected servicemember is involved with the misconduct. As an illustration, in the Coast Guard, the executive officer (XO) normally reviews the report of misconduct and if a factual basis exists to support the allegations, the XO will inform the coastguardsman under investigation of the allegations, identify a preliminary inquiry officer, and name a representative to assist the servicemember. Based upon the PIO's recommendation and findings, the XO may dismiss the matter if delegated this authority or forward it to the commanding officer with a recommendation for further action.[13]

In all branches of the military, witnesses may be interviewed or the inquiry may be based on available documents, written statements and reports, including those prepared by law enforcement officials. After the investigation is complete, the commander determines whether the evidence is adequate to support the allegation against the servicemember and whether a different disciplinary option should be used. The decision as to how to proceed is a personal one and cannot be dictated by a superior commander. MCM, Part V, ¶ 1(d)(2). Unique to the army, commanders elect between "formal" or "summarized" NJP proceedings, the latter possessing greatly reduced punishment potential and, concomitantly, few rights for the servicemember. Commanders may consult with a judge advocate prior to electing to proceed by NJP; the air force specifically encourages such consultation.[14]

Once the commander elects to proceed by Article 15, the suspect servicemember is informed of the commander's intention to impose NJP, advised of his or her legal rights, and provided a copy of the applicable service document describing the offense. Additionally, the army specifically requires that the servicemember receive a copy of all supporting documents and statements, the air force provides a right to examine any statements or evidence made available to the commander, while the navy and marines permit examination of all supporting evidence but only upon request.[15] The servicemember is then afforded a reasonable period of time to see an attorney, if applicable, and respond to the commander. The army permits at least forty-eight hours for a formal Article 15; seventy-two hours in the air force; and the Coast Guard, navy, and marines set no specific time period.[16] Commanders may grant additional time upon request.

However, the right to consult an attorney for NJP purposes is not unlimited. Because NJP is not a criminal proceeding, there exists no constitutional right to an attorney. Further, the right to an attorney is not rooted in Article 15 itself; instead, it is found in implementing service regulations. Soldiers do not enjoy the right to counsel for summarized Article 15 proceedings because of the reduced punishment potential, and the Coast Guard specifically denies the right to counsel to personnel attached to or embarked in a vessel.[17] Sailors and marines possess no right to consult an attorney at all during the NJP process, although commanders of the naval services are still encouraged to permit consultation, subject to availability and military exigencies.[18]

If not attached to or embarked in a vessel, servicemembers may elect between agreeing to proceed by NJP or demand a court-martial. Significantly, an election to proceed by NJP is not an admission of guilt. Servicemembers merely permit their commanders to fairly determine their guilt or innocence and, if applicable, impose a sentence. By accepting an Article 15 the servicemember makes a tradeoff between accepting fewer procedural rights than found at a court-martial, but avoiding a federal conviction and greatly limiting the potential punishment if found guilty.

Servicemembers should be forewarned that an Article 15 may be used later by the military as the basis for adverse administrative actions, such as a bar to reenlistment or an administrative discharge. Additionally, Rule for Courts-Martial 1001(b)(2) permits the trial counsel (prosecutor) to introduce as sentencing evidence personnel records indicating the nature of the accused's prior service. Records of NJP qualify as personnel records if they are properly made and maintained in accordance with applicable regulations. Trivial administrative mistakes will not preclude admission of otherwise proper Article 15s; however, an Article 15 may not be offered against an accused at sentencing if the document does not indicate that the accused had first been afforded more important legal rights, such as the opportunity to consult with an attorney or the opportunity to appeal.[19]

Once having elected to proceed by NJP, servicemembers may request a hearing, or submit evidence in their behalf, or waive both rights in which case the commander may immediately impose punishment. If evidence is submitted or an Article 15 hearing is held, the commander must determine the servicemember's guilt or innocence and what, if any, punishment to impose. A hearing is normally open to other members of the unit and to the general public, although all or part of it may be closed upon request of the servicemember, subject to the discretion of the imposing commander. In practice, however, persons not directly connected with a NJP hearing rarely attend.

At the hearing the servicemember may present evidence to establish innocence, explain the misconduct (extenuation), or reduce the amount of possible punishment (mitigation). The formal military rules of evidence do not apply. However, the servicemember does retain the constitutional right to remain silent and cannot be compelled to provide incriminating testimony or evidence.

Because some members of the armed forces are inarticulate, nervous in the presence of superiors, or unnerved by the NJP process itself, the servicemember may desire a spokesperson or personal representative at the hearing. No prohibition against using a spokesperson exists. Indeed, the U.S. Army, Coast Guard, Navy, and Marine Corps specifically authorize a person of the servicemember's choosing to speak on the servicemember's behalf.[20] Further, although a servicemember has no right to an attorney at the NJP hearing, no blanket prohibition against their participation exists in any service. In their discretion, commanders may permit an attorney to serve as a spokesperson during the hearing, and may permit the attorney or servicemember to examine any witnesses or, in the alternative, the commander may accept suggestions regarding appropriate areas of inquiry.[21] As a practical matter, however, attorneys rarely participate in an NJP hearing.

The standard of proof to find a servicemember guilty of an Article 15 offense varies by service. Army commanders must be convinced of guilt "beyond a reasonable doubt," which is the highest standard known to the law and the same standard imposed at a court-martial.[22] Naval and marine NJP authorities only require the less burdensome "preponderance" of evidence standard, which requires a determination that the servicemember more likely than not engaged in the misconduct.[23] The air force and Coast Guard impose no particular standard of proof on their commanders, but the air force appears to encourage its commanders to use the same "beyond a reasonable doubt" standard seen at a court-martial.[24]

If the commander determines that the servicemember committed the offense an appropriate punishment is determined and announced. The commander may explain why a particular punishment was chosen, but is not required to do so. Once punishment is imposed, the servicemember may appeal the Article 15 punishment to the next higher commander. Art. 15(e). An appeal is presumed late, and may be rejected, if not initiated within a reasonable time, which is normally five days.[25] NJP punishment may not be increased on appeal. MCM, Part V, ¶ 1(f)(2). Pending resolution of the appeal, the commander is not required to suspend execution of the punishment. However, if after five days no action on the appeal has been taken and the offender requests that the remaining punishment not be executed, the commander must grant the request. MCM, Part V, ¶ 7(d).

Limitations

Not all officers are authorized to impose nonjudicial punishment. Generally, only a "commander" enjoys Article 15 authority. In the army, a commander for NJP purposes includes both commissioned and warrant officers.[26] The air force, navy, and marines limit NJP command authority to commissioned officers only; naval and marine officers must be a commander or designated as "an officer in charge."[27] In the Coast Guard, provisions exist to permit officers, warrant officers, and enlisted "officers-in-charge" to impose NJP.[28]

Commanders may only impose NJP on current members of their commands. Implementing service regulations differ slightly, but generally a member of the command includes not only assigned members of a unit or organization, but also may include those personnel accompanying or attached to the unit, including those on temporary duty. A member of another branch of the service may still be considered part of the command. Because they are all part of the Department of the Navy, sailors and marines are considered part of the same service. Generally, joint or multiservice commanders possess NJP authority over all members of the command, regardless of branch of service, but may elect to designate separate service commanders for NJP purposes. The army and air force prohibit the imposition of NJP over military academy cadets; the air force reserves such authority to the academy.[29] Civilians are immune to NJP.

Commanders also retain the authority to withhold NJP authority from a subordinate commander. For example, a commander may elect to withhold all NJP authority from a subordinate commander under investigation or pending relief for cause. In the army and Coast Guard, a superior commander may withhold NJP authority over specific categories of personnel (e.g., all enlisted personnel in the pay grade of E-9), particular offenses (e.g., DUI), or particular cases.[30] The air force permits a superior commander to withhold all or part of a subordinate commander's NJP authority, which should be accomplished in writing.[31] Withholding authority in the navy and marines requires the secretary of the navy's approval.[32]

Misconduct punishable by Article 15 is subject to a "statute of limitations," which means that NJP must be imposed within a certain period of time after the misconduct occurred. The UCMJ mandates that a servicemember may not be punished pursuant to Article 15 "if the offense was committed more than two years before imposition of the punishment." Art. 43(b)(2), UCMJ. However, the two-year clock does not run during the period that the servicemember is AWOL, fleeing, in the custody of civilian authorities, a prisoner of war (POW), or in a country where the United States lacks apprehension authority. Art. 43(c) and (d).

Normally the Constitution and the Manual for Courts-Martial prohibit a person being tried or punished twice for the same misconduct. For example, an accused found not guilty in one court-martial cannot be retried in a second proceeding for the same misconduct. This restriction is known as the prohibition against double jeopardy, and is contained in the Fifth Amendment to the United States Constitution and Article 44 of the UCMJ. The Manual for Courts-Martial prohibits twice imposing NJP on a servicemember for the same misconduct. MCM, Part V, ¶ 1(f)(1).

However, an Article 15 does not preclude a later court-martial for the same misconduct if the accused is charged with a serious, rather than a minor, offense.[33] Art. 15(f). Generally, a minor offense is of the type normally tried at a summary court-martial, but does not include offenses punishable by a dishonorable discharge or confinement greater than a year.[34] A minor offense is roughly synonymous with a civilian misdemeanor. If the servicemember does go to a court-martial for the same misconduct, the prior Article 15 may not be used by the government for any purpose and, if convicted, the accused must be afforded full credit for any prior punishment.[35]

Permissible Punishment

If a servicemember is determined to have committed an offense, the commander must then determine the appropriate level of punishment. Article 15 dictates the general limitations on punishment. An officer or warrant officer may be placed on restriction, and suspended from duty, for up to 30 days, and suffer a reprimand. Art. 15(b)(1)(A). If NJP is imposed by a general/flag officer or general court-martial convening authority, an officer may be restricted to quarters for up to 30 days, forfeit up to one-half a month's pay for two months, be placed on restriction and suspended from duty for up to 60 days, and suffer detention of one-half a month's pay for three months. Art. 15(b)(1)(B).

The maximum permissible punishment for enlisted personnel depends upon the rank of the imposing NJP authority. An officer below the rank of major or lieutenant commander has far less punishment authority than does a higher-ranking officer and may actually refer the matter to a higher commander if circumstances indicate that the imposing officer's punishment authority is insufficient. Subject to certain restrictions regarding combinations of punishments and to service specific limitations on quantum, the maximum permissible punishment for enlisted servicemembers, by rank, is as follows:

	Imposed by Lower-ranking Officer	Imposed by Higher-ranking Officer
Correctional custody	7 days	30 days
Forfeiture of pay	7 days	one-half of 1 month's pay for 2 months
Loss of rank	1 grade (if within promotion authority)	unlimited grades or 2 grades (E5–E9)
Extra duty	14 days	45 days
Restriction	14 days	60 days

Additionally, commanders may reprimand or admonish the offender, and if the servicemember is attached to or embarked in a vessel, Article 15(a) authorizes a maximum of three consecutive days of confinement on bread and water or diminished rations.

Additional restrictions are imposed by specific service regulations and instructions. For example, the army and navy limit the bread and water punishments to servicemembers in the bottom three enlisted ranks; the air force and Coast Guard prohibit the punishment altogether.[36] Further, under the army's summarized NJP procedure, a soldier faces relatively light sanctions. The maximum permissible punishment is fourteen days' extra duty, fourteen days' restriction, an oral reprimand or admonition, or any combination of the three.[37]

In addition to the authority to impose punishment, commanders and their replacements ("successor-in-command"), as well as superior commanders on appeal, may suspend, reduce, or set aside previously imposed punishments. Suspending punishment is similar to putting the offender on a form of probation. If the offender stays out of trouble for the specified period of time, that portion of the punishment suspended is canceled. The suspension should be initiated at the time of imposition of punishment, or within four months for any reduction in grade or forfeiture of pay, and suspended for no longer than six months or the end of the enlistment period, whichever is shorter. MCM, Part V, ¶ 6(a). If the offender violates the terms of the suspension, the commander should give the offender an opportunity to explain what happened and, if the explanation proves inadequate, may reinstate the original punishment. The commander may also take additional disciplinary action to punish the new misconduct. MCM, Part V, ¶ 6(a)(5). The manual suggests that punishment suspension may be appropriate for "first time offenders or when significant extenuating or mitigating matters are present." MCM, Part V, ¶ 1(d)(3).

The commander may mitigate, or reduce, the severity of the punishment to reflect the offender's subsequent good conduct or if, upon reflection, the commander determines that the original punishment was too harsh. For example, reduction in grade may be reduced to a forfeiture of pay, if accomplished within four months of the original imposition of punishment. MCM, Part V, ¶ 6(b). For the same reasons justifying a reduction of punishment, the commander may elect to remit or cancel the remaining uncompleted punishment. MCM, Part V, ¶ 6(c).

Finally, the entire NJP may be set aside, or canceled, and all rights, rank, privileges, and property returned to the servicemember. This action should be taken if a "clear injustice" has occurred. MCM, Part V, ¶ 6(d). The army regulation defines clear injustice as the existence of "an unwaived legal or factual error which clearly and affirmatively injured the substantial rights of the soldier."[38] The most obvious illustration of clear error is evidence establishing that the servicemember did not commit the offense. The air force also offers a catch-all "best interests of the Air Force" exception.[39] Examples of reasons not to set aside Article 15 punishment — at least for the army — include the adverse affect of NJP on a servicemember's promotion potential and subsequent exemplary work performance.[40]

The Vessel Exception

Generally, a servicemember may reject an Article 15 and demand trial by court-martial, and this right of refusal exists up to the time that the punishment is actually announced. Art. 15(a), UCMJ. The single exception to this rule, known as the vessel exception, occurs when the servicemember is "attached to or embarked in a vessel," which includes a member of the armed forces who is "assigned or attached to the vessel, is on board for passage, or is assigned or attached to an embarked staff, unit, detachment, squadron, team, air group, or other regularly organized body." MCM, Part V, ¶ 3. The vessel exception is not limited to the navy and marines but extends to any member of the armed forces in that status.[41]

The exception remains a controversial one and is susceptible to abuse.[42] Two cases illustrate this point. In *United States v. Jones,* a sailor was acquitted at court-martial of drug-related conspiracy and dereliction of duty charges.[43] Based on the same evidence, Jones was then subjected to Captain's Mast for slightly different offenses while attached to a vessel and administratively discharged based on the NJP. Although the military appellate court determined that they were without the legal power to act, one judge referred to the "unseemly manner in which this nonjudicial punishment arose" and the court as a whole commented that the "case foreshadows unreasonable-abuse of command disciplinary powers which cannot be tolerated in a fundamentally fair military justice system."[44]

In *Fletcher v. Covington,* a sailor tested positive on a urinalysis for the presence of cocaine and was processed for court-martial.[45] When the military judge ordered the navy, over its objections, to either produce a report addressing employee misconduct at the navy's drug-screening laboratory or stop the court-martial, Fletcher's commander dismissed the charges and NJP proceedings were immediately initiated against Fletcher for the same offense.[46] Because Fletcher was assigned to a vessel he could not refuse the NJP and demand trial by court-martial, despite the ship being in port.[47] In a written opinion disagreeing with the decision of the U.S. Court of Appeals for the Armed Forces not to review the case, Chief Justice Sullivan observed that there "is something that smells in this case."[48]

The vessel exception certainly is at the height of its legitimacy when the servicemember commits minor misconduct while embarked in a ship in port about to depart or actually at sea. In these situations, a demand for court-martial would disrupt the efficiency of the ship if granted by requiring members of the ship's crew to remain ashore for the proceedings, or undercut the captain's ability to maintain good order and discipline if disciplinary action is postponed until the ship can return to port.

Conversely, the exception seems unjustified when the ship is in port for an extended period of time with ample legal resources in close proximity ashore and—as in the *Fletcher* and *Jones* cases—the command has actually made use of those resources. In some instances use of the exception is downright unconscionable, such as when a commander deliberately assigns a servicemember to a vessel in order to deny the alleged offender the right to demand a trial or deliberately waits until the offender is assigned to a vessel before initiating NJP. This deliberate circumvention of the right to trial is made possible by the rule that a servicemember's right to refuse an Article 15 is determined at the time NJP is imposed rather than at the time the offense is committed or discovered.

Casting a jaundiced eye on the procedure in a rare instance when the issue was before it, the military's appellate court system has imposed some limitations of this controversial procedure. In *United States v. Edwards,* the military's highest appellate court limited the exception "to situations such as where service members were aboard a vessel, in the immediate vicinity and in the process of boarding, or attached to vessels and absent without authority in foreign ports."[49] A sailor technically attached to a ship who normally performs duties and receives NJP ashore may still enjoy the right to demand a trial. Further, to be a "vessel" the ship should be in an operational status. The court suggested that a ship incapable of being used as a means of transportation, such as one undergoing a long-term overhaul, may not be considered a vessel unless a compelling reason to maintain "discipline at sea" is found.[50] Without deciding, the court suggested that the vessel exception may still apply to a ship rendered inoperative by reason of being "a casualty at sea, accidental grounding or collision, or wartime damage."[51]

6

The Court-Martial Process

The court-martial process begins with the discovery of a real or perceived crime and the subsequent notification of commanders or military law enforcement officials. Anyone may report an offense to military authorities, and such information frequently comes from civilians, military dependents, servicemembers, and state, federal, and foreign law enforcement bodies. A commander who receives such a report is required to conduct a preliminary inquiry into the truth of the allegations or forward them to military investigators, who then gather evidence and present their findings to commanders and military judge advocates (lawyers) for review. RCM 303. Frequently, judge advocates advise investigators about the strength of the evidence and suggest additional evidence necessary to successfully prosecute the case.

After the preliminary inquiry or investigation is complete, the suspect servicemember's immediate commander makes the initial decision as to how the matter should be handled unless a higher level commander has withheld such discretion for certain types of crimes. RCM 306(a). The commander may take no action at all, handle it administratively, hear the case under Article 15, or recommend that the servicemember be court-martialed. RCM 306(c). If charges have been sworn-out (preferred), they are forwarded through the accused's chain of command to determine the proper disposition of the case. Each commander may dismiss the charges, forward them with a recommendation, or refer them to court-martial if that commander is the appropriate convening authority. RCM 401(c).

Superior commanders are not generally bound by the decisions of their subordinates. RCM 306(a), Discussion.

In determining the proper disposition of cases, commanders frequently seek the advice of their assigned judge advocates. Military lawyers may suggest a particular level of court-martial, but no commander may be pressured into making a specific decision or recommendation. Alternatively, judge advocates may advise against prosecution for a variety of reasons. Insufficient evidence may exist, the facts and circumstances surrounding the misconduct may create an overly sympathetic accused such that a panel would be unlikely to convict despite evidence of guilt, the circumstances may be such that a court-martial conviction would be too severe given the minor nature of the misconduct, or the prosecution may be stretched thin and unable to devote its limited resources to the case.

Preferral of Charges

In the military an individual files charges against a servicemember by "preferring" them. Anyone subject to the UCMJ may prefer charges against another servicemember. RCM 307. Indeed, following the conviction of Lieutenant Calley for the Vietnam-era My Lai massacre, a military defense lawyer for one of Calley's men filed charges against Gen. William Westmoreland, which were later dismissed by the secretary of the army.[1]

The preferrer of charges must have personal knowledge of the misconduct or must have investigated it. The preferrer then signs the charge sheet under oath before a duly authorized commissioned officer. RCM 307 (b). In practice, a military lawyer normally drafts the charges and specifications, and then a legal clerk prepares the charge sheet. The legal clerk forwards the completed charge sheet to the servicemember's immediate commander, who prefers the charges and is listed as the accuser. The immediate commander is responsible for notifying the accused of the charges and of the accuser's identity, which is usually done by presenting the accused with a copy of the charge sheet. RCM 308.

A "charge" refers to the specific article of the UCMJ alleged to have been violated and a "specification" describes factually each specific violation of that particular article. For example, a servicemember alleged to have gone AWOL on one occasion and to have assaulted a superior commissioned officer on three different occasions will see a charge sheet with

Charge I alleging a violation of Article 86, and a single specification under that charge; and Charge II alleging a violation of Article 90 with three specifications under the second charge.

In the federal system, a defendant is not normally indicted and tried for factually unrelated crimes.[2] Conversely, in the military an accused may be charged with several factually unrelated offenses and is usually prosecuted for all known offenses in a single court-martial. RCM 307(c)(4); 601(e)(2). The military system is efficient in terms of time and the use of resources and discourages the government from taking multiple bites at the court-martial apple by repeatedly levying charges at a servicemember until it finally achieves a conviction. However, despite these obvious benefits, the military procedure risks unfairly increasing the likelihood of a conviction by painting the accused as a bad person through the "stacking" of unrelated charges or by encouraging a panel to assume the accused is guilty of one crime because evidence establishes guilt of another.

The Article 32 Investigation

After preferral of charges if a general court-martial is contemplated, Article 32, UCMJ, requires the convening authority to first ensure "a thorough and impartial investigation." This investigation is loosely analogous to a civilian grand jury proceeding, but the military accused enjoys infinitely more rights than a civilian defendant.

Any commander with court-martial convening authority may appoint the investigator—known as the investigating officer (IO)—who must be an impartial commissioned officer with the rank of major/lieutenant commander or above. RCM 405(c) and (d)(1). In practice, all branches of the armed forces, except the army, prefer to use military lawyers for this duty. In the army, the IO is usually an experienced line officer with little, if any, formal legal training, in the grade of major/lieutenant commander or above.[3] A line officer's lack of formal legal training is considered unimportant because the IO makes largely factual determinations and when legal issues do arise an impartial judge advocate can be appointed to provide legal advice.[4] Although the IO is required to make note of any legal issues or objections raised during the investigation, a legal determination of those issues is not normally required. Further, because a line officer presumably thinks more like the potential pool of panel members than like a lawyer, the line officer IO's perception of the evidence will arguably give the convening authority and the prosecution a good sense for how the panel members (jury) will view the case.[5]

The Article 32 investigation is designed to serve four purposes: (1) to inquire into the truth of the charged misconduct, (2) to review the form of the charges, (3) to generate a recommendation from the IO concerning the disposition of the case, and (4) to provide an opportunity for the defense to gather evidence. Art. 32, UCMJ; RCM 405(a), Discussion. A significant difference between the military and civilian systems is that without the permission of the grand jury a civilian prosecutor cannot go forward with the case. Conversely, in the military the IO's recommendation is only that — a recommendation. The convening authority may refer the matter to a general court-martial even when the IO recommends that all charges be dismissed.

In the federal system, the prosecutor controls the presentation of the evidence to the grand jury and is not required to present evidence favorable to the defendant, let the defendant attend, or even notify the defendant of the existence of an investigation. Many times, a civilian's first official notification of the government's investigation occurs after the prosecutor presents an indictment to the grand jury, who formally charges the defendant with a crime. The next step in the process for the civilian defendant is to appear in federal court to be read a copy of the charges, enter a plea, and be scheduled for trial.

Conversely, a military accused can convince the convening authority to dismiss the charges or pursue a lesser form of discipline by pointing out the weakness of the government's evidence during the Article 32 hearing. As part of the IO's investigation the accused must be informed of the preferred charges, be notified of the evidence and witnesses (including the identity of the accuser) known to the IO, and be permitted to attend all parts of the investigatory hearing with the assistance of an attorney, cross-examine the government's witnesses and challenge its evidence, and present favorable witnesses and evidence. RCM 405(f). The accused may make a statement in any form, sworn or unsworn, written or oral. RCM 405(f)(12).

The accused is entitled to a free military attorney, either detailed to the accused or of the accused's choosing, if available, or to a civilian attorney at the accused's expense. RCM 405(d)(2). It is not uncommon for an accused to enjoy the services of both civilian and military counsel. In 1997 an unusually long Article 32 investigation of Sgt. Maj. of the Army

Gene McKinney saw the exercise of all these rights. SGM McKinney enjoyed the assistance of both civilian and military counsel; his Article 32 hearing lasted some nine weeks and involved the examination of more than 30 witnesses.[6]

The IO controls the investigation, making determinations as to the availability of requested witnesses and controlling the questioning by the attorneys. The IO may prevent an attorney from harassing a witness or move things along when the attorney repeatedly asks the same or similar questions. Normally the hearing is open to the public, but the IO may close the hearing in order to obtain testimony from reluctant, embarrassed, or sensitive witnesses. RCM 405(h)(3), Discussion.

If the defense fails to object, the IO may consider almost any evidence except information covered by the limited number of evidentiary rules applicable at the Article 32 stage. Excluded evidence includes confidential communications between the accused and his/her attorney, spouse, or clergymen, and certain information regarding a victim's past sexual history. RCM 405(g)(4) and (i). If a witness or evidence is unavailable the defense can limit the IO's consideration of certain evidence, generally restricting it to sworn prior testimony or statements, authenticated copies of documents or photographs, and live testimony describing evidence. RCM 405(g)(4) and (5). These restrictions are relaxed during wartime.

Any legal advice the IO receives must come from a neutral source, which does not include the trial counsel, and should be made known to both the defense and prosecution. Frequently, in the army a judge advocate from a noncriminal section of the staff judge advocate's office is appointed to assist the IO with any legal issues. To avoid the appearance of impropriety, the IO should never discuss any substantive issues with one side alone; all discussions should be in the presence of both trial and defense counsel.

Referral of Charges and Convening the Court-Martial

The convening authority will "refer" or order the charges prosecuted at a specified level of court-martial once having personally determined, or having been advised by a military lawyer, that reasonable grounds exist to believe that the accused committed the charged offense, a proper offense is alleged, and the court-martial has jurisdiction. RCM 406, 601(a) and (d)(1).

Next, the convening authority orders the court-martial to be assembled. The accused may elect to be tried by a military judge alone, by a panel (jury) of officers, or, if the accused is enlisted, by an enlisted panel consisting of at least one-third enlisted personnel. RCM 503, 903. Panel members are chosen by the convening authority based on "age, education, training, experience, length of service, and judicial temperament." Art. 25(d)(2), UCMJ. A general court-martial must have at least five members; a special court-martial must have at least three. RCM 501. Often several panels are appointed to serve on courts-martial for a fixed period of time. Accordingly, panel members may serve on several different courts-martial during this period of duty.

The Contested Trial

Assuming the accused elects not to plead guilty, the first step in the actual trial process is called the arraignment. The military judge will have the charges and specifications read to the accused, unless the accused chooses to waive the reading, based on having been previously provided with a copy of the charge sheet. RCM 904. The judge will then ask the accused to enter a plea. The accused may plead guilty, guilty but only to certain charges or to facts different from those alleged, not guilty, guilty but reserving the right to appeal an adverse legal ruling (if the judge and prosecution agree), or remain silent. Unlike the civilian system, the military does not permit an *Alford* plea, one in which the defendant concedes that the prosecution has enough evidence to convict, but the defendant still refuses to admit guilt. Art. 45, UCMJ.

If the accused stands mute (remains silent), the military judge must enter a plea of not guilty on the accused's behalf. RCM 910. Standing mute may serve as a jurisdictional defense in prolonged AWOL/desertion cases when the prosecution cannot prove the identity of the accused, that is, that the person standing next to the defense attorney is actually someone subject to the UCMJ. RCM 201(b)(4). Usually a specific date for trial will be announced; counsel for both sides may be told informally of the date before arraignment.

In addition to kicking off the beginning of the court-martial, the arraignment is important for various legal reasons. First, it stops the speedy trial clock, which is discussed below.[7] RCM 707(b)(1). Second, an accused who elects not to attend the court-martial — usually by virtue of being AWOL — may be tried "in absentia" (while absent). RCM 804(b). The effect of a trial in absentia is that the defense counsel defends an empty chair at the court-martial. Further, after arraignment no additional charges may be referred to that particular court-martial unless the accused consents. RCM 601(e)(2); 904, Discussion.

Prior to or after the arraignment, the defense may make a motion (request) that the judge throw out certain charges, order the prosecution to provide the defense with additional evidence or clarify the charges, split the charges into multiple trials, or keep out certain evidence. RCM 905–907. Motions are usually argued by counsel to the judge prior to trial or outside the presence of the panel during the trial. The outcome of these motions impact on trial strategy and are frequently dispositive in the accused's decision either to go to trial or to cut his or her loses and pursue a plea agreement with the government.

Usually the government has 120 days to get the accused to trial. The time counted subtracts out delays resulting from actions by appellate courts, the unauthorized absence of the accused, and delays authorized beforehand by a lawful authority such as the military judge (after referral), or the convening authority (before referral). RCM 707.[8] It is unclear whether an Article 32 officer is such a lawful authority when acting without the express permission of the convening authority.[9] The defense may challenge the excusable delays, attacking both the decision to grant them and the reasonableness of their duration.[10]

The 120-day speedy trial clock begins to run from the preferral of charges, the imposition of restrain, or a reservist's entry on active duty for UCMJ purposes, whichever occurs first. RCM 707(a).[11] Failure to meet the 120-day rule results in dismissal of the charges. RCM 707(d). If the charges are dismissed "without prejudice," the government may start the court-martial process over again. If dismissed "with prejudice," the accused cannot be made to stand trial again for the same offenses. Although the federal system operates under similar time constraints, in practice military members accused of an offense usually go to trial much faster than their federal counterparts.

The actual court-martial is divided into two phases: guilt/innocence and sentencing. Prior to trial the accused must elect between a trial by judge alone, by an officer panel, or by an enlisted panel. This decision is usually a tactical one. The defense guesses as to whether a judge or panel is more likely to be sympathetic, believe the accused's version of the facts, or impose a lighter sentence if convicted.

If the accused elects not to be tried by a military judge alone, the first phase begins with counsel questioning the panel members in a process called "voir dire" to determine if any member is biased or possesses some quality favorable or disfavorable to their side. For example, the defense may seek a panel member who has been the object of a false report of misconduct in the past, or who has been cleared after suffering through an official investigation, because such a person may be more sympathetic to an accused who denies committing the crime. Additionally, attorneys frequently craft questions to educate the panel members about some aspect of the law that they consider to be important, such as the burden of proof or the relative value of different types of evidence.

Any panel member may be challenged, and removed, "for cause." Grounds for removal include being improperly detailed, having had prior involvement in the case, exhibiting an inflexible attitude concerning the accused's guilt or as to the severity of sentences for particular crimes, and the catch-all "in the interest of having the court-martial free from substantial doubt as to legality, fairness, and impartiality." RCM 912(f). In *United States v. Minyard*,[12] the military judge committed legal error by failing to grant the defense challenge of a panel member whose Air Force Office of Special Investigations (AFOSI) agent/husband had investigated the case. The government must disclose any known grounds for a causal challenge and military judges should liberally grant any legitimate challenges.[13]

Additionally, counsel for both sides may use a "peremptory challenge" or "strike" to remove a member for any reason at all, so long as the challenge is not based on improper considerations such as the panel member's race or gender. RCM 912(g).[14] Peremptory challenges are usually tactical decisions. Trial counsel may seek to remove the young and naïve, whereas the defense may want to remove the seasoned member who has grown cynical or intolerant. Counsel often make their challenge based on reputation or their own stereotypical views of certain classes of panel members. Commanders, particularly from combat arms or line units, are often favored by prosecutors because they are reputed to be staunch disciplinarians and more likely to hold an accused responsible for misconduct. Conversely, prosecutors disfavor junior officers, members with social worker–type backgrounds, and members serving in administrative-type branches of the service because they are reputed to be more inclined to forgive or sympathize with the accused's motivation for committing the crime.

Occasionally, defense counsel use their peremptory strike in order to "play the numbers," that is to gain a slight mathematical advantage given that a two-thirds vote is required for conviction. For example, with nine members on the panel, the prosecution needs six votes for a conviction. If the defense strikes a member—leaving the panel with eight members—the prosecution still needs six votes to convict because two-thirds of eight is slightly more than five. Since a fraction of a panel member only exists in the minds of statisticians, rounding up to the next whole number is required, which is six. The prosecution has a slightly greater burden mathematically to convince a panel of eight than to convince a panel of nine.

After the panel members are selected, the attorneys make opening arguments to the panel. The arguments are designed to provide a road map of what each side expects the evidence to show, emphasizing a particular interpretation of the facts. For tactical reasons the defense may wait until the prosecution puts on its evidence before making an opening statement. Because of the importance of the opening statement, particularly in cases with a panel, defense counsel rarely exercise this option.

The government goes first in its presentation of witnesses and other evidence. This phase of the trial is called the government's "case-in-chief." If the trial counsel fails to provide evidence of every part (element) of each charge and specification, the military judge may throw out that part of the case. When the prosecution is finished, the defense is permitted to offer its own witnesses and evidence. The prosecution may then offer additional witnesses and evidence to contradict or "rebut" the defense. After all evidence is presented, both sides argue their interpretation of the facts and law to the judge or panel, depending on who is deciding the case. Because the government must prove the charges beyond a reasonable doubt, it argues first and last. Finally, in a panel case the judge will read an explanation (instruction) of applicable portions of the law to the panel members before they meet to discuss the evidence and vote on the accused's innocence or guilt.

Throughout the trial, the evidence and testimony that comes into the trial is governed by the military rules of evidence, which are similar in many respects to the federal rules. Essentially the rules are designed to filter out evidence that has nothing to do with the issues being decided at trial (irrelevant), evidence that may cause a panel to improperly convict (prejudicial), evidence that is not sufficiently trustworthy (hearsay, unauthenticated, lacking foundation, beyond the witness' personal knowledge or expertise), and confidential communications between the accused and selected individuals that society has determined should be protected (privileged). For example, an accused's confidential conversations with a attorney or priest cannot be divulged to the court even if the accused admits to committing the crime to such a person.

During the court-martial, panel members may take notes and may request that certain evidence and witnesses be produced. RCM 913(c)(F); 912; MRE 614(a); Art. 46, UCMJ. Further, members may request that witnesses be asked particular questions by submitting written questions to the judge via the attorneys, giving the attorneys the opportunity to object. MRE 614(b). Indeed, in *United States v. Hill,* a Coast Guard panel submitted over 125 questions.[15] The military judge may also question witnesses and call a witness to testify. MRE 614.

After both sides make their arguments and the judge instructs them on the law, the panel leaves the courtroom and reassembles with their notes, any written legal instructions, and any physical evidence in a separate room. After fully discussing the evidence, the panel members vote in secret with the junior member present collecting and counting the votes. RCM 921. Superiors may not "pull rank" on military inferiors; any effort to do so may constitute unlawful command influence. A conviction requires a two-thirds vote of the panel; anything short of that number results in an acquittal. Art. 52(a)(2), UCMJ; RCM 921(c)(3). There are no "hung juries" in the military. The panel may return with a finding of not guilty, guilty, or guilty of a lesser form of the crime or with a slightly different factual basis (guilty by exceptions and/or substitutions). RCM 918(a)(1). If the insanity defense is raised, the panel may find the accused "not guilty only by reason of lack of mental responsibility." RCM 921(c)(4).

If the accused is convicted of any crime then the second phase of the court-martial begins. The trial counsel begins and may offer the accused's service data from the charge sheet, military records showing the nature of the accused's prior service, prior military and civilian convictions, any aggravating circumstances surrounding the commission of the crime, opinion evidence concerning the accused's previous performance in the military, and potential for rehabilitation as a useful member of society. RCM 1001 (a) and (b). The accused's juvenile convictions are inadmissible.[16] The trial counsel cannot solicit testimony from the accused's chain of command as to whether the accused should be discharged from the service or returned to the unit. RCM 1001(b)(5)(D).

The defense then presents E&M (extenuation and mitigation) evidence, which serves to rebut the trial counsel's evidence, explain the circumstances that caused the accused to engage in the misconduct, and persuade the sentencing judge or panel that little if any punishment should be imposed or that clemency should be recommended. RCM 1001(c). The military judge may relax the rules of evidence during this portion of the sentencing hearing. RCM 1001(c)(3). Accordingly, the judge may accept such items into evidence as letters from the accused's friends, doctor, and business associates; unauthenticated copies of certificates, bills or other documents; affidavits; and photographs.

Matters in extenuation explain the commission of the crime and may include the fact that the crime was committed under the stress of combat, upon provocation, while suffering from minor mental problems, or because of financial and family problems. Matters in mitigation focus on the accused rather than the crime. They include prior acts exhibiting good military or civilian traits, the accused's marital status and number of children, that the accused is pregnant, financial information, and the fact that the accused was previously punished under Article 15 for the same or similar misconduct. RCM 1001(c)(1)(B). Retirement-eligible accused, and those on the verge of retirement, may present evidence that a discharge or dismissal would deprive them of significant retirement benefits.[17] Further, the accused may testify under oath, subject to cross-examination, or offer an unsworn statement, which may not be cross-examined. RCM 1001(c)(2).

After the presentation of any rebuttal evidence and the final arguments by counsel, the sentencing judge or panel, as applicable, leaves the courtroom to determine the appropriate sentence. If a panel is sentencing the accused they vote on the proper punishment, which may include no punishment at all. Subject to the maximum punishments permitted by the level of court-martial and specific UCMJ article, authorized punishments include: a reprimand, forfeiture of pay and allowances, a monetary fine, reduction in grade for enlisted personnel, restriction, hard labor without confinement, incarceration, dismissal for an officer, and either a dishonorable or a bad conduct discharge for enlisted personnel. RCM 1003. A limited number of crimes authorize imposition of the death penalty. The sentence is determined by a two-thirds vote of the panel. A sentence of more than ten years requires agreement of three-quarters of the panel, and the death penalty requires a unanimous vote. RCM 1006(d)(4).

Pursuant to Article 58a, UCMJ, as soon as the convening authority approves any sentence of an enlisted person that includes a punitive discharge, confinement, or hard labor without confinement, the enlisted person is automatically reduced to the lowest enlisted rank. Retired enlisted servicemembers may not be reduced in rank either by operation of Article 58a or as part of a sentence.[18] Unlike active-duty enlisted personnel, officers, warrant officers, cadets, and midshipmen cannot be reduced in rank. RCM 1003(c)(2)(A)(i). However, in times of war or national emergency, a dismissal may be commuted to service in the enlisted ranks. Id.

In the sea services, an appropriate punishment for officers includes "loss of numbers, lineal position, or seniority." RCM 1003(b)(4). Accordingly, in cases in which officers are not dismissed, they may suffer a loss of position or seniority within their rank, which will affect their date of eligibility for future promotions. Such a sentence was imposed on Capt. Charles McVay III of the heavy cruiser USS *Indianapolis,* which was sunk by a Japanese submarine at the end of World War II and is remembered largely for the number of shark attacks on its crew as they struggled to survive for five days in the water. Convicted of hazarding his vessel by failing to steer a zigzag course, a navy court-martial sentenced McVay to lose one hundred numbers each in his temporary rank of captain and his permanent rank of commander.[19]

After sentencing, the accused's first avenue of relief is with the convening authority, who may disapprove findings of guilt and dismiss the charges, order a rehearing, or reduce the severity of the sentence. RCM 1107. The accused may submit virtually anything that may affect the convening authority's decision including recommendations for clemency from the panel members. RCM 1105. Additionally, the convening authority may approve the sentence but suspend execution of all or part of it, effectively placing the accused on a form of probation. RCM 1108.

A court-martial conviction is automatically submitted for review to a court of criminal appeals from the accused's branch of service, if the sentence includes death, dismissal, a dishonorable or bad conduct discharge, or confinement of at least one year. RCM 1201(a). These courts are composed of senior military lawyers, who may review both the factual and legal basis for the conviction. Servicemembers receive the services of a detailed military appellate lawyer free of cost or may hire a civilian attorney at no expense to the United States. Less severe sentences from general court-martial convictions will be reviewed by the Office of the Judge Advocate General, which may throw out or reduce the findings of guilt and/or the sentence. RCM 1201(b).

If unsuccessful the accused may then seek review by the U.S. Court of Appeals for the Armed Forces, again with the assistance of a detailed military attorney. This court is made up of five civilian judges but does not possess the fact-finding authority of the courts of criminal appeals. The CAAF may accept review of a case if two judges vote to do so, but it must accept review in death penalty cases and cases in which a service's top military lawyer presents an issue to the court. Finally, the accused may ask the U.S. Supreme Court to review the conviction, but such review is rare.

The procedure differs in "capital" cases, those in which the accused may be sentenced to death. The accused cannot plead guilty, cannot be tried by a judge alone, and cannot waive any appeal rights. RCM 903(a)(2); 910(a)(1); 1110. Further, before an accused may be sentenced to death four requirements must be satisfied. First, the entire panel must agree that the accused is guilty. Art. 52, UCMJ; RCM 1004(a)(2). Second, the panel must unanimously find the existence of at least one "aggravating factor," such as the offense was committed in the enemy's presence, national security was endangered, or that a murder was committed for money or while participating in a robbery, rape, or mutiny. RCM 1004(b)(4) and (c). Third, all panel members must agree that any positive circumstances (extenuation and mitigation) are outweighed by the negative (aggravating) aspects of the crime. RCM 1004(b)(4). Finally, the entire panel must vote for the death penalty. RCM 1006(d)(4).

The military, which uses lethal injection to execute its servicemembers, presently has seven enlisted men on death row, including four soldiers, two marines, and one airman.[20] The last military execution occurred in 1961, when Pvt. John Bennet was hanged for the rape and attempted murder of a young girl.[21] In 1996, the Supreme Court ruled that the military's system of capital punishment was constitutional, but four of the nine judges queried whether a servicemember could be put to death by the military for a crime having no military connection.[22] That question remains unanswered.

Historical Illustration:
The Court-Martial of Billy Mitchell

Although the court-martial system has changed considerably since Mitchell's day, his trial serves as an interesting illustration of how the process works. In 1925 airpower advocate Brig. Gen. William "Billy" Mitchell was prosecuted for conduct that was service discrediting and prejudicial to good order and discipline because he publicly denounced the army and navy's handling of the development of military aviation, accusing the services of incompetency, treason, and criminal negligence. Sitting in judgment of Mitchell were the highest-ranking military members ever assembled for an American military trial—including Brig. Gen. Douglas MacArthur—and the court-martial was personally convened by no less than the president of the United States, Calvin Coolidge.[23]

Mitchell was represented by both civilian and military attorneys, including civilian attorney Frank Reid, a sitting member of Congress, and Col. Herbert White, the detailed military defense counsel.[24] The Mitchell defense team successfully challenged three of the twelve court members for prior statements indicating a bias against the accused.[25] After an unsuccessful defense motion to dismiss the charges, both sides presented their witnesses and evidence. Defense witnesses included World War I ace Eddie Rickenbacker, Congressman (later mayor of New York City) Fiorello La Guardia, and future air force giants Maj. Carl Spaatz and Maj. Hap Arnold.[26] Unfortunately, the story did not have a happy ending. Mitchell was convicted of all charges and specifications and sentenced to suspension from the service for five years.[27] The lone vote for acquittal was that of MacArthur, who also persuaded the other members not to dismiss Mitchell.[28]

Plea Agreements

After having an opportunity to examine the government's evidence, an accused may seek to enter into a plea agreement to limit the possible punishment. A plea agreement is essentially a contract between the government and the accused in which the accused agrees to plead guilty to one or more crimes in exchange for some benefit, such as a particular sentence, withdrawal of other charges, or referral to a lower level of court-martial. RCM 705(b)(2). Such agreements are common in both the military and civilian systems.

The plea agreement procedure is particularly beneficial to the military accused. Acting through a defense counsel, the accused reaches an agreement with the government, which must be approved by the convening authority. RCM 705(c)(3). This agreement is usually negotiated with the assigned trial counsel and places a limitation on the maximum sentence that the accused may receive. After capping the sentence, the accused enters a plea of guilty to some, all, or alternate charges, and proceeds to a sentencing hearing in which the sentencing authority (either a judge or a panel) is unaware of the terms of the plea agreement. The sentencing authority renders a specific sentence which is then compared to the plea agreement; the *lower* sentence is the actual sentence imposed. In effect, the accused gets two bites at the sentencing apple.

In addition to requiring the accused to plead guilty to certain charges, the government may also require additional concessions as part of the plea agreement. The prosecution may require the accused to agree to the existence of certain facts, cooperate and testify against another accused, agree to specific conditions of probation, pay a certain amount of money to any victims, waive an Article 32 investigation, be sentenced by a panel rather than by a judge alone (or vice versa), and waive the personal appearance of certain sentencing witnesses. RCM 705(c)(2). Provisions requiring the accused to pay a fine or to waive an administrative separation board if not sentenced to a discharge are permissible.[29] In *United States v. Davis*,[30] a marine sergeant's unusual plea agreement requiring him to plead not guilty but to agree to a stipulation of facts amounting to a confession and to waive the right to present evidence in his defense in exchange for a sentence limitation was permitted.

However, the government's ability to impose terms upon an accused is not without limitations. Any term not freely and voluntarily agreed to is unenforceable. RCM 705(c)(1)(A). An accused cannot be made to agree to a blanket waiver of all motions.[31] Further, an accused cannot waive certain rights, such as the right to counsel, due process, attacks upon the court's jurisdiction, a speedy trial, complete sentencing, and appeal. RCM 705(c)(1)(B).

Effect of a Court-Martial Conviction in the Civilian Sector

The effects of a court-martial conviction are not limited to the accused's relationship with the armed forces or the entitlement to veteran's benefits. For instance, some civilian criminal statutes require a prior felony conviction as part of the substantive criminal offense. Court-martial convictions may serve as the requisite predicate offense. As a further example of the impact of a military conviction in the civilian world, in the federal system section 922(g) of title 10, United States Code, makes it a crime for a convicted felon to possess a firearm. In *United States v. McDonald*,[32] the United States Court of Appeals for the Ninth Circuit determined that a forty-year-old army court-martial conviction for "fraudulent enlistment, failure to obey a lawful order, and sale of a 'liberty' pass" was a sufficient prior felony conviction to support the felon-in-possession charge.

Unlike the military, the federal court system determines a defendant's sentence through the use of sentencing guidelines. The sentence is determined on a point system, assigning points for the type of offense and then adding or subtracting points based on various aggravating or mitigating circumstances. A defendant with a prior history of brushes with the law is placed in certain criminal history categories; the higher the category, the greater the potential sentence. In calculating a defendant's criminal history category the federal guidelines include convictions imposed by general and special courts-martial; summary court-martial convictions and the results of nonjudicial punishment are excluded.[33]

On the flip side, for years the federal courts debated whether a positive military record should justify a reduction in a defendant's sentence. In 1991, the federal sentencing guidelines specifically resolved that issue against former members of the armed forces. Currently, a servicemember's favorable military record is "not ordinarily relevant in determining whether a sentence should be outside the applicable guideline range."[34]

Clearly, a court-martial conviction will have a significant impact on the accused's postmilitary rights and opportunities. The decision to subject a servicemember to the court-martial process should not be made lightly.

7

Military Crimes

The Uniform Code of Military Justice regulates a much broader spectrum of conduct than does civilian criminal law; as a result, it may at times seem a bit heavy-handed. In the civilian sector, there is no criminal sanction for missing work; in the military a servicemember can be prosecuted for being absent without leave. Similarly, the UCMJ contains other punitive articles punishing conduct not considered criminal elsewhere, such as using foul language (Article 134, Indecent Language), having an intimate relationship with an employee who works for you (Article 134, Fraternization), and failing to behave as an officer and gentleman (Article 133).

A comprehensive examination of all military crimes is beyond the scope of this book. However, several punitive articles addressing uniquely military offenses are topical, commonly encountered, or simply interesting and warrant some explanation.

Disobeying Orders

Obedience to orders is essential to the efficient operation of the armed forces. While the military preserves democracy, it does not always practice it. More often than not, leaders possess neither the time nor inclination to debate the wisdom of their orders. Disobedience may be punished pursuant to Article 90(2), Disobeying a Superior Commissioned Officer; Article 91(2), Disobeying a Warrant, Noncommissioned, or Petty Officer; and Article 92, Failure to Obey Order or Regulation.

Unless "palpably illegal on its face," military orders are presumed to be legal and servicemembers disobey an order at their peril.[1] Generally, to be a legal order, it "must relate to those activities which are reasonably necessary to safeguard and protect morale, discipline, and usefulness of members of the command and directly connected with the maintenance of good order in the service."[2] In short, the order must possess a legitimate military purpose. The military courts have upheld the legality of a wide variety of orders. Servicemembers have been convicted for disobeying orders to wear United Nations insignia,[3] not to consume alcohol,[4] to give blood samples for a DNA registry,[5] to wear a condom and notify sexual partners of HIV positive status,[6] and to present a military identification card.[7]

Albeit rare, orders that are "palpably" or obviously illegal enjoy no presumption of legitimacy and must be disobeyed. The modern standard is whether a person "of ordinary sense and understanding would know it to be illegal."[8] In the most famous case involving an unsuccessful obedience to orders defense, Lt. William Calley was convicted of the premeditated murder of twenty-two civilians from the village of My Lai, Republic of South Vietnam.[9]

A lesser-known case predating *Calley* in which a soldier was convicted under this standard bears repeating. In *United States v. Griffen,* an infantry platoon of the 1st Cavalry Division captured a Vietcong soldier and was unable to evacuate him to the rear. The accused, S. Sgt. Walter Griffen, overheard a radio transmission in which the company commander ordered the prisoner to be killed. Griffen's platoon leader in turn ordered the accused to "take him down the hill and shoot him."[10] Griffen and another soldier marched the Vietcong prisoner, whose hands were bound behind his back, to an embankment, where they shot him to death.

At trial, Griffen claimed that he was merely following orders, which he believed to be legal. Griffen explained that he had received a direct order from his platoon leader and that the security of the unit would have been jeopardized by keeping the prisoner because they were in a hostile area and under Vietcong observation.[11] The army appellate court upheld Griffen's court-martial conviction, characterizing the platoon leader's order as obviously illegal on its face and stated, "It is difficult to conceive of a military situation in which the order of a superior would be more patently wrong."[12]

To be legally enforceable, an order must be a positive command or demand, "a communication, delivered orally, or in writing, or by signal, which *tells* the service person receiving the order what to do or what not to do."[13] Merely offering advice or expressing a wish or desire is not an order.[14] However, the legality of an order is not diminished merely because it is proceeded by "please" or stated in a friendly, polite, or diplomatic manner.[15]

The timing for compliance with the order determines whether it has been disobeyed. When obedience to an order requires immediate compliance, the order is disobeyed if the accused either expresses an intention not to obey or if the accused fails to make any effort to immediately execute the order. MCM, Part IV, ¶ 14c(2)(g). For example, an order to "stop and come back here" is a positive command requiring immediate obedience.[16] If the order does not expressly or implicitly indicate when compliance is required, a reasonable delay in carrying out the order is acceptable. Id.

Disrespect and Insubordination

Disrespectful conduct serves as a direct challenge to military authority and, if left unchecked, will undermine the unit's morale and discipline. Article 89 punishes anyone who behaves in a disrespectful manner to a superior commissioned officer in either the officer's official or personal capacity. Although comments made in a private conversation are not normally prosecuted, the officer need not be present for the article to be violated; and truth is not a defense. MCM, ¶¶ 13c(3) and (4).

To illustrate, in *United States v. Claytor,* a seaman on the USS *Midway* remarked to a petty officer that the seaman thought their division chief "could act like an asshole sometimes."[17] Although the division chief was not present and the division chief may indeed have been a difficult supervisor to work for, Claytor was convicted of disrespect.

In addition to statements, certain acts may constitute disrespect. As examples, the manual "includes neglecting the customary salute, or showing a marked disdain, indifference, insolence, impertinence, undue familiarity, or other rudeness in the presence of the superior officer." MCM, ¶ 13c(3). In *United States v. Ferenczi,* the Court of Military Appeals upheld the disrespect conviction of a soldier "for contemptuously turning from and leaving the presence of the [officer] while said officer was talking to him."[18]

Generally, to determine if the victim is a superior commissioned officer of the accused, the law looks at the relationship between the two in terms of grade, command, and, if in different armed forces, position in the chain of command. MCM, ¶¶ 13c(1)(a) and (b). A higher-ranking officer who is inferior in command may not qualify as a superior commissioned officer for purposes of this article. MCM, ¶ 31c(1)(a).

Article 91 is similar to Article 89 except that it protects warrant officers, noncommissioned officers, and petty officers from disrespect, rather than commissioned officers. Both articles require knowledge of the victim's status. MCM, ¶¶ 13c(1)(2) and 15c(2). However, unlike Article 89, here the disrespect must be within sight or hearing of the victim. MCM, ¶ 15c(5).

Dereliction of Duty

In June 1994 a B-52 at Fairchild Air Force Base crashed, due to the unsafe flying of a pilot with a reputation for reckless and daredevil antics. The colonel commanding the group was court-martialed, and convicted, of dereliction of duty for allowing the pilot to fly after receiving information that he was reckless and for failing to inquire into the pilot's reckless reputation.[19]

The charge of dereliction in the performance of duties is contained in Article 92(3). To obtain a conviction, the trial counsel (prosecutor) must establish three elements: (1) the existence of a duty, (2) knowledge of the duty, and (3) the failure to perform the duty through willfulness, neglect, or culpable inefficiency.

The potential sources of a duty are many and proving one at trial is not difficult. The UCMJ provides that a "duty may be imposed by treaty, statute, regulation, lawful order, standard operating procedure, or custom of the service." MCM, ¶ 16c(3)(a). A medical standard of care may serve as the basis for a "duty."[20]

Dereliction requires that the act or omission be performed either willfully, negligently, or by culpable inefficiency. Willfulness means intentional and purposeful conduct. MCM, ¶ 16c(3)(c). For example, a member of a flag detail who blew his nose on the American flag was convicted of being willfully derelict in his duty to protect the flag.[21]

Negligence refers to conduct falling short of what one would expect of a reasonably prudent person in similar circumstances. In *United States v. Lawson,* a marine lieutenant was convicted of being negligently derelict in his duties for failing to post road guides in pairs and failing to maintain a roster of guides.[22] Because the marines were engaged in night movements as part of a desert field exercise, Lawson's command had stressed strict accountability and use of the buddy system for the guides. Lawson failed to post several marines in pairs and neglected to maintain the required roster. As a result, one of the marine guides was forgotten for over forty hours and eventually died of exposure.[23]

The manual defines culpable inefficiency as "inefficiency for which there is no reasonable or just excuse." MCM ¶ 16c(3)(c). Previously, the term was associated with faulty performance of duty, rather than nonperformance; however, the courts have appeared to blur any distinction between this term and negligent dereliction of duty.[24]

Ineptitude is a valid defense to a dereliction of duty charge. MCM, ¶ 16(c). Generally, an ineptitude defense is a fact specific inquiry into the accused's *ability* to accomplish the duty, taking into consideration the servicemember's level of training and circumstances under which the duty is to be performed.[25] As an illustration of cognizable ineptitude, the manual offers the situation of a recruit who fails to qualify on the rifle range despite his best efforts. MCM, ¶ 16c(3)(d). Other examples include the squad leader who gets his squad lost on maneuvers despite diligent efforts to maintain the proper direction, and the battery commander who earnestly attempts to train his battery well but it nonetheless fails a live-fire evaluation.[26]

Unauthorized Absences

On January 31, 1945, a twelve-man army firing squad executed Pvt. Eddie D. Slovik. With that rifle volley, Slovik acquired the dubious—and no doubt undesired—distinction of being the first and last American executed for desertion since the Civil War.[27] Slovik's execution reflected the army's frustration at its inability to stem the flood of deserters during World War II.[28]

In 1979, the General Accounting Office (GAO) completed a comprehensive study of the AWOL problem confronting all branches of the post-Vietnam military. The GAO found over 608,000 AWOLs exceeding twenty-four hours in length during a four-year period, resulting in a projected cost to the United States in excess of a billion dollars.[29] AWOL was "the most frequently committed crime in the military," which threatened to significantly undermine military effectiveness.[30]

Three articles are available to punish unauthorized absences: Article 85 (Desertion), Article 86 (AWOL), and Article 87 (Missing Movement). Servicemembers are AWOL if they fail to go to, or improperly leave, their appointed place of duty, unit, or organization at a time when they are required to be there. MCM, ¶ 86a. The punishment for AWOL increases with the length of the absence, when the absence is terminated by apprehension rather than voluntary surrender or when the servicemember has left a particular type of duty (guard duty, watch, etc.) or departed with the intent to miss a maneuver or field exercise. MCM, ¶ 10c(4). Servicemembers who are properly on leave, pass, or liberty are not AWOL merely because they fail to follow the proper signing out procedures, exceed certain geographic limitations, or are unable to return through no fault of their own.[31]

Desertion is an AWOL coupled with an intention either to remain away permanently, to avoid hazardous duty, or to shirk important service. MCM, ¶ 85a. The accused's intent—not the length of time in an AWOL status— is the key factor in determining if a servicemember is a deserter. The court determines the existence of a hazardous duty or important service on a case-by-case basis, depending upon the specific circumstances. Military actions taken in response to war or national emergency are likely to be considered important service. The manual provides that "such services as drill, target practice, maneuvers, and practice marches are not ordinarily 'hazardous duty or important service.'" MCM, ¶ 9c(2)(a). A servicemember may be convicted of desertion even if the unit did not actually depart to engage in hazardous duty or important service.[32] Further, the accused's moral and ethical concerns about the appropriateness of the duty or service is not a defense.[33]

Missing movement is a form of AWOL in which the servicemember, either deliberately or through neglect, misses a military movement involving a particular ship, aircraft, or unit. MCM, ¶ 87a. Unlike desertion, a missing movement conviction requires that the movement actually occurred.[34] The physical inability to make the movement is a defense to the charge.[35]

Contempt toward Officials

Article 88 prohibits a commissioned officer from using "contemptuous words against the President, the Vice President, Congress, the Secretary of Defense, the Secretary of a military department, the Secretary of Transportation, or the Governor or legislature of any State, Territory, Commonwealth, or possession in which he is on duty or present." This prohibition can be traced to the British Articles of War of 1765, which prohibited "the use of 'traitorous or disrespectful words against the Sacred Person of his Majesty or any of the Royal Family.'"[36] It first appeared in its Americanized version in the code of 1776, prohibiting "traitorous or disrespectful words against the authority of the United States in Congress assembled . . . or the Legislature of any of the United States in which he may be quartered."[37]

In his classic treatise of military law, *Military Law and Precedents,* Colonel Winthrop noted that earlier courts-martial under Article 88's predecessor, Article 19 of the Articles of War, had been of a political nature, most prosecutions arising as a result of comments aimed at President Lincoln during the Civil War. Prosecutions based upon contemptuous comments against Congress, the vice president, or a state governor were almost nonexistent.[38]

In *United States v. Howe,* a second lieutenant at Fort Bliss, Texas, was convicted of Article 88 after carrying a sign during an anti–Vietnam War protest which read "Let's Have More than a Choice Between Petty Ignorant Fascists in 1968" on one side and "End Johnson's Fascist Aggression in Viet Nam" on the other.[39] In upholding the conviction, the court of review held that Article 88 did not violate Howe's constitutional right to free speech, was not too vague to be unenforceable, and explained that the Article's purpose was to avoid "the impairment of discipline and the promotion of insubordination."[40]

To obtain a conviction the government must prove that the accused was a commissioned officer; used contemptuous words against an enumerated official or legislature which became known to someone else; or, if the object of the contempt was a governor or legislature, acted while in that governor or legislature's state, territory, possession, and so on. MCM, ¶ 88b. The official or legislature must be in office at the time of the offense, and the article does not apply to comments about individual members of a legislature or a lieutenant governor. MCM, ¶ 88c.

The manual provides that opinions expressed during private conversations "should not ordinarily be charged," and that the article does not apply to opinions expressed during political discussions so long as the opinion is not "personally contemptuous." MCM, ¶ 88c. Truth is not a defense. MCM, ¶ 88c. The maximum punishment is dismissal, total forfeitures, and confinement for one year. MCM. ¶ 88e.

Mutiny

The term "mutiny" conjures up images of an unruly mob of sailors seizing the HMS *Bounty* from Captain Bligh or relieving Captain Queeg of command in Herman Wouk's novel *The Caine Mutiny*. Ironically, the majority of reported cases of mutiny have been from the army, rather than the navy, and have generally involved military inmates. Further, there has never been a successful mutiny aboard a United States warship.[41]

The two largest mutiny cases were not precipitated by harsh conditions at sea; rather, they grew out of racially motivated disparate treatment of African American servicemen. During World War I, African American soldiers of the Twenty-Fourth Infantry Regiment rioted in Houston, Texas, after being provoked by local, white civilians, resulting in seventeen white civilians and two black soldiers being killed. Fifty-four soldiers were court-martialed and convicted of murder and mutiny; thirteen were hanged and the remainder imprisoned.[42]

In 1944, the navy used untrained African American seamen to load ammunition onto Liberty ships at Port Chicago, near San Francisco. After an explosion that killed 320 men, over 200 African American sailors refused to continue loading the ammunition, citing unsafe conditions. Fifty of the sailors were then court-martialed and convicted of mutiny, receiving sentences of between eight to fifteen years.[43]

The most recent military case involving a mutiny occurred at the United States Disciplinary Barracks (USDB), Fort Leavenworth, Kansas. In May 1992, a group of disgruntled prisoners refused to obey the evening lockdown order, built barricades, and ransacked portions of the cell block.[44] One of the ringleaders, José Sanchez, was convicted of mutiny for failing to obey the orders of the USDB commander and for organizing other inmates to join Sanchez in defying the order.[45]

Article 94(a) prohibits two forms of mutiny: (1) "by creating violence or disturbance" and (2) "by refusing to obey orders or perform duty." Both types require that the accused act "with intent to usurp or override lawful military authority." MCM, ¶ 18b(1)(b) and (2)(c). The mere intent to defy or invoke military authority is insufficient.[46] The requisite intent "may be declared in words or inferred from acts, omissions, or surrounding circumstances." MCM, ¶ 18c(1)(b).

The second form of mutiny is a form of conspiracy requiring that the accused act together with at least one other person; the mutineers must share a common purpose.[47] The misconduct need not be violent or planned; it may be a passive refusal to obey orders or perform assigned duties. MCM, ¶ 18c(1)(b).

Historically, mutiny has been viewed "as the gravest and most criminal of the offenses known to the military code."[48] Under the UCMJ, mutiny may be punished by death or any lesser form of punishment that the court-martial directs. The potential for the death penalty reflects the seriousness with which the military views this crime.

Misbehavior before the Enemy

Historically, misbehavior referred to not only cowardice but also any conduct "not conformable to the standard of behavior before the enemy set by the history of our arms."[49] Article 99 sets out nine categories of misconduct that are punishable when accomplished "before or in the presence of the enemy." MCM, ¶ 23(a). The nine categories are: (1) running away; (2) failing to properly defend a command, place, unit, or property; (3) endangering the safety of a command, unit, place, or property; (4) casting away weapons or ammunition; (5) cowardice; (6) leaving a place of duty to plunder or pillage; (7) false alarms; (8) avoiding enemy contact; and (9) failing to assist American or allied forces engaged in battle. MCM, ¶ 23a.

Military courts treat the terms "before" and "in the presence of" as being synonymous.[50] Generally, "if an organization is in position ready to participate in either an offensive or defensive battle, and, its weapons are capable of delivering fire on the enemy and in turn are so situated that they are within effective range of the enemy weapons, then that unit is before the enemy."[51]

For purposes of this article, "enemy" refers to any force engaged in combat against American forces, regardless of whether a formal declaration of war exists.[52] The term is broad enough to include not only an organized military force but any hostile body to include a "rebellious mob."[53] The April 1992 Los Angeles rioters would constitute the "enemy" for purposes of this article. A servicemember called out to suppress a riot, who throws away his weapon and runs away from the rioters, could be court-martialed for misbehavior before the enemy.

Subordinate Compelling Surrender

Article 100 provides that a servicemember may be put to death for compelling, or attempting to compel, a commander to surrender to the enemy. No reported cases exist to explain this article, but the manual does provide some guidance.

The offense is very similar to mutiny except that the specific object of the misconduct is to surrender to the enemy rather than the more generic purpose of overriding lawful military authority. MCM, ¶ 24c(1)(a). Further, concert of action is not required. Words alone are not enough to violate the article; the accused must take some affirmative step to effectuate a surrender. MCM, ¶ 24c(1)(c). Examples of such acts include the unauthorized lowering of the flag and sending an emissary with an offer to surrender. MCM, ¶ 24c(3)(a) and (b). Historically, the open refusal to participate in defensive measures has been construed as a means of compelling surrender.[54] Success is not a prerequisite for conviction. The article is still violated if the surrender effort fails, if the enemy does not receive the overture, or receives it and rejects it. MCM, ¶ 24c(3)(b).

The article takes into consideration the realities of battle. Lower-level leaders who determine that further resistance is pointless *and* who are unable to contact higher authority may surrender without committing a criminal offense. MCM, ¶ 24c(3)(b).

Aiding the Enemy

Article 104 provides:

> Any person who —
> (1) aids, or attempts to aid, the enemy with arms, ammunition, supplies, money or other things; or
> (2) without proper authority, knowingly harbors or protects or gives intelligence to or communicates or corresponds with or holds any intercourse with the enemy, either directly or indirectly; shall suffer death or such other punishment as a court-martial or military commission may direct. (MCM, ¶ 28a.)

The MCM defines the term "enemy" broadly to include not only organized military forces but also all citizens of a belligerent nation and any hostile force opposed by U.S. forces, including "a rebellious mob or a band of renegades." MCM, ¶¶ 23c(1)(b), 28c(2). As a general rule, it is not a defense that the accused aided the enemy in an effort to gain better treatment for others, but such motivations may be considered in determining the appropriate sentence.[55] The maximum permissible penalty for a violation of this article is death. MCM, ¶ 28e.

As an exception to the rule, military personnel may provide enemy POWs with basic subsistence items, for example, food, shelter, and medical aid. MCM, ¶ 28c(3). This exception reflects the obligations imposed on detaining powers under international law.

Following the Korean War, an army court-martial convicted Maj. Ronald Alley of communicating with the enemy while a POW and sentenced him to dismissal from the service, total forfeitures, and ten years at hard labor — the only officer in this century to be imprisoned for such an offense.[56] Captured in North Korea in December 1950, Alley spent more than two and a half years in captivity. Allegedly in an attempt to gain better treatment for the Americans, Alley prepared, and encouraged others to fill out, a questionnaire to give information to the Chinese.[57] Further, Alley provided information on American manuals, acted as a "monitor" at indoctrination sessions, openly advocated socialism and questioned American participation in the war, supplied pro-communist speeches and articles and encouraged other POWs to sign a "Peace Petition."[58]

The most recent case involving a charge of aiding the enemy is *United States v. Garwood*. Marine PFC Robert Garwood was captured by the Vietcong outside of Da Nang, Republic of South Vietnam, in September 1965 and returned to U.S. control in 1979 after contacting a United Nations delegate in a Hanoi hotel cocktail lounge.[59] Based on intelligence reports and information received from former POWs, the marines initiated an investigation of Garwood's activities, culminating in his court-martial.

Specifically, Garwood's misconduct included acting as an indoctrinator, interpreter, and group discussion leader during communist indoctrination sessions; informing on fellow POWs; serving as an armed guard; assaulting a fellow POW; and assisting in the interrogation of POWs.[60] The marine panel convicted Garwood of several charges, including "communication and holding intercourse with the enemy, in violation of Article 104," and sentenced Garwood to a dishonorable discharge, total forfeitures, and reduction in grade to private.[61]

Misconduct as a Prisoner

Congress enacted Article 105 in the wake of mistreatment of American prisoners of war by their fellow countrymen during World War II.[62] The article seeks to punish those prisoners who attempt to improve their own situation at the expense of other POWs and to preclude abuse of prisoners by those acting in positions of authority. MCM, ¶¶ 29c(3)(a) and (4)(b).

However, reflecting the widespread torture that American POWs have suffered in Korea and Vietnam, military officials have rarely used this article. Following the Korean War only four reported cases were prosecuted.[63] At the end of the Vietnam War, the services declined to prosecute any returning POWs for propaganda statements and related conduct, which was broadly defined.[64] Garwood, who returned to the United States six years later in 1979 during a different presidential administration, was the only returning Vietnam-era POW charged with violating Article 105; however, Garwood was convicted only of the lesser offense of assault upon a fellow American POW.[65]

Pursuant to Article 105, a servicemember may be sentenced to any punishment, except the death penalty, if while in the custody of enemy forces during time of war:

> (1) for the purpose of securing favorable treatment by his captors acts without authority in a manner contrary to law, custom, or regulation, to the detriment of others of whatever nationality held by the enemy as civilian or military prisoners; or
>
> (2) while in a position of authority over such persons maltreats them without justifiable cause. (MCM, ¶ 29a)

An attempt to escape from captivity that causes the enemy to punish remaining POWs is not a crime. MCM, ¶ 20 29c(3)(b). Indeed, the Code of Conduct requires an American POW to attempt escape.

Malingering

Article 115 punishes any servicemember "who for the purpose of avoiding work, duty, or service . . . (1) feigns illness, physical disablement, mental lapse or derangement; or (2) intentionally inflicts self-injury." MCM, ¶ 40a. The article covers conduct ranging from faking a stomach ache to avoid a physical training run to shooting yourself in the foot to avoid combat. To illustrate, in *United States v. Kersten,* an army sergeant was convicted of malingering after he persuaded another soldier to drop a rock on Kersten's foot so that he could miss a field exercise.[66]

Merely being prone to sickness or injury does not constitute malingering; the accused must fake an illness or intentionally cause an injury to himself. Failing to perform certain duties because of an inability to bear pain associated with an actual injury does not constitute malingering.[67] However, any act or omission that causes, prolongs, or aggravates an illness or injury may constitute malingering so long as the accused's purpose is to avoid work, duty, or service. In what must be considered the outer edge of the article's reach, an army sergeant was convicted of malingering after he attempted to hang himself in order to avoid his court-martial.[68]

Conduct Unbecoming an Officer and Gentleman

Officers have always been held to a higher standard of conduct than enlisted members of the services.[69] Reflecting that heightened standard, Article 133 criminalizes any acts or omissions that, under the particular circumstances, constitute conduct unbecoming an officer and gentleman. The offense targets only commissioned officers, including commissioned warrant officers, and cadets and midshipmen at the Military, Naval, Air Force, and Coast Guard Academies. MCM, ¶ 59a; UCMJ art. 1. The offense applies to both men and women. MCM, ¶ 59c(1). Possible punishment includes dismissal from the service, total forfeitures, and a period of confinement. MCM, ¶ 59e.

Conduct violative of this article may occur in either the officer's official or unofficial capacity, and must be of such severity that it dishonors and disgraces the officer, compromising that person's character or standing as an officer. MCM, ¶ 59c(2). The manual offers several examples of sanctionable conduct, including making false official statements, cheating on examinations, opening and reading someone else's mail, publicly associating with prostitutes, crimes of moral turpitude, and failing to financially support the officer's family. MCM, ¶ 59c(3).

Case law provides additional guidance of impermissible conduct. Such misconduct includes writing sexually lewd letters to a young schoolgirl,[70] adultery with an enlisted woman,[71] smoking pot with enlisted members,[72] publicly associating with a known drug smuggler,[73] soliciting someone to violate the law,[74] and writing over two hundred worthless checks.[75] Even purely private conduct may violate Article 133.[76]

Article 134: The General Article

Article 134 is the catch-all provision that criminalizes certain misconduct not specifically mentioned elsewhere in the Uniform Code of Military Justice. The article can be traced back to the Articles of the Earl of Essex in

1642, which provided: "All other faults, disorders and offenses, not mentioned in these Articles, shall be punished according to the general customs and laws of war."[77] In 1775 the Continental Congress adopted British Article of War twenty-three, which punished "all Disorders or Neglects . . . to the Prejudice of good Order and Military Discipline."[78]

The current version of Article 134 punishes "all disorders and neglects to the prejudice of good order and discipline in the armed forces, all conduct of a nature to bring discredit upon the armed forces, and crimes and offenses not capital." MCM, ¶ 60a. Not all misconduct is prejudicial to good order and discipline; the acts must be directly prejudicial. MCM, ¶ 60c(2)(a). Further, violation of a longstanding military custom may violate this portion of the article. MCM, ¶ 60c(2)(b). Examples of misconduct prosecuted under this clause of article 134 includes a chief petty officer cross-dressing in public view,[79] an army sergeant who exposed his buttocks ("mooned") to the wife of a fellow servicemember in a trailer park,[80] and a seaman who used shipboard phones to make unauthorized long-distance telephone calls.[81]

Article 134's second clause punishes conduct of a nature to bring discredit upon the armed forces. Misconduct satisfies this criteria if it "has a tendency to bring the service into disrepute or which tends to lower it in public esteem." MCM, ¶ 60c(3). For example, engaging in carnal copulation with a chicken has been held to be service discrediting,[82] whereas engaging in sexual intercourse on a public beach under circumstances where the act was unlikely to be seen by others is not service discrediting.[83]

In paragraphs 61–113 of the MCM, several specific offenses are listed that are prejudicial to good order and discipline or are service discrediting. Such offenses include: adultery, bribery and graft, making or uttering worthless checks, dishonorably failing to pay a debt, fraternization, gambling with subordinates, indecent language, straggling, and wearing unauthorized awards. MCM, ¶¶ 62, 66, 68, 71, 83, 84, 89, 107, 112.

Article 134's third clause permits a servicemember to be court-martialed for federal crimes and a limited number of state crimes by assimilating these offenses into the UCMJ. For example, under this article, in *United States v. Rayford* a soldier was convicted of using a telephone to facilitate a drug sale.[84] However, a legal rule called the preemption doctrine precludes the use of any state or federal statute if the same conduct is punished elsewhere in the UCMJ. MCM, ¶ 60(5)(a). Further, an offense punishable by death may not be prosecuted under Article 134. MCM, ¶ 60c(5)(b).

Unauthorized Awards

Napoleon is reputed to have once said that men will die for a bit of ribbon. While Napoleon's statement may be hyperbole, the tragic suicide of Adm. Jeremy "Mike" Boorda, Chief of Naval Operations, in response to allegations that he improperly wore two "V" devices[85] on Vietnam-era awards highlights the significance that the military community attaches to its awards system. Often the only recognition that members of the military receive for long periods of separation, hazardous duty, or the loss of life or limb is "a bit of ribbon."

Established by Gen. George Washington in 1782, the Purple Heart was America's first decoration for heroism in combat.[86] It was not until 1932, for the army, and 1943, for the navy and marines, that the Purple Heart was awarded exclusively to servicemembers wounded in action.[87]

In 1862 Congress authorized the second decoration to recognize gallantry in action: the Congressional Medal of Honor.[88] Originally, the medal was awarded freely; prior to World War I, 2,625 had been awarded.[89] During the Civil War, the army awarded George Custer's younger brother, Thomas, two Medals of Honor within a four-day period for capturing Confederate battle flags.[90] A veteran of several Civil War battles, Dr. Mary Walker, the only woman to ever receive the Medal of Honor, was presented the medal in 1866 in recognition of her wartime service.[91]

Gradually, the types of medals awarded to military members began to proliferate. During World War I, the Distinguished Service Cross, the Navy Cross, and the Silver Star were created to recognize heroism not justifying an award of the Medal of Honor.[92] The Distinguished Flying Cross — first awarded to Capt. Charles Lindbergh — appeared in 1926 and World War II saw the creation of the Bronze Star and Air Medal.[93]

Reflecting the importance that the armed forces puts on its decorations, Article 134(113) criminalizes the wearing of unauthorized awards. To obtain a conviction, the United States must prove that the accused wrongfully wore an unauthorized award on his uniform or civilian clothing under such circumstances that the misconduct was prejudicial to the military's good order and discipline or service discrediting. MCM, ¶ 113b. An unauthorized award may include "insignia, decoration, badge, ribbon, device, or lapel button." MCM, ¶ 113b(1). A servicemember convicted of this offense may be sentenced to a bad conduct discharge, total forfeitures, and six months confinement. MCM, ¶ 113e.

8

Substantive Crimes

Like its civilian counterparts, the Uniform Code of Military Justice contains offenses punishing crimes against people and property. In addition to these commonplace crimes, the UCMJ contains certain offenses which, if not unique to the military, are certainly unusual. While a comprehensive discussion of all such crimes is beyond the scope of this book, a representative slice of those offenses are provided, emphasizing the military idiosyncracies when applicable.

Sex Crimes

Like any other criminal system, the military punishes certain types of sexual crimes, such as rape, statutory rape, and indecent assaults. Unlike other criminal systems, however, the military penalizes various social and sexual relationships — even consensual ones — that often have no civilian analogue. Adultery and fraternization are two notable examples. These differences reflect the military justice system's primary focus on the maintenance of good order and discipline, rather than as a pure system of criminal law.

Although frequently challenged as draconian or archaic, the punitive articles criminalizing improper sexual relationships are justifiable in light of the military's unique mission, the unusual demands placed on military personnel, and the higher standards of conduct that this country has expected of its military leadership. For example, adultery frequently involves some amount of deceit, the violation of a marital oath by at least one participant with knowledge of the violation by the other, and casts doubt on the judgment and integrity of the participants.

No one can seriously argue that adulterous conduct or fraternization is compatible with an officer's or NCO's obligation to lead by personal example. When either offense becomes public or the subject of rumors, they detract from a military leader's stature with subordinates, compromising the ability to lead. Adulterous conduct is particularly egregious when one of the participants is married to another servicemember. In the relatively tight-knit communities found on military bases, such misconduct inevitably becomes known to others, causing morale problems among a force that frequently faces deployments away from their families for extended periods of time. In a profession in which lives, property, and indeed the security of the nation depend upon such intangible factors as morale, unit cohesion, and discipline, such misconduct cannot be dismissed lightly.

Through its justice system, the military is able to legally impose, and enforce, higher standards of personal conduct on its members than is seen in the civilian sector. Further, rather than merely tolerating the criminal enforcement of the military's elevated moral precepts, the nation's highest civilian court has staunchly defended them. In upholding the convictions of an army officer, who insulted Special Forces soldiers and encouraged various enlisted men to oppose the Vietnam War, for conduct unbecoming and prejudicial to good order and discipline, Supreme Court Justice Harry Blackmun defended the military's strict standards of acceptable behavior stating: "In military life there is a higher code termed honor, which holds its society to stricter accountability; and it is not desirable that the standard of the Army shall come down to the requirements of a [civilian] criminal code."[1]

To the extent a weakness exists in the military justice system, it is the lack of real, or at least perceived, uniformity in the enforcement of these punitive laws. With some measure of legitimacy, critics have pointed to the disparity of enforcement between the upper and lower ranks.[2] In 1997, the air force preferred fraternization charges against a lieutenant for dating a female airman he later married, despite having 461 officer-enlisted married couples on active duty.[3] On the eve of his court-martial, former sergeant major of the army Gene McKinney alleged that twenty-three senior soldiers, including ten general officers, were accused of similar misconduct but were not prosecuted.[4] Further, sexual misconduct by servicemembers on liberty at a foreign port or border town, or serving unaccompanied tours of duty on such far-flung outposts as Korea or Okinawa, are not viewed with the same critical eye as similar misconduct committed in the United States.[5]

Obviously the facts of each case are different and not all sexual misconduct finds its way to trial. Regardless of the system's shortcomings, real and perceived, the UCMJ's punitive articles criminalizing sexual misconduct are frequently prosecuted and deserve some discussion.

Rape

Largely recognized as a crime of violence rather than one of passion, rape is punishable under Article 120a. To achieve a conviction the prosecution must prove that the accused had sexual intercourse with another person "by force and without consent." MCM, ¶ 45a(a). The slightest amount of sexual penetration is all that the law requires. MCM, ¶ 45a(c).

Article 120a is gender neutral which means than a woman can also be convicted of raping a man. Further, in 1992 the UCMJ was amended to make Article 120a a marital rape offense, eliminating the requirement that the victim not be the accused's wife or husband. Accordingly, an accused may now be convicted of rape for nonconsensual sexual intercourse with his or her spouse.

The "by force and without consent" portion of a rape charge is frequently the most contested part of a rape charge. The amount of force required to constitute rape varies with the circumstances. In cases where the victim is unable to resist, resistance is futile, or the accused has threatened the victim into acquiescing, the mere force required to achieve penetration is sufficient. MCM, ¶ 45c(1)(b). In military law this is known as the doctrine of "constructive" force, which has been extended to "the unique situation of dominance and control presented by [the rapist's] superior rank and position."[6] This doctrine contributed to the rape convictions of Drill Sgt. Delmar Simpson of the army during the recent Aberdeen court-martials. The military judge in that case determined that drill sergeants wield so much power over trainees that no threat of harm or display of weapons need be shown to establish the force component of a rape charge.[7]

The victim's lack of consent does not require evidence of physical resistance; the victim can indicate unwillingness in other ways, including requests for the accused to stop coupled with limited physical gestures such as turning the victim's face away when the accused seeks a kiss.[8] However, in a particularly controversial ruling the army's appellate court overturned a rape conviction because the victim did not make her lack of consent known, despite her repeated efforts to stop the accused's sexual advances. In *United States v. Pierce,* the army court reasoned that the accused — characterized as "more persistent than forceful" — could have reasonably believed that the victim was giving in because, after multiple requests that he stop, the victim returned the accused's French kiss in the hopes that he would then leave her alone and she failed to call for help when an NCO knocked on her barracks door.[9] At the time the accused had locked the victim's door, pulled down the victim's sweatpants against her will, and was laying on top of her.

The victim must consent not only to the act of intercourse but also consent to sex with a particular person. In *United States v. Traylor,* a male soldier engaging in vaginal intercourse from the rear with the victim was replaced by the accused, without the victim's knowledge or consent.[10] Traylor was subsequently convicted of rape because the woman never consented to having sex with him.

As a matter of law, some victims are incapable of giving their consent. For example, it is considered rape when the accused engages in sexual intercourse with someone lacking mental or physical faculties, such as a sleeping, unconscious, or heavily intoxicated person, or the mentally handicapped. MCM, ¶ 45c(1)(b).[11] The Manual for Courts-Martial specifically notes that a young child is legally incapable of consent. MCM, ¶ 45c(1)(b).

One of the strangest cases to come out of this area asked whether an accused could be convicted of attempted rape when the victim, unknown to the accused, was dead. In *United States v. Thomas,* three sailors met a woman at a bar who subsequently passed out while dancing with them.[12] The three volunteered to take the woman home, but they instead decided to take advantage of her unconscious state and engaged in sexual intercourse with her in their car. Unknown to the three, the woman had not passed out but had actually died in the bar of a heart-related illness.[13] The court upheld Thomas's attempted rape conviction, ruling that rape required a live victim but attempted rape did not.[14]

Depending on the specific facts of the case, various UCMJ articles are available to prosecute sexual misconduct falling short of rape. Article 134 punishes an assault with the intention of committing a rape and indecent assaults. Article 128 covers the more generic assault charges and Article 80 would be used to prosecute an attempted rape. To illustrate, a naked soldier who attempted to pull the pants off a sleeping female soldier was convicted of assault with intent to commit rape, and an NCO who grabbed a female airman from behind and rubbed his groin against her buttocks was convicted of indecent assault.[15]

Carnal Knowledge

Known as "statutory rape" in the civilian legal community and as the "jail bait" offense in the barracks, carnal knowledge criminalizes consensual intercourse with a person under the age of sixteen, pursuant to Article 120(b). Like rape, carnal knowledge is a gender-neutral offense, meaning that both male and female servicemembers may be convicted. To obtain a conviction, the prosecution need only prove sexual intercourse with (1) someone who is not the accused's spouse and (2) someone under sixteen years old. MCM, ¶ 45(b)(2).

An increasing number of defenses may be raised against a carnal knowledge charge. First, Article 120(b) does not prohibit intercourse with an underage spouse. Additionally, in 1996 the UCMJ was amended to permit a mistake of fact defense. Now, as long as the victim was at least twelve years old, the accused can defend against a carnal knowledge charge by presenting evidence that the accused reasonably believed the minor was at least sixteen.[16] The defense may offer evidence that the victim looked older, possessed false identification, and engaged in conduct normally associated with an adult, such as smoking, drinking, hanging out in a bar, or driving an automobile. However, if the victim is less than twelve, carnal knowledge remains a "strict liability" offense. This means that all the court is concerned about is whether the accused had sex with the minor; a mistake as to the minor's age is no defense.

Military law recognizes a mistake of spouse or mistaken identity defense. In *United States v. Adams,* an army sergeant pled guilty to carnal knowledge after engaging in sexual intercourse with his underage niece.[17] Adams challenged his conviction based on his mistaken belief that he thought he was having sexual intercourse with his wife rather than his niece, who had climbed into bed with the accused in a dark bedroom and initiated the sexual relations. Adams admitted that he noticed "there was something peculiar about his 'wife's' body structure and hair; but he insisted that, in the midst of intercourse, he really 'did not pay attention to it.'"[18] The court threw out the conviction, determining that these facts raised a legitimate defense that had not been properly addressed at Adam's court-martial.[19]

Adultery

Adultery is a military crime of relatively recent vintage. It was not listed by name in the Manual for Courts-Martial until 1949, although it had been charged under the predecessor to Article 134 since at least 1937 in the navy and 1940 in the army.[20] Despite its controversial nature, adultery has been regularly prosecuted. Between 1992 and 1996 over 858 servicemembers were charged with having committed adultery.[21] In 1997 the continued vitality of the military's prohibition against adultery contributed to the resignation in lieu of court-martial of the air force's first female B-52 pilot, Lt. Kelly Flinn, and the career derailments of two general officers after admitting to past transgressions.

In practice the offense is rarely charged by itself. Prosecutors may throw in adultery as an alternative charge in a rape trial in the event the prosecution cannot prove lack of consent beyond a reasonable doubt.[22] Additionally, adultery is more likely to result in a court-martial if the servicemember lies about the misconduct, refuses an order to cease it, or engages in the adulterous misconduct in a particularly notorious and public manner so that it embarrasses the military or compromises an officer's or NCO's stature within the command.

Significantly, not all acts of adultery are punishable under the UCMJ. To obtain a conviction, the prosecution must show that the accused engaged in sexual intercourse with another person (1) at a time when one of the two was married to another and (2) under circumstances that were service discrediting or prejudicial to good order and discipline. MCM, ¶ 62(b). The requirement that the adultery be either prejudicial or discrediting provides the dividing line between an overly puritanical concern with extramarital affairs and a legitimate criminal prohibition.

Service-discrediting conduct must be of a type to injure the armed forces' reputation; it must have "a tendency to bring the service into disrepute or which tends to lower it in public esteem." MCM, ¶ 60(c)(3). The focus here is on the civilian community's reaction to the affair. For the conduct to be discrediting, both the accused's military status and the adulterous misconduct must be of a public nature; "wholly private conduct is not generally service discrediting."[23] Further, the courts will look to see if the misconduct violated local laws or community standards, recognizing "that imposition of punishment for adultery has become alien to the civilian's concept of criminal law."[24]

Determinations of prejudicial conduct is the more likely dividing line in determinations of criminality. The courts focus on the impact of the adulterous conduct on the military community, noting that unlike the civilian community, "adultery is not . . . alien to the soldier's concept of criminal law."[25] To be prejudicial the adultery must have a "direct and palpable" impact on military order and discipline. MCM, ¶ 60(c)(2)(a).

The army's appeals court found prejudicial conduct when the adultery occurred in the barracks, in the presence of a third person, following heavy drinking and drug use, only hours before the beginning of a duty day. Conversely, the court determined that no prejudice existed when the accused, who was separated from his wife, privately had sexual intercourse with a civilian woman in her off-post residence, and no working relationship existed between the two.[26]

Interestingly, at least one intermediate appellate court has recognized the offense of attempted adultery. In *United States v. St. Fort,* a husband returned home to find his wife clad only in a bathrobe and the accused hiding in a closet wearing nothing but a smile.[27] To convict the accused of attempted adultery, the government only had to establish that St. Fort specifically intended to commit adultery, and that he took some step beyond mere preparation in that direction. The army appellate court determined that the evidence was sufficient to convict the accused, rejecting his argument that the facts equally could have shown that he was present to commit some other unnamed offense, that he abandoned his intention of committing adultery—presumably upon the unexpected arrival of the husband—or that he was merely there to make a "social call."[28]

Wrongful Cohabitation

Article 134 criminalizes instances in which the accused openly lives with someone, who is not the accused's spouse, presenting themselves as a married couple, under circumstances that are prejudicial to the good order and discipline of the armed forces or service discrediting. MCM, ¶ 69(b). In the vernacular, it prohibits servicemembers from openly "shacking-up" with another person and then fraudulently wrapping themselves in the protective blanket of matrimony.

Unlike adultery, to prove wrongful cohabitation the prosecution is required to prove neither sexual intercourse nor the marital status of any of the offenders. MCM, ¶ 69(c). However, the offense requires more than merely sharing the same home, residing with another as an extended houseguest, or frequently visiting someone over an extended period of time.[29] The pair must present themselves as a married couple.

Reported convictions for this offense are rare, but they nevertheless do exist. The military courts have found wrongful cohabitation when an officer lived with an enlisted man's wife for sixteen months and when an officer brought a woman to live with him at his new duty station, introducing her as his wife to other officers and their wives.[30]

Bigamy

Bigamy has been prosecuted in the military since at least 1879.[31] It occurs when a person who is lawfully married to one living spouse marries a second person. As soon as the second marriage ceremony is finished, the accused is a bigamist.[32] It is not necessary that the second marriage be a valid one so long as the couple participates in some form of marriage ceremony with the mutual desire of being joined in matrimony.[33] Also, to be punishable under Article 134, the prosecution must prove that the accused's conduct was prejudicial to the good order and discipline of the armed forces or service discrediting. MCM, ¶ 65(b).

Several defenses are available to defend against a bigamy charge. First, the statute of limitations runs out five years after the second wedding ceremony is completed. Art. 43(b)(1), UCMJ. Second, even if unknown to the accused, if the earlier marriage is not legally recognizable or has been terminated through death or divorce, then there exists only one valid marriage and no crime has been committed. Third, if the accused has been forced into a "shotgun wedding," then the defense of duress exists. RCM 916(h).

Finally, the accused can claim a mistake of fact defense, arguing that the accused mistakenly thought the first marriage had been terminated. Such a defense would be successful if the accused honestly and reasonably believed that the first spouse had either died or the two had been divorced.

RCM 916(j). In determining if the accused's belief was an honest one, the panel (or military judge as applicable) may consider the accused's education, intelligence, age, and life experience. The honesty of the professed belief is more believable for the young servicemember with limited education and minimal experience in life than for a military lawyer who is trained, if not experienced, with such legal matters.[34]

To determine if the belief is objectively reasonable, the court will look to see if the accused made an effort to determine whether the first spouse actually died or whether a divorce actually took place.[35] Merely relying on assurances that a divorce will occur at some future date and then not following up on the matter after that date is insufficient to meet the legal standard of reasonableness.[36] Significantly, the mistake must be *both* honest and reasonable to succeed as a defense.

Sodomy

People have engaged in, and been punished for, sodomy since at least biblical times. The term is derived from the biblical city of Sodom, destroyed by God for the innumerable sinful pursuits of its inhabitants.[37] Further, sodomy has been no stranger to the military. Indeed, Winston Churchill of England reputedly referred to British naval tradition as resting upon "nothing but rum, sodomy, and the lash."[38]

In the United States sodomy first appeared as an offense in the 1917 Manual for Courts-Martial, punishable under Articles of War 93 (assault with intent to commit sodomy) and 96 (sodomy charged under the General Article).[39] The offense was limited to bestiality and anal sex, specifically excluding fellatio from its coverage until the manual was revised in 1920 to include fellatio and to make sodomy a separate offense under Article 93.[40]

The current sodomy provision, Article 125, criminalizes "unnatural" forms of sex with another person of the same or opposite gender, or with an animal. Such unnatural sexual acts include at least fellatio, cunnilingus, anal intercourse, and acts of bestiality. MCM, ¶ 51c. However, the article is written broadly enough to encompass virtually any unorthodox sexual activity exceeding penile-vaginal intercourse. The crime is completed by the slightest penetration, but some penetration must be proven. MCM, ¶ 51a(a). Increased punishment is available if sodomy is committed by force and without the consent of the victim, or if done with a child less than sixteen years old. MCM, ¶ 51e.

Private, noncommercial, consensual acts between heterosexual adults falls within the scope of this punitive article.[41] In *United States v. Fagg,* a young airman "cut a rather wide swath through the pubescent female population of Althus, Oklahoma," and was convicted of engaging in both fellatio and cunnilingus, despite such acts being voluntarily engaged in and not performed for money.[42]

The most infamous sodomy case in military law is unquestionably the Sanchez chicken case in which a soldier committed foul acts with a fowl, although it was inexplicably charged under the general article. In *United States v. Sanchez,* a soldier out for a night of beer and singing at the local Gasthaus stopped off at a chicken coop while returning to the barracks.[43] In his pretrial statement, Sanchez explained that he grabbed a chicken, "did something to the chicken . . . put his penis in it," and left the chicken at the coop after he was finished with it.[44] However, the accused was quick to explain that he only got urges to do this sort of thing after drinking.[45]

The next morning Frau Kalsch discovered her dead and apparently ravished chicken next to Sanchez's khaki cap, and Sanchez's roommate noticed bloodstains on the accused's trousers and underwear. At trial, the ever vigilant trial counsel presented scientific evidence establishing that the blood was, in fact, chicken blood and that chicken feathers were found on the accused's clothing.[46] A German veterinarian who performed a postmortem examination on the deceased chicken was brought in as an expert witness to establish the cause of death, opining that the victim's rectum had been penetrated by a dull object causing internal bleeding that resulted in the chicken bleeding to death.[47] Sidestepping the issue of whether Sanchez's misconduct should have properly been charged as sodomy, the court upheld the conviction determining that indecent acts with a fowl constituted an offense under Article 134.[48]

Indecent Exposure

Intentionally exposing private body parts to the public constitutes an offense under Article 134. However, not all public nudity or exposure of private parts constitutes a criminal offense. Unintentional exposures, such as being observed walking naked from a shower to the bedroom in private quarters or discretely urinating in the forest while on a field exercise are not crimes. In *United States v. Caune,* a soldier who had grown tired of being in the army stripped naked outside the headquarters commandant's office, but made no gestures, was in a semiprivate outer office area, and was only observed by other male soldiers.[49] Reversing Caune's indecent exposure conviction, the military court reasoned that nudity by itself was not indecent and there was nothing inherently lewd or morally offensive about a male soldier appearing naked in front of other males in a semiprivate area.[50]

The prosecution can prove that the exposure was purposeful by showing that the accused took some action to draw attention to his/her au naturel condition or the exposure occurred in a place where observance by the public was so likely that the court can presume it was intentional.[51] For example, in *United States v. Moore,* a Coast Guardsman who exposed his penis to a shipmate while simultaneously making "indelicate remarks and gestures" was convicted of indecent exposure although the incident occurred in a small compartment of a ship in the Antarctic.[52] The gestures and exposure in a compartment of the ship occupied by other personnel established that the misconduct was both intentional and prejudicial to good order and discipline. Similarly, the military courts upheld the conviction of a sailor who repeatedly stood naked in his open garage waiving and greeting his neighbors as they passed by.[53]

Pandering and Prostitution

Article 134 criminalizes prostitution (sex in exchange for something of value) and pandering (pimping). MCM, ¶ 97. Although most frequently associated with females, prostitution may be committed by either a man or a woman. MCM, ¶ 97(c). The article's plain language appears to limit a prostitution conviction to one who receives compensation for sex, as opposed to the person paying for it—the "John." However, the "John" could be convicted of soliciting prostitution pursuant to Article 82. MCM, ¶ 6(c)(3).

A pandering conviction requires that the accused wrongfully cause someone to engage in sex for hire while under the accused's direction or that the accused arranged for a person to engage in sex with a third person, all under circumstances that were prejudicial to good order and discipline or service discrediting. MCM, ¶ 97(b). Pandering does not require that the accused arrange for the sex in order to make some sort of profit.

In *United States v. Gallegos* a marine was convicted of pandering after arranging for three fellow marines to have sex with his wife so that he could watch.[54] However, a pandering conviction does require that more than two people be involved in the misconduct.[55] Further, merely offering to transport soldiers to a whorehouse for a fee, without arranging for the sexual intercourse itself, is not enough to warrant a conviction.[56]

Indecent Language

One would think that the last institution on the face of the earth to punish indecent language would be the military. However, Article 134 punishes that exact offense. To be considered "indecent" the language must be "grossly offensive to modesty, decency, or propriety, or shocks the moral sense, because of its vulgar, filthy, or disgusting nature, or its tendency to incite lustful thought." MCM, ¶ 89(c). The language must be "calculated to corrupt morals or excite libidinous thoughts" as measured by the standards of the military community.[57] In short, the language must be *really* "obscene."[58]

The language is examined in light of the context in which it occurs. Private, sexually oriented conversations between consenting adults is permissible, whereas the same type of language addressed toward a child or an adult finding such language offensive would be improper. Merely asking another adult to begin a sexual relationship is normally permitted, unless the inquiry suggests a particularly vulgar sexual act, is presented in a filthy manner, or is an offer to buy sexual favors.[59]

Coming as no great shock to anyone who has ever served in a line unit or attended basic training, the courts have indicated that the UCMJ does not prohibit "coarse language among soldiers" or the "language used daily in line units, motor pools and the like" which "certainly [is] not the 'parlor or drawing room' language heard in polite society."[60] Further, an NCO's jokeful bragging about his sexual prowess to a female servicemember, in an environment where such joking was common and engaged in by the female, was not violative of the UCMJ.[61]

Also, language may be insulting, but fall short of being criminally indecent or obscene. In *United States v. Linyear,* calling a female marine a "swine" was not deemed indecent, but it was enough to convict the accused of the lesser offense of provoking speech in violation of Article 117.[62]

When the military courts have taken a foul-mouthed servicemember to task, it has usually involved a child-victim, an unwanted and ill-mannered request for sex, or a solicitation to engage in some form of illegal activity such as prostitution. Examples of language held to be indecent include a request by a stepfather to climb into bed with his stepdaughter, comments during an extortion attempt that the accused wanted to "butt F———" a woman who was trying to break off an adulterous sexual relationship, and calling an eight-year-old girl "a little bitch" and a "cunt."[63]

Fornication

The act of sexual intercourse between two unmarried persons is known as fornication. It is not usually punished in the military unless committed under "conditions of publicity or scandal."[64] In other words, the intercourse must have been committed in the presence of other people or in a place where there is a substantial risk that others will see it, such as in the barracks. The following cases illustrate this critical distinction.

In *United States v. Carr,* a marine corporal engaged in sexual intercourse with a woman, at night, on a secluded beach, behind a canvass tent, approximately a quarter mile from any known person.[65] The intermediate appeals court set aside Carr's conviction for indecent acts because the intercourse was unlikely to be seen by anyone. Conversely, in the World War II–era case of *United States v. Lineberger,* an army lieutenant's conviction was upheld when he was observed by a police officer and cab driver attempting to have sex with a woman up against the side of a house at night in a residential neighborhood.[66] Obviously, sexual intercourse is much more likely to be observed in a residential neighborhood than on a secluded beach.

Permissible Sexual Conduct

Given the broad sweep of military law in this area a servicemember may ask, What can I do? The military courts have held that oral foreplay, in private, between two consenting adults, not amounting to adultery or sodomy, is legal.[67] Further, private sexual intercourse between two consenting, unmarried, heterosexual adults is permissible.[68] However, private acts of oral copulation between two consenting heterosexual adults is in violation of military law.[69]

In short, private, nonperverted, noncommercial, voluntary, heterosexual, penile-vaginal sexual intercourse or simple foreplay between two consenting adults, not in an improper senior-subordinate relationship, not married to another, not involving an animal, and not occurring while improperly holding themselves out as husband and wife is okay under military law.

Violent Crimes

Homicide

Homicide, the killing of another person or human being, is punished under a hierarchical system of punitive articles: Article 118 (murder), 119 (manslaughter), and 134 (negligent homicide). At the top of the hierarchy is premeditated murder, which imposes the heaviest elements of proof on the prosecution and concomitantly authorizes the most severe punishment: death. Descending down the levels of homicide, the burden on the prosecution gradually decreases, but so too does the amount of potential punishment.

Before discussing the unlawful death of a human being one must first determine how military law defines both "death" and a "human being." The army appeals court has determined that a person is legally dead for purposes of the UCMJ when either the victim's (1) heart and lungs have stopped working or (2) brain has permanently stopped functioning.[70] Accordingly, a servicemember can be prosecuted for killing someone who, although brain dead, was sustained for a period of time on a respirator.

Military law has yet to define if and when a fetus becomes a recognized person. Because of the medical difficulty in determining both the health and existence of a fetus, early civilian and military law did not recognize a fetus as a human being until it was "born alive," that is, that it existed independent of the mother.[71] As a result of either legislation or reinterpretation of existing law, the majority of states now recognize some form of fetal homicide. It appears likely that military courts would permit the homicide prosecution of an accused who injures a fetus that is later born alive but subsequently dies of the prenatal injury.[72] What remains uncertain is whether the military courts, in the absence of legislation, will join with the growing number of states who have rejected the born alive rule and permit prosecution for killing a fetus.

Murder

Article 118 describes four types of murder: premeditated, unpremeditated, acts inherently dangerous to others, and felony murder. Only premeditated and felony murder may result in the death penalty. MCM, ¶ 43(e).

Premeditated murder is the unlawful killing of another human being when the accused's actions were deliberate and the accused consciously thought about taking the victim's life beforehand. The accused need only reflect on taking the victim's life for an instant. Premeditation can be shown by things the accused said or by looking at the circumstances surrounding the crime.

In *United States v. Schap,* after learning that another soldier had impregnated his wife, Schap tracked the man down, kicked and cut off his head with a knife, and, while holding the victim's head by its hair, announced, "This is what happens when you commit adultery."[73] Schap then presented the head to his wife. Based on Schap's statements and the circumstances of the killing, the army determined that the murder was committed "in a cold and calculating manner" and upheld the premeditated murder conviction.[74]

Worth noting, under the legal doctrine of "transferred intent" the accused's premeditation to kill intended victim A may be transferred for purposes of convicting the accused for the murder of unintended victim B. MCM, ¶ 43(c)(2)(b). So if the accused shoots at A and misses but hits and kills B, the accused may be convicted of the premeditated murder of B. In *United States v. Corey,* for example, a GI in search of a prostitute during the Korean War was chased away from a house of ill repute by a pistol-toting sergeant.[75] Private Corey returned with his carbine and fired into the hooch, killing not only the sergeant but also the sergeant's female companion. In upholding two convictions for premeditated murder, the army court reasoned that Corey's premeditation to kill the sergeant transferred to the female victim as well, even if Corey had not intended to kill her.[76]

Unpremeditated murder occurs when the accused kills someone while trying to kill or seriously injure that person, but without prior consideration of the murderous act. Usually the intent to kill or injure occurs at the time of the act. The lack of prior consideration distinguishes this offense from premeditated murder. The Manual for Courts-Martial offers the example of an escaping burglar who sees and kills the homeowner in the same instant. MCM, ¶ 43(c)(3)(a).

Murder While Doing an Inherently Dangerous Act does not require proof that the accused intended to kill the victim. Indeed, the accused may be convicted of this offense even if he truly hoped that no one would be killed. MCM, ¶ 43(c)(4). To obtain a conviction, the prosecution need only prove that the accused, while acting in an inherently dangerous manner and failing to exhibit any concern for the safety of others, caused a death while aware that death or serious injury was a likely consequence of his actions. MCM, ¶ 43(b)(3). Examples of such misconduct include jokingly throwing a grenade at the victim, flying extremely low to scare people on the ground, and firing a rifle in a populated area as part of a "sham" firefight. MCM, ¶ 43(c)(4)(a).[77]

Felony Murder is committed when someone is killed while the accused is involved in the commission, or attempted commission, of certain specific offenses: burglary, sodomy, rape, robbery, and aggravated arson. MCM, ¶ 43(b)(4)(d). That the death was accidental or unintentional is no defense. MCM, ¶ 43(c)(5). Further, it is no defense that the accused was not the actual killer. In *United States v. Borner,* three soldiers involved in a rape fled and one fired a shot at the victim, killing her.[78] Although it could not be determined which of the three killed the woman, all were convicted of felony murder because the victim was killed as part of the rape in which all three soldiers had participated.[79] All three were equally guilty of felony murder although only one actually killed the woman.

Manslaughter

Article 119 encompasses two types of manslaughter: voluntary and involuntary. Voluntary manslaughter involves a killing while "in the heat of passion caused by adequate provocation," by an accused who intended to either kill or seriously injure the victim. MCM, ¶ 44a(a) The classic example involves the husband who returns home to find his unfaithful wife in bed with another man and, in an uncontrolled fit of rage, kills the spouse and/or her lover. When a homicide is committed in emotional or passionate circumstances, it is not unusual to see a conviction of manslaughter rather than murder.

However, the law places limits on what constitutes adequate provocation. The provoking event must "excite uncontrollable passion" and may be the result of either fear or rage, but it cannot have occurred so far prior to the killing that the accused should have calmed down. MCM, ¶ 44(c)(1)(a) and (b). In addition to adultery, the provocation requirement may be satisfied by unauthorized imprisonment, serious bodily harm, and other offenses. MCM, ¶ 44(c)(1)(b). Actions that do not qualify as adequate provocation include giving someone the finger, a slap, damaging personal property, refusing to engage in sexual intercourse with the victim's fiancée, racial insults, and a run-of-the-mill domestic argument. MCM, ¶ 44(c)(1)(b).[80]

Involuntary manslaughter occurs when the accused unintentionally kills another (1) while committing, or attempting to commit, against a particular victim, an offense other than the five associated with felony murder or (2) while acting in a grossly careless manner indicating an utter disregard for the foreseeable consequences of the accused's actions. MCM, ¶ 44(c)(2). In *United States v. Richardson,* the court found that the accused acted with "an utter disregard for human safety" when he shot a soldier while playing quick-draw with a loaded pistol.[81] The manual notes that engaging in target practice in front of someone's home or leaving poison out unattended illustrate the required level of carelessness. MCM, ¶ 44(c)(2)(a)(i).

Negligent Homicide

Punishable under the general article, negligent homicide makes up the bottom rung of homicide's hierarchical ladder. Whereas premeditated murder is punishable by death, negligent homicide's maximum punishment is a Bad Conduct Discharge, total forfeitures, and three years' confinement. MCM, ¶ 85(e).

Negligent homicide is similar to involuntary manslaughter, except that this offense requires a lower degree of negligence (lack of care). To be convicted of negligent homicide the accused must have significantly contributed to or caused the victim's death while failing to exhibit the level of care or caution that the average Joe Sixpack off the street would have been expected to exhibit in those circumstances. MCM, ¶ 85(b) and (c). Further, the prosecution must show that the accused violated a legal duty to use due care that caused the death, such as the duty a parent has to provide medical care for a child or the duty of an armed servicemember in a combat zone to determine if he is shooting at an enemy or friendly soldier.[82] The prosecution need not show that the accused intended to kill or harm the victim. MCM, ¶ 85(c)(1).

The military justifies a homicide offense based on this lower level of negligence by virtue of the heightened danger to life and limb inherent in everyday military operations. "The danger to others from careless acts" is so much greater in the military "because of the extensive use, handling and operation in the course of official duties of such dangerous instruments as weapons, explosives, aircraft, vehicles, and the like."[83]

Comparing Degrees of Homicide

At the risk of oversimplification, the following illustrates the distinctions between the various degrees of homicide. Premeditated Murder: Private

Smith plans to kill Airman Jones, waits for Jones to cross the street and then deliberately runs over Jones, killing him. Unpremeditated Murder: Smith intentionally tries to kill Jones, and succeeds, but did not really consider it before acting. Felony Murder: Smith runs over Jones while acting as the getaway driver after a bank robbery. Voluntary Manslaughter: Smith chases Jones out of his house after finding him in bed with Mrs. Smith, jumps in his car and while in a state of rage, floors the gas pedal and kills Jones with the car. Involuntary Manslaughter: Smith runs a red light while driving twenty miles over the speed limit, knowing he has bad brakes, and after consuming large quantities of alcohol, hits Jones as he crosses the street. If Smith's disregard for the safety of others is slightly more extreme, such as running several lights, driving without a license, and hitting a prior car or person, Smith could be convicted of murder under the theory that he engaged in acts inherently dangerous to others.[84] Negligent Homicide: Without bad brakes and sober, Smith hits Jones after running a red light while speeding.

Assaults

Similar to homicide, the military uses a hierarchical system of offenses and punishments. Under Article 128, the severest form of the offense is an assault intentionally inflicting serious injury using a firearm, which is punishable by loss of all pay and allowances, a dishonorable discharge, and ten years' confinement. MCM, ¶ 54(e)(9)(a). The lowest form is a "simple assault," which does not require actual contact and is punishable by three months' confinement and loss of two-thirds pay per month for three months. MCM, ¶ 54(e)(1).

Article 128 also provides a sliding scale of punishments depending upon the victim's status. In addition to forfeiture of all pay and allowances, assault upon a commissioned officer not in the execution of military duties may result in a dishonorable discharge and three years' confinement; eighteen months' confinement and a dishonorable discharge for an assault upon a warrant officer; and six months' confinement and a bad conduct discharge for an assault upon a petty or noncommissioned officer. MCM, ¶ 54e.

Assault offenses are found in other punitive articles. Articles 90 and 91 criminalize assaults upon a superior commissioned officer, a warrant officer, and a petty or noncommissioned officer while performing military duties. Article 134 punishes various types of indecent touching and assaults carried out while intending to commit other offenses.

On the lowest rung of the assault hierarchy, a simple assault may be accomplished by two different means: offer and attempt. Assault by offer "is an unlawful demonstration of violence" that creates a reasonable fear or apprehension of being harmed in the mind of the victim. MCM, ¶ 54c(1)(b)(ii). A mere verbal threat by itself; threats of violence at some future date; and conditional threats indicating no intention of injuring the victim, such as "If you weren't already so ugly I'd punch you in the face," are not assaults.[85] Conversely, displaying a deadly weapon in a menacing manner, with or without accompanying threats of violence, constitutes an assault if the victim is placed in danger of injury.

An assault by attempt occurs when the accused intentionally takes some action designed to injure the victim. MCM, ¶ 54c(1)(b)(i). It is not a defense that the victim was not injured or even that the victim was unaware of the accused's efforts. MCM, ¶ 54c(1)(b)(i) and (iii)(A). Accordingly, if an accused tries to hit a sleeping person, but misses, an assault has occurred.

Once the slightest, offensive body contact has been made, the accused moves up to the next rung and may be prosecuted for "assault consummated by battery." Examples of a battery include spitting on someone, an unwanted kiss, slapping or punching, and a male unbuttoning a button on the blouse of an unwilling female.[86] Further, the offensive touching can be accomplished indirectly. Indirect batteries include striking a horse so that it throws its rider and causing a dog to attack and bite another. MCM, ¶ 54c(2). However, innocent touching is not a crime, such as when you accidently bump into a person or touch that person's shoulder to get their attention, or when you jerk back a person who is about to step in the path of an oncoming car. MCM, ¶ 54c(2)(d).

Aggravated assault sits on the upper end of the hierarchy. One controversial application of the assault article has been to an accused infected with the human immunodeficiency virus (HIV). For an aggravated assault conviction, the government must prove that the accused assaulted someone with a means "likely to produce death or grievous bodily harm." MCM, ¶ 54b(4)(a)(iv). The Manual for Courts-Martial notes that such "means" are not limited to things normally considered a weapon, and these "means" are "likely" to produce the requisite harm when death or grievous bodily harm is the "natural and probable consequence" of the conduct. MCM, ¶ 54c(4)(a)(ii).

The human immunodeficiency virus (HIV) qualifies as a means likely to cause death because the accused has no control over HIV once sexual intercourse has occurred, and acquired immunodeficiency syndrome (AIDS)—and eventually death—are the natural consequences of HIV infection.[87] To illustrate, in *United States v. Bygrave,* an HIV-positive sailor was convicted of two specifications of assault with a means likely to cause death or grievous bodily harm after engaging in unprotected sexual intercourse with two female sailors, both of whom later tested positive for HIV.[88] Significantly, the court also determined that the knowing consent of the victim was not a defense, taking the position that the law will simply not recognize a victim's consent to an act that will likely result in death or serious injury.[89]

Maiming

Also known as the offense of mayhem, this offense is rooted in the old English prohibition against inflicting an injury upon a man's body of such seriousness that "the act permanently disables the person 'to fight in defense of the King and Country; and as a soldier to protect himself on the field of battle.'"[90] Article 124 significantly broadens the offense to protect any person's "natural completeness and normal appearance of the human face and body," rather than focusing on the military effectiveness of potential or actual military members.[91] Recently, the offense has been extended to cover severe cases of child abuse. In *United States v. Outin,* a marine was convicted of maiming an eight-week-old infant by placing her in scalding hot water, which caused third-degree burns and permanent scarring, and in *United States v. Spenhoff* an airman was convicted of maiming a two-year-old girl after burning her buttocks with a steam iron.[92]

The punitive article requires that the accused intended to injure the victim, but does not require an intent to maim. MCM, ¶ 50(c)(3). The accused cannot defend against a maiming charge by claiming that the more serious injury was unintentional or accidental.[93]

Article 124 prohibits three types of injury. First, injuries that seriously disfigure the victim and detract from the victim's "comeliness" or attractive appearance, such as cutting off an ear, lip, tongue, or nose or throwing acid in someone's face. Second, the destruction or disabling of a person's internal organs or certain portions of that person's body, including the loss of an eye, tooth, finger, foot, hand, or testicle and the smashing of the victim's skull. Third, injuries to internal organs that "seriously diminish [the victim's] physical vigor," that is they sap the victim's strength and energy.

MCM, ¶ 50(a) and (c).[94] The odd emphasis on protecting teeth probably reflected the need for soldiers to be able to tear open paper cartridges for use with muskets, a requirement that lasted at least through the American Civil War.[95]

Although maiming requires long-term injuries, it is no defense that the injuries may eventually be corrected through surgery or other medical treatment. MCM, ¶ 50(c)(1). The offense is broad enough to include disfiguring injuries that are not easily observed, such as injuries to the back, breasts, or buttocks even though these areas of the body are normally covered by clothing.[96] However, the injuries must be of a severe, relatively permanent nature. Injuries such as simple fractures of a cheekbone, bites on a hand or forearm that break the skin, and black eyes do not constitute maiming.[97]

Dueling

American military law has prohibited dueling since the birth of the nation, contained in Article 11 of the Code of 1775 and carried over into the Continental Articles and Rules for the Better Government of the Troops of 1776.[98] Military figures, such as Generals Gates and Cadwalader, have engaged in duels since the Revolutionary War, and court-martial convictions for such misconduct date back to at least 1814.[99]

Although at first blush the offense appears to be a relic from the past, dueling remains an offense punishable under the UCMJ with modern applications. The prohibition against dueling encompasses more than the stereotypical version of two gentleman who stand back-to-back with pistols, take ten steps, and then turn and fire. The manual defines the act as "combat between two persons for private reasons fought with deadly weapons by prior agreement." MCM, ¶ 39(c)(1). Accordingly, two servicemembers who, based upon a prior agreement, meet at some private location to settle their differences with knives or baseball bats are engaging in a duel.

The requirement for a prior agreement separates dueling from a run-of-the-mill fight generated in the heat of passion. This same agreement should serve as evidence of premeditation for a murder charge should a death occur in the subsequent confrontation. Further, dueling requires the use of "deadly weapons," which includes pistols and swords, but is otherwise undefined. MCM, ¶ 39(f)(1). However, an instrument that satisfies the definition of a "dangerous weapon" for purposes of Article 128(4) (aggravated assault) should normally satisfy the definitional requirements of dueling.

Article 114 not only prohibits duels, but also criminalizes the active encouragement and failure to prevent or report them. MCM, ¶ 39. This provision of the article appears to reflect earlier civil and military law in which "seconds" and others present at the duel who assisted or encouraged the duelists—to include attending surgeons—were held criminally responsible.[100]

Property and Economic Crimes

The UCMJ contains numerous articles dealing with the theft, destruction, or damage of property and money. Some provisions, such as embezzlement, are well established in military law, whereas other provisions, such as espionage, are relatively new. Albeit more properly labeled as a national security crime, I have included espionage in this section because it basically prohibits the sale or transfer of a unique form of property—information.

As an historical aside, West Point's first African American graduate, Henry Ossian Flipper, was court-martialed for property crimes. An 1877 graduate of the United States Military Academy, Flipper was assigned to Fort Davis, Texas, when he was charged with two charges: a single specification of embezzlement and five specifications of conduct unbecoming an officer and a gentleman, including one specification of what is now commonly known as a bad check offense.[101] Although acquitted of embezzlement, Flipper was convicted of conduct unbecoming and dismissed from the army.[102] Coincidentally, sitting in judgment of Flipper at the court-martial was Col. Galusha Pennypacker. As a brevet major general during the Civil War, Pennypacker was the youngest general of the war, and possibly the youngest army general ever, becoming a general officer at the age of only seventeen.[103]

Bad Check Offenses

Bad check offenses are addressed by Articles 123a (Making, drawing, or uttering check, draft, or order without sufficient funds) and 134 (Check, worthless, making and uttering—by dishonorably failing to maintain funds). The two offenses are distinguished by proof of the accused's knowledge and intent at the time the check is created or delivered.

Basically Article 123a prohibits the writing of a check to obtain an item of some value or to pay a debt, knowing that insufficient funds are available to cover the check and thus intending to defraud or deceive the check's recipient. The offense also includes delivering or offering to deliver a worthless check to someone, even if the accused does not personally prepare and sign it. MCM, ¶ 49c. In comparison, for an Article 134 conviction the prosecution must prove neither an intent to defraud or deceive, nor knowledge that the accused had enough money in the bank to cover the check at the time it was prepared or by the time it arrived for payment. MCM, ¶ 68c. However, the misconduct must be "dishonorable" and service discrediting or prejudicial to good order and discipline. MCM, ¶ 68b.

The maximum sentences of the two offenses reflect the accused's relative culpability required for conviction. Article 123a, which requires a knowing and intentionally fraudulent act, authorizes a dishonorable discharge, loss of all pay and allowances, and five years in jail, assuming the check is for one hundred dollars or more. If less than one hundred dollars, Article 123a mirrors Article 134, which only requires that the accused acted in bad faith or with gross indifference, both offenses providing for a bad conduct discharge, total forfeiture of pay and allowances, and six months' confinement. MCM, ¶¶ 49, 68.

Several possible defenses exist to bad check charges. First, an honest but mistaken belief that adequate funds existed in the bank to cover the worthless check is a defense to an Article 123a charge.[104] Credible evidence that the accused simply did not understand checking accounts may establish that the accused did not intend to defraud or deceive as required by Article 123a or did not act in bad faith or with gross indifference for purposes of Article 134.[105]

Because the service-discrediting nature of the Article 134 offense stems from the failure of the bank to accept or honor the check, overdraft protection for worthless checks precludes a finding that the accused's misconduct was service discrediting.[106] Further, the UCMJ may not be used to enforce worthless checks written to facilitate gambling or to pay off gambling loses, at least to the extent the checks are written at a government facility and the government is aware the checks are being used for that purpose.[107]

DITY Move Fraud

Few financial programs are more susceptible to fraud than the Do-It-Yourself (DITY) Move Program. The DITY Move Program is designed to reduce the military's cost of moving a servicemember's household goods by providing a financial incentive to members of the armed forces to move their own possessions. Annually, approximately 150,000 servicemembers take advantage of the program, in which the government pays the servicemember a percentage of what it would pay a moving company to pack and transport the goods.[108]

Because installation transportation offices rarely possess the resources necessary to double check the validity of all DITY Move claims, some servicemembers attempt to take advantage of the system by inflating the weight of the goods moved or, particularly for those exiting the military, claim a move that never occurred. Since discharged servicemembers are no longer subject to the UCMJ, any prosecution of the latter group is usually handled through the federal system. However, because DITY Move fraud is usually a low dollar crime, federal authorities may be reluctant to devote their limited resources to these offenses.

Under the UCMJ, the fraudulent claim for reimbursement of the inflated or nonexistent move, and any supporting documentation, may be prosecuted under Article 132 (Frauds against the United States). In *United States v. Parks,* an army staff sergeant inflated the weight of his household goods by placing "trash and building materials" in his rental truck, weighed it, and then submitted the inflated weight tickets with a claim for reimbursement of his DITY move.[109] Under this scenario, the claim for reimbursement would violate Article 132(1)(B) as a presentation for payment of a claim against the United States. Alternatively, submission of the inflated weight tickets would constitute the making or use of a false or fraudulent writing in violation of Article 132(2)(A).

Hazarding a Vessel

During the evening of 30 July 1945, a Japanese submarine torpedoed the USS *Indianapolis,* sinking the ship. The surviving crewmembers drifted helplessly for five days, succumbing to the elements, lack of water, and incessant shark attacks. Of the 1,200-man crew, only 316 survived the ordeal. Five months later, in a highly controversial court-martial, the ship's captain, Charles McVay III, was convicted of "suffering a vessel to be hazarded through negligence" because he failed to order that the ship steer a zigzag course.[110] More recently, in *United States v. Lynch,* the commanding officer of a Coast Guard buoy tender was also convicted of negligently hazarding a vessel after the ship grounded itself on a rock shoal in Lake Superior.[111]

Article 110 criminalizes the hazarding of an American military vessel through intentionally wrongful actions or through the absence of due care under the circumstances. To "hazard" the vessel means to place it "in danger of loss or injury," and conclusive evidence exists that the ship was placed in harm's way when the vessel runs aground, runs upon a shoal or rock, or collides with another ship. MCM, ¶ 34c(1). However, merely hazarding a vessel or causing it to run aground is not by itself an offense; the prosecution must prove intentional or negligent (absence of due care) conduct, and that such misconduct caused the hazarding.[112]

The law places a heavy duty on those responsible for the safety and well-being of a vessel: "The duty is to take all necessary precautions; to exercise due care and external vigilance."[113] However, Article 110 fails to identify who is subject to this legal duty. It is beyond dispute that as a matter of military custom and historical precedent a vessel's commanding officer shoulders this mantle of responsibility, even where no specific duty is found in service regulations.[114] Significantly, in *United States v. Adams,* the navy's Court of Military Review extended the article's scope to *any* service-member who willfully or negligently hazarded a vessel, rejecting the argument that the offense was limited to those "specifically entrusted" with "the navigational or operational activities of a vessel," and upheld the conviction of a sailor who deliberately started a fire in a compartment of the USS *Austin*.[115] The court's ruling in *Adams* has been followed in a more recent case, sustaining the conviction of a seaman who set fire to a paint locker on a moored Coast Guard ship.[116]

Espionage

Article 106a makes espionage and attempted espionage a *peacetime* criminal offense, punishable by death in certain circumstances. The wartime version of the offense, called spying, is punished under Article 106. Added in 1985 and modeled after federal espionage law, Article 106a was needed to give the military a vehicle for prosecuting peacetime espionage because the military could not assimilate the federal law, which authorized the death penalty, under Article 134(3) as "crimes and offenses not capital."[117]

To be convicted of espionage the accused must transport or communicate documents or other information relating to national security to a foreign entity, knowing that such information would be used either to harm the United States or to help the foreign country. MCM, ¶ 30ab(1). Even the passing of unclassified information may sustain a conviction.[118] Further, the accused may be sentenced to death if the information disclosed deals with "(1) nuclear weaponry, military spacecraft or satellites, early warning systems, or other means of defense or retaliation against large scale attack, (2) war plans, (3) communications intelligence or cryptographic information, or (4) any other major weapon systems or major element of defense strategy." MCM, ¶ 30ab(3).

In *United States v. Schoof,* a sailor was convicted of espionage-related charges when he tried to sell classified information to the Soviet embassy.[119] The conviction was upheld on appeal despite the classified material having been superseded, and thus posing no real threat to national security; the accused's desire to avoid "serious" injury to his country; and Schoof's decision not to complete the transfer of the stolen classified material to the Soviets.[120] Similarly, in *United States v. Wilmoth,* a sailor from the USS *Midway* was convicted of attempted espionage after he tried to pass classified naval messages dealing with future deployments of the *Midway* to a Soviet agent.[121] It was of no consequence that Wilmoth was unable to transfer the messages because he could not find his Soviet contact.[122]

Principals, Accessories, and Conspirators

Even if the accused did not directly commit a crime, he or she may still suffer a conviction under a number of legal theories.

Law of Principals

Article 77, which is not itself an offense, codifies the law of "principals." Generally, a servicemember who "causes a [criminal] act to be done" or "aids, abets, counsels, commands, or procures its commission" is just as guilty of the crime as the person who actually commits it. For example, an officer who commands a soldier to execute an enemy prisoner is as guilty of murder as the soldier who pulled the trigger, even if the officer is out of the area when the execution actually occurs.

To be guilty of an offense the aider and abettor must know of, and share in, the effort to commit the offense, and possess the requisite level of criminal intent. MCM, ¶ 1b(2)(b) and (4). A servicemember who gives a friend a ride to the bank, unaware that the friend intends to rob it, is not guilty of an offense. If the servicemember actively assists the robbery, both individuals would be equally responsible for the robbery and for any associated crimes considered to be a "natural and probable consequence" of the robbery, such as shooting the bank guard. MCM, ¶ 1b(5).

For crimes distinguished by the level of criminal intent, or type of guilty mind, an aider and abettor may be convicted of a greater or lesser form of that crime. In the case of a homicide, the actual killer who acts in the heat of passion may be guilty of only manslaughter, but the aider and abettor who encourages and arms the actual killer may be guilty of premeditated murder. MCM, ¶ 1b(4).

Sometimes doing nothing can run afoul of the law. In *United States v. Crouch,* a soldier pulling guard duty at a motor pool was convicted of larceny and unlawful entry as an aider and abettor when, having learned of the intended crime earlier, the accused did not prevent his roommate and another soldier from breaking into the motor pool and then lied to a military policeman about the ownership of the two thieves' vehicle.[123] However, unless the accused has a duty to stop a crime, merely being present at the scene of a crime and standing idle is not a UCMJ offense.[124]

Accessory after the Fact

The UCMJ also criminalizes as "an accessory after the fact" the actions of a servicemember who protects a lawbreaker from the authorities. Art. 78, UCMJ. To be convicted of this offense, Article 78 requires that the accused, knowing that a certain person had committed an offense "punishable" under the UCMJ, helps that person "for the purpose of hindering or preventing the apprehension, trial, or punishment of the offender." MCM, ¶ 2b. The crime need only be one that could be punished under the UCMJ if a servicemember had committed it; the accused may still be convicted as an accessory after the fact when the actual lawbreaker is not subject to the UCMJ. For example, in *United States v. Michaels,* a soldier was convicted as an accessory to larceny—a crime punishable under the UCMJ—even though the actual thieves were Korean civilians.[125] Additionally, it is no defense that the actual lawbreaker is acquitted at trial.[126]

Forms of prohibited assistance include efforts to help a lawbreaker's escape from authorities; concealing the lawbreaker's whereabouts; or hiding evidence of the crime itself, such as the murder weapon or stolen property. MCM, ¶ 2c(1). In *United States v. Davis,* a sailor was convicted of being an accessory after the fact to larceny when he provided misleading information to military police, intending to shift the focus of their investigation away from the accused's friend and on to an innocent sailor.[127]

Generally, this article is not violated by the failure to report a crime. MCM, ¶ 5(c)(2). However, in *Michaels,* the accused was convicted as an accessory for accepting hush money to keep quiet about thefts of property under his control after he discovered the larcenies.[128]

Conspiracy

Finally, military law punishes those who enter into an agreement to commit an offense and then take some step (an overt act) toward accomplishing the object of that agreement. Article 81 states that a conspiracy is established by proving (1) that the accused was part of an agreement with at least one other person to commit a UCMJ offense and (2) that while the accused was part of this agreement *any* of the coconspirators performed an overt act designed to bring about the goal of the agreement. MCM, ¶ 5b. Unlike aiding and abetting, conspiracy is an offense by itself. An accused may be convicted of conspiracy to distribute drugs and punished as a drug distributor, without ever being charged or convicted of drug distribution.

The offense gives the prosecutor a great deal of leeway in terms of proving a conspiracy. First, an overt act need not be illegal. MCM, ¶ 5c(4). Purchasing bolt cutters to break into a motor pool or ski masks in preparation of a bank robbery would serve as the required overt act for a conspiracy charge. Proving the existence of an overt act shows that the conspirators were doing more than just thinking about committing a crime; at least one of them has taken a step toward accomplishing the illegal objective. Further, the government is not required to prove the identities and roles of all other conspirators, need not show that the agreement was anything more concrete than "a common understanding," nor prove that the conspirators were even capable of successfully carrying it out. MCM, ¶ 5(c). Additionally, the courts have ruled that attempted conspiracy is a UCMJ offense and that the accused may still be found guilty of conspiracy even if his or her alleged coconspirator has been acquitted in a separate trial.[129]

Once part of the conspiracy, the servicemember is criminally responsible for the actions of other conspirators. MCM, ¶ 5c(5). A servicemember may escape a conviction by withdrawing from the conspiracy, but withdrawal must be completed before any overt act in furtherance of the conspiracy has been accomplished. If withdrawal occurs after an overt act, the accused may still be convicted of the conspiracy charge because the crime is complete at the moment of the overt act, but the accused will not be held responsible for crimes committed by other conspirators after the point of withdrawal. MCM, ¶ 5c(6). Nonparticipation in further acts of the conspiracy is not enough to withdraw from the conspiracy, the service-member must take some action that is inconsistent with the conspiracy's goal and cut all ties with the other conspirators. MCM, ¶ 5c(6).

The conspiracy offense does not apply to crimes that necessarily require the participation of the two alleged conspirators. Known as "Wharton's Rule," this limitation applies to such crimes as dueling, bigamy, incest, adultery, and bribery. MCM, 5c(3). If more than two persons are involved in the illegal agreement, then the accused can be convicted of conspiracy. Additionally, the accused may not be convicted of conspiracy when the only other conspirator is a government agent.[130]

9

Defenses

Military law groups criminal defenses into two basic categories: special defenses (also known as affirmative defenses) and all other defenses. A special defense is one that denies criminal responsibility for the crime, but does not deny that the accused committed the conduct itself. RCM 916(a). All defenses listed in Rule for Courts-Martial (RCM) 916 are special defenses. Other defenses deny that the accused committed the misconduct or deny some portion (element) of the offense.

Special Defenses

Unless the evidence is unbelievable, a military judge must give an instruction to the panel explaining the legal aspects of any special defense raised at trial. Except for a lack of mental responsibility defense (insanity), once an affirmative defense is established the government then assumes the burden of disproving the defense beyond a reasonable doubt. RCM 916(b). The accused retains the burden of proving insanity by clear and convincing evidence. Those special defenses not discussed elsewhere appear below.

Justification: The Parental Discipline Example

The Manual for Courts-Martial states that a "death, injury, or other act caused or done in the proper performance of a legal duty is justified and not unlawful" and offers the examples of a police officer who must use reasonably necessary force to arrest a criminal and a soldier who kills the enemy in battle. RCM 916(c) and Discussion.

111

A commonly cited justification defense in child abuse cases is the right of parental discipline. Military law recognizes the right of parents to discipline their children. Accordingly, certain conduct that would otherwise constitute a form of criminal assault, such as spanking, may be justified by the parental duty to discipline a child.[1] As a defense to criminal charges, this defense also extends to those acting in the place of parents, such as a babysitter or a step/foster parent.

However, the right of parental discipline is not without limitations. Parental force is permissible only if properly motivated and applied in a reasonable degree and manner. Parental discipline may only serve as a defense if the force is (1) "used for the purpose of safeguarding or promoting the welfare of a minor, including the prevention or punishment of his misconduct;" and (2) "not designed to cause or known to create a substantial risk of causing death, serious bodily injury, disfigurement, extreme pain or mental distress or gross degradation."[2]

Because no bright line test exists between permissible and impermissible levels of discipline, a review of applicable case law helps establish the parameters of acceptable parental discipline. Military courts have posited that the following conduct is not inherently unreasonable: (1) hitting a twelve-year-old boy on the legs with an army uniform web belt, after removing the buckle and tip, not resulting in serious injury; and (2) striking an eight-year-old child six to ten times on the buttocks and thighs with a leather belt, causing welts and bruises.[3] Conversely, and not surprisingly, the following forms of discipline have been found excessive: (1) forced immersion in scalding hot water; (2) tying a minor's hands and feet and then placing a plastic bag over his head; and (3) repeatedly beating a three-year-old with an electrical cord, belt, and belt buckle, which caused permanent scars and a deep cut.[4]

Even if the force applied does not appear excessive, the parental discipline defense may fail if the parent possesses an improper motivation for striking the child. In *United States v. Brown*,[5] the accused struck his seven-year-old stepson with a belt and switch, causing welts and bruises. The force itself was not inherently excessive and Brown testified that he was merely disciplining the boy for stealing. However, a panel rejected the defense after receiving evidence that the accused disliked his stepson, regularly took out his hostility on the child, and was angry at the time of the beating because of work-related problems.[6]

Self-Defense and Defense of Others

Military law recognizes a limited right to defend yourself and others. The level of permissible force that may be used in self-defense is dependent upon the level of harm that the accused reasonably fears and the amount of force necessary to avoid injury.

In homicide or aggravated assault cases, the accused is justified in killing or seriously injuring another only if (1) acting in reasonable fear that a similar level of harm was about to be inflicted on him and (2) the force used in self-defense was necessary to prevent such harm. RCM 916 (e)(1). For simple assault and battery, the accused may inflict nonlife-threatening injury if (1) he reasonably feared bodily injury to himself and (2) the force used was not likely to cause death or serious injury and he believed such force was necessary to escape the perceived harm. RCM 916(e)(3). In aggravated assault cases in which injury is threatened, but not inflicted, the accused must (1) be in reasonable fear of bodily harm and (2) be threatened with force capable of causing death or serious injury in an effort to deter the other combatant. RCM 916(e)(2).

The defense may be available to the instigator of a fight if the level of hostilities increases. For example, if A slaps B causing the two to brawl, A cannot claim the right of self-defense. However, if after being slapped B then threatens A with a knife or pistol, the level of hostilities has escalated and A may be able to use an equivalent level of force in self-defense.

To illustrate, in *United States v. Cardwell,*[7] a soldier brought a chicken dinner into the barracks. The accused, Private Cardwell, grabbed the dinner. The owner retrieved his dinner, made a few choice remarks, and approached Cardwell. The accused reacted by punching the soldier, who then choked Cardwell, who in turn struck the soldier on the head with a beer bottle. Although the accused was the initial aggressor, at the point the soldier raised the level of force by choking Cardwell, the accused had a right to increase his level of force in self-defense.

Further, the defense may be available to the instigator who withdraws from the confrontation and expresses a desire to avoid further hostilities. For example, if after punching his fellow soldier, Cardwell had apologized and left the area, he would be able to claim the right of self-defense during any subsequent confrontation. However, if the two soldiers had instead agreed to meet later for a fight, neither would be able to claim the defense because military law does not recognize the right of self-defense between mutual combatants.

The right to stand your ground and use deadly force to defend yourself can be traced back to the manslaughter trial of Wild Bill Hickock, who successfully claimed self-defense after killing Dave Tutt in a Springfield, Missouri, gunfight.[8] Likewise, military law does not require a service-member to exhaust all avenues of retreat prior to inflicting death or serious injury upon an attacker. However, the failure to retreat when that option exists may be considered when evaluating the reasonableness of the accused's fear of harm and sincerity of the accused's position that deadly force was necessary. RCM 916(e)(4), Discussion.

Servicemembers who use force in the defense of others only enjoy the same right to self-defense as those they assist. RCM 916(e)(5). If a service-member erroneously comes to the assistance of the aggressor, believing him to be the innocent victim, the servicemember may *not* claim defense of others. Neither may an accused claim self-defense after intervening in a mutual fight because neither of the original combatants can claim the defense.

Coercion/Duress

The fear of a third party inflicting immediate death or serious injury to the accused, or another innocent person, if the accused does not break the law may excuse any resultant criminal misconduct. In military slang, this situation is known as being between a rock and a hard place.

To raise the defense, the accused must establish (1) the misconduct was caused by a reasonable fear that the accused or another innocent person would suffer immediate death or serious injury if the accused did not commit the crime; (2) the fear of death or serious injury continued throughout the course of the criminal activity; and (3) the accused had no reasonable opportunity to stop engaging in the misconduct without subjecting himself or the innocent third party to that harm. RCM 916(h). The defense allows the accused to protect *any* innocent person; such as the accused's family, friends, shipmates, or even a complete stranger. However, the defense envisions the accused protecting an innocent party from *physical* injury; committing a crime to protect property, reputation, or to prevent someone from going to jail does not raise the defense.[9] Further, "financial duress" is not a recognized defense under military law. Accordingly, an army appeals court rejected the duress defense of a soldier who attempted to justify drug dealing by using his illicit profits to help rebuild his mother's house destroyed in a hurricane and to pay medical bills associated with his son's birth.[10]

Military courts have allowed some flexibility in the "immediate" harm requirement, depending upon the specific facts of the case. For example, in *United States v. Roberts,*[11] a sailor's AWOL was justified by fear of a demeaning initiation ceremony expected to occur the next day. In *United States v. Roby,*[12] a marine accused properly raised the defense to an unlawful absence charge when three fellow marines threatened to severely beat him the next time he was seen on base.

For a successful duress defense, the law requires that the fear of harm be reasonable. In *United States v. Logan,*[13] the accused sought to have his larceny and conspiracy convictions overturned, alleging that he engaged in the misconduct in Korea only after an unidentified caller threatened to harm his family, located in the United States, if he refused to participate. The appeals court rejected his arguments, reasoning that there was no basis "for a well-grounded apprehension of immediate death or serious bodily harm if he did not participate in the venture."[14]

In *United States v. Rankins,*[15] a soldier challenged her missing movement conviction based upon a duress defense. The court found her claim, that her husband might have a heart attack at some point in the future without anyone to assist him at home, failed all three elements of the duress defense. Albeit the accused's husband suffered from a minor heart ailment, no evidence existed suggesting that he was in immediate danger of a heart attack, thus failing the immediacy and reasonableness prongs.[16] Further, the accused could have avoided missing movement by purchasing her husband an electronic alert device, failing the third prong.[17]

Military law recognizes two significant exceptions to the defense. First, reflecting the military's unique function, duress is not a defense to the failure to obey an order to perform dangerous military duties.[18] Second, conforming to the generally accepted principle of law, duress is never a defense to killing an innocent person. RCM 916(h). Interestingly, the first conviction before the United Nations war crimes tribunal for crimes committed in the former Yugoslavia involved a Bosnian-Serb soldier who participated in the execution of hundreds of Muslim civilians near Srebrenica, Bosnia-Herzegovina. The soldier had offered a duress excuse for the murders, telling the tribunal that if he had refused to kill the civilians, he would have been shot.[19]

Accident

RCM 916(f) provides that "A death, injury, or other event that occurs as the unintentional and unexpected result of doing a lawful act in a lawful manner is an accident." In order to present this defense, the accused must meet a three-part test by showing that the act: (1) was not prohibited by a law, regulation, or order; (2) was performed in a proper manner; and (3) was accomplished without any improper intent.[20]

In *Moyer v. United States,*[21] a soldier who shot his troop commander in Vietnam challenged his murder conviction on the grounds that the death was an accident. Opposed to returning to the field, Moyer pointed his finger in his captain's face and began arguing with the officer. Prosecution witnesses testified that Moyer raised his M-16 and fired a burst of automatic fire into the officer's chest. Defense witnesses testified that the officer bumped Moyer while swatting the hand away, causing Moyer to accidently fire the weapon.[22]

The Army Court of Military Appeals rejected Moyer's accident defense, finding that he failed the first two portions of the test. First, at the time of the incident, Moyer was carrying a loaded weapon on the firebase, in direct violation of the unit's weapons SOP. Second, Moyer acted in a careless manner, carrying the rifle with the safety off, a round chambered and the selector switch on automatic.[23] Moyer's conduct was both prohibited by an order (weapons SOP) and performed in a careless (improper) manner.

Entrapment

Commonly known as "sting" operations, police regularly and legitimately use trickery to set traps for criminals intent on committing misconduct. However, military law recognizes that overzealous law enforcement efforts may cause otherwise law-abiding servicemembers to engage in misconduct that would not have occurred in the absence of police enticements.

To present an entrapment defense the accused must establish that (1) the idea to commit the crime originated with agents of the government, which include confidential informants and cooperating witnesses; and (2) the accused was not otherwise predisposed to the misconduct. RCM 916(g). The defense is not raised merely because governmental agents repeatedly approach the accused,[24] or provide the opportunity and means necessary to commit the offense. RCM 916(g), Discussion.

Once the defense raises an entrapment defense, the prosecution must prove that the accused was predisposed to committing the offense. Proof of predisposition may include evidence of similar misconduct, the lack of a personal relationship between the government informant and the accused, that the accused committed the crime after only a single contact or suggestion, the existence of a profit motive, or that government agents merely provided the accused with an opportunity to commit the crime but did not otherwise encourage it.[25]

Even if predisposed to a crime, an entrapment defense may still survive if the government's conduct was so outrageous that it violated the accused's constitutional right to due process. Although the success of a due process defense is rare, three of the five appellate judges in *United States v. LeMaster*[26] found outrageous government conduct and threw out the accused's conviction for attempted possession of cocaine. In *LeMaster,* an informant working with the Air Force Office of Special Investigations enticed a young, emotionally distraught, alcoholic woman, stationed in Montana, whose husband and children had just left her, into attempting to purchase cocaine from an AFOSI undercover agent. With AFOSI's knowledge, the informant had oral and anal sex with the accused, joked with AFOSI about her stupidity and emotional state, and—acting with the AFOSI undercover agent—initiated and coordinated all aspects of the drug sale.

Inability

Financial or physical inability serves as a defense to the refusal or failure to perform a duty or obey an order. However, the inability must be the actual cause of the accused's misconduct and cannot be the result of some fault of the accused. RCM 916(i).

Military courts have posited that the physical inability defense was established when a soldier with a hand injury failed to tie sandbags, by a guard with narcolepsy who fell asleep on guard duty, when a soldier with frostbitten feet refused to return to his fighting position on a nearby hill, and by a sailor who missed the sailing of his ship because he was mugged and rendered unconscious.[27] Conversely, the defense failed to an AWOL charge when the accused was confined by civilian police solely because of his own misconduct.[28]

A financial inability defense has seen some success in the military system. In *United States v. Pinkston,*[29] a marine sergeant's conviction for failure to obey an order to purchase two required uniforms by a specific date was reversed because the accused did not possess the financial ability to purchase the uniforms. Upon receipt of the order, Sgt. Pinkston, who was broke, made several unsuccessful efforts to draw advance pay and to borrow money from members of his unit. Pinkston's inability to timely comply with the order was the result of circumstances beyond his control.

The Manual for Courts-Martial offers as an example of a failed defense the situation of an accused who receives an order to obtain a haircut but then spends his money on nonessential items. RCM 916(i), Discussion. Additionally, published cases show that the financial inability defense has failed when the accused ignored the debt, and when he intentionally accumulated a large debt knowing that he could not, and would not, be unable to satisfy it.[30]

Insanity and Other Mental Responsibility Defenses

The military's insanity defense is identical to that found in the federal criminal system, reflecting changes to the law dictated by the Insanity Defense Reform Act of 1984.[31] To prove insanity the accused must establish that at the time of the misconduct he or she suffered from a "severe mental disease or defect" that caused her to be "unable to appreciate the nature and quality or the wrongfulness of the acts." Art. 50a(a), UCMJ. Procedurally, the panel first votes on the issue of guilt or innocence (two-thirds vote) and then votes on the insanity issue (majority vote). Art. 50a(e). If successful, the accused will be found "not guilty only by reason of lack of mental responsibility." Art. 50a(c) and (d).

Not all mental problems satisfy the legal standard for insanity; they must be "severe." Unfortunately, the manual fails to define the term but does indicate that it does not include "an abnormality manifested only by repeated criminal or otherwise antisocial conduct, or minor disorders such as nonpsychotic behavior disorders and personality defects." RCM 706(c)(2)(A). Further, the courts have determined that an intermittent explosive disorder, compulsive gambling, and a moderate personality disorder do not meet the severity requirement.[32]

The severity requirement may be satisfied in cases of multiple personality disorder, severe postpartum psychosis, involuntary intoxication, and post-traumatic stress disorder when the accused disassociates himself from reality.[33] A psychosis is not required.[34] However, even if the accused suffers from a severe mental disease or defect, insanity is not established unless the accused proves he was unable to understand the nature and quality or wrongfulness of his acts.

Although Article 50a(a) and RCM 916(k)(2) specifically preclude a partial mental responsibility defense, the courts have permitted an accused to attack the *mens rea* (guilty mind) element of an offense. Accordingly, an accused may present evidence of psychological impairment to negate a premeditated design to kill or a specific intent to commit a crime.[35] For example, voluntary intoxication, which is normally not a defense, can be used to cast reasonable doubt on the prosecution's evidence that the accused acted with the requisite knowledge, intent, willfulness, or premeditation.[36]

Successfully negating the mental condition can result in a complete acquittal or a conviction for a lesser form of the offense. Assume the accused is charged with unpremeditated murder, which requires the prosecution to prove a specific intent to kill or inflict serious bodily harm. Art. 118(b)(2). A conviction for unpremeditated murder may result in a life sentence. However, if successful in negating the mental condition of specific intent, the greatest offense that the accused can be convicted of is involuntary manslaughter, which is not a specific intent crime. Art. 119(b)(2). Involuntary manslaughter is punishable by a maximum period of incarceration of only ten years.

Voluntary Abandonment

Voluntary abandonment was initially recognized as a special defense to an attempt charge in *United States v. Byrd.*[37] The defense exists when the accused voluntarily abandons efforts to commit a crime; however, voluntary abandonment fails as a defense if the accused stops as a result of unexpected circumstances, fear of detection, or a lack of success.[38] Under such circumstances the accused's abandonment is considered involuntary and the law will not permit the accused to reap a windfall from failed efforts.

To illustrate, in *United States v. Miller,*[39] a sailor attempted to break restriction and leave his ship disguised as a food service worker, but aborted the effort after seeing a shipmate who could identify him standing topside. Because Miller abandoned his plan as a result of his fear of detection, the defense did not apply.

Voluntary abandonment also fails as a defense if the accused has progressed too far along the path of success before stopping efforts to commit the intended crime, particularly when the accused has caused substantial harm. In *United States v. Collier*,[40] an air force major who was having an affair attempted to murder his wife by drugging her and then pouring Tylenol elixir down a nasogastric tube into her stomach. After Collier's wife awoke, the accused left to obtain an antidote for her. The wife required emergency room care and recovery in intensive care. The Air Force Court of Military Review rejected Collier's voluntary abandonment defense, reasoning that the court had to draw a line at which the accused could no longer raise the defense. The court determined that the defense no longer existed once injury had occurred as a result of the accused's conduct.[41]

Similarly, the defense failed to a charge of attempted carnal knowledge in *United States v. Smauley*.[42] In that case a marine sergeant's conscience caused him to stop short of penetrating his stepdaughter after he fondled her breasts and vaginal area, undressed her and placed his penis against her vagina. Although stopping short of consummating his intended act of sexual intercourse, the accused had already indecently assaulted the victim and caused substantial psychological injury.[43]

Ignorance or Mistake of Fact

Although an accused's ignorance of the law is generally not a defense, the accused's ignorance of the true state of affairs may provide a partial or complete defense to certain crimes. RCM 916(j) provides that if the accused engaged in misconduct while operating under a mistaken belief as a result of being ignorant or mistaken as to certain facts, then a defense to the charge is raised when no crime would have existed if the facts were as the accused believed them to be. For example if Private Smith picks up the wrong gym bag and exits the post gymnasium believing herself to be in possession of her own gym bag, she would be able to raise a mistake of fact defense to any theft charges. If the facts were as she believed them to be—she took her own bag—she would have not committed a crime.

The requirements of the defense vary depending upon the type of crime. First, if the crime requires proof of "premeditation, specific intent, willfulness, or knowledge of a particular fact" then the mistake need only be an honest one. Second, if the crime requires proof of the lesser mental states of a general intent or knowledge, then the mistake must not only have honestly existed in the accused's mind but also have been objectively reasonable. RCM 916(j). A court may consider age, education, and experience when evaluating the honesty of the accused's mistaken beliefs.[44]

However, mistake of fact is not a defense to crimes in which the accused's knowledge or intentions are of no consequence. The manual provides two examples of such crimes: (1) Carnal Knowledge, because the accused's knowledge of the victim's age is not necessary to a determination of guilt or innocence if the victim is under the age of twelve; and (2) Improper Use of a Countersign, because it is not a defense that the accused did not know that the recipient of the countersign was not authorized to receive it. RCM 916(j) and Discussion.

In *United States v. Pierce,*[45] the defense was successful to a rape charge because the victim gave conflicting signals to the accused as to whether or not she actually consented to the sexual intercourse. Conversely, in *United States v. Traylor,*[46] the defense failed when the accused took the place of another soldier who was engaged in vaginal intercourse from the rear with the victim, without her knowledge of or consent to the switch. The court determined that Traylor's trickery negated any claim as to the honesty of his mistaken belief that the victim consented to intercourse with him and determined that the woman would consent to sex with the accused, without knowing his identity, "was patently unreasonable."[47]

The "self-help" defense is similar to, and often develops into, a mistake of fact defense. The self-help defense is limited to situations in which the accused takes property from another in order to satisfy a debt. In *United States v. Gunther,*[48] the defense was limited to instances in which the debtor agrees to permit the accused to take property either to satisfy or secure the debt. When no such agreement is in effect, but the accused honestly believes that an agreement did exist or that he could take the debtor's property, then a mistake of fact defense arises. Significantly, the self-help defense does not justify attempts to retrieve illegal goods, such as narcotics, and the value of the property taken must be similar to the amount of the debt.[49]

Miscellaneous Defenses

Although not specifically listed in the MCM, numerous defenses to military crimes have developed. A detailed discussion of all such defenses is beyond the scope of this book, but several such defenses warrant mentioning.

Divestiture

In the eyes of the law, commissioned, warrant, petty, and noncommissioned officers enjoy a special status by virtue of their rank and position. When they engage in behavior unbefitting of that elevated status they are considered to have abandoned it. Divestiture (also called abandonment of office or abandonment of rank) then serves as a defense to crimes in which the officer/NCO status is implicated, such as Articles 89 (Disrespect toward a superior commissioned officer), 90 (Assaulting or willfully disobeying superior commissioned officer), 91 (Insubordinate conduct toward warrant officer, noncommissioned officer, or petty officer), and 128(3)(a) (Assault upon a commissioned, warrant, noncommissioned, or petty officer).

A popular example, often seen on television or in the movies, revolves around the tough sergeant and the recalcitrant private who set their rank aside to settle their differences in a manly fashion. In *The Sands of Iwo Jima,* when Sergeant Striker (John Wayne) pummels PFC Thomas (Forest Tucker) for abandoning two squad mates in order to enjoy a cup of coffee, Striker has abandoned his status as an NCO.[50]

A similar situation (also involving marines) arose in *United States v. Stuckman,*[51] in which Pvt. Stuckman stated during a nonjudicial punishment hearing that he "would like to see the Marine Corps flat on its back with its heels in the air." Stuckman's commanding officer replied that he represented the Marine Corps and challenged Stuckman to put the officer on his back, which Stuckman did. Because the marine officer had abandoned his position and rank, Stuckman's court-martial conviction for assaulting the officer was reversed.

The existing body of case law defines the parameters of this defense. The use of racially offensive epithets may serve as a complete defense to a disrespect charge, but only a partial defense to an assault charge.[52] Instead of being convicted of assault upon an officer or NCO, the accused would be convicted of a lesser form of assault. Art. 128(b). Profanity, even if used in a heated fashion, will not normally result in divestiture.[53]

The divestiture defense is not raised by the mere fact that military superiors exceed their authority. The courts have determined that superiors did not abandon their status merely because they conducted unlawful searches or violated regulations by assisting in the repossession of the accused's automobile.[54] Undue familiarity between a superior and subordinate may serve as a defense to a disrespect charge, but is unlikely to work for assault or disobedience charges.[55]

Amnesia

Historically, military courts have rejected amnesia defenses, viewing the accused's inability to remember merely as a symptom of a mental problem, but not as a defense itself.[56] Further, an inability to remember the crime does not by itself render the accused incompetent to stand trial, although the courts have conceded that such a mental state may place the accused at a slight disadvantage.[57]

A narrow exception to the general rejection of the amnesia defense arises in cases of unauthorized absences or missing movement. In *United States v. Wiseman*,[58] a sailor was convicted of being an unauthorized absentee (UA) for almost two years, despite having testified that he could not remember portions of the UA period, including its inception. The navy appellate court adjusted the time period reflected in Wiseman's conviction, holding that the panel should have been informed that the sailor could not be convicted of UA for those periods of time that he was temporarily without knowledge that he was in the navy.[59]

Automatism

In *United States v. Berri*,[60] the U.S. Court of Military Appeals reaffirmed automatism as a valid defense in the military. Also known as the "unconsciousness" defense, automatism refers to actions taken without thinking about them. Sleepwalking is an example of conduct performed in an unconscious or semiconscious state. Because the condition is not dependent upon a mental disease or defect it is not considered a defense based on a lack of mental responsibility.

In one of the earliest recorded successful uses of the defense, a man sleeping in a hotel lobby reacted instantaneously to the efforts of a porter to awake him by shooting the porter. A Kentucky court reversed the man's murder conviction because he had not been permitted to put on evidence that he was a sleepwalker and had acted in an unconscious state.[61]

The only reported military case of a successful automatism defense occurred during World War II. In *United States v. Braley*,[62] a drunken merchant marine sailor serving with the navy suffered a head injury after being knocked unconscious by the ship's sentry, whom the sailor had challenged to fight. While being carried to his room, Braley awoke in a confused and irrational state, pulled out a pistol and shot the ship's master, referring to the latter as a "Nazi Jap."[63] The navy reversed Braley's murder conviction, finding that he had engaged in "automatic behavior" as a result of his head injury.[64]

Defenses to Drug Use

Although chemical hair analysis has been accepted as a legitimate means of proving unlawful use of narcotics,[65] most drug use courts-martial are generated as a result of a positive urinalysis. Coming up "hot" on a urinalysis creates a permissible inference that the accused wrongfully used that drug.[66]

Testing laboratories check primarily for by-products of cocaine and marijuana (called "metabolites") but are also capable of testing for LSD, barbiturates, opiates, PCP, and amphetamines. These metabolites are not naturally produced by the body absent the presence of the illicit drug. The ability to detect the metabolite varies with each drug. Because cocaine is water soluble, it dissipates quickly and is detectable for a shorter period of time than marijuana, which is fat soluble and dissipates slowly.

In testing urine for drugs, two tests are commonly used: (1) radio-immunoassay (RIA) and (2) gas chromatography/mass spectroscopy (GC/MS). RIA is an initial screening test that will result in a presumptive positive. It involves adding a radioactive substance that competes with the drug metabolites to bind with antibodies in the urine and then measuring the level of radioactivity in a sampling of that mixture. The level of radioactivity in the sample is inversely related to the amount of drug in the urine. High radioactivity indicates little or no drug metabolites because the sample only contains what was put into it: the radioactive substance. Conversely, low radioactivity indicates the presence of an illicit drug because the sample contains a higher percentage of nonradioactive material: the drug metabolite.

If the sample satisfies the RIA nanogram level, it then proceeds to the GC/MS confirmatory test. The GC/MS testing procedure is based on an analysis of the unique ion fragmentation of each drug. The urine is heated to a gaseous state, bombarded by ions, and then clocked by a computer to measure its speed as it runs along a glass tube. The speed of the gas varies with each drug.

The Department of Defense has set cut-off levels for both tests, varying by specific drug, which must be satisfied before a sample is declared positive. The cut-off levels are measured in nanograms (parts per billion) per milliliter. Even if the presence of metabolites for a prohibited drug are discovered, if either test result measures below the prescribed nanogram level, the sample is declared negative for illicit drugs.

The accuracy and quality of laboratory testing has progressed to such a state of proficiency that attempting to establish laboratory error rarely succeeds. Further in *United States v. Mance,*[67] the court specifically rejected the melanin defense, which is based on the premise that pigmentation in dark-skinned people can cause a false positive for marijuana.

However, other defenses to a positive urinalysis based court-martial remain viable. Such defenses, used singularly or in combination, include: good military character, passive inhalation, and innocent ingestion.[68] The latter defense is rooted in Article 112a's requirement that the accused knowingly use the illegal drug. MCM, ¶ 37(c)(10). In *United States v. Williams,*[69] the court explained that the defense would be raised when someone secretly places a drug in the accused's drink, when the accused eats a brownie that he does not know contains marijuana, or when the accused puts a white powdery drug into his coffee thinking it to be sugar even though it is actually cocaine.

Recently, the United States Supreme Court closed the door to the possibility of admitting evidence that the accused had passed a polygraph denying the use of drugs. In *United States v. Scheffer,*[70] the Supreme Court upheld Military Rule of Evidence 707, which creates an absolute prohibition against the use of polygraph evidence at courts-martial.

Various procedural errors may serve to undercut the prosecution's case. Examples of possible defenses include: the potential for tampering as evidenced by an unexplained break in the urine sample's chain of custody; the improper destruction of the urine sample, precluding an opportunity for the defense to retest the sample;[71] and improperly targeting an individual under the guise of a random urinalysis (subterfuge testing is discussed in chapter 4).

Jury Nullification

Jury nullification is not a recognized defense; rather, it is more a state of affairs. The term refers to the power of a jury (or panel) to refuse to convict even though the accused is clearly guilty of the crime. Such power exists because a military judge cannot direct a guilty verdict, the trial counsel cannot appeal an acquittal, and an accused cannot be court-martialed twice for the same crime.

Acting as the conscience of the military community, a panel may refuse to convict merely because they believe the law is unjust, view the prosecutor or command as overzealous or vindictive, sympathize with the accused, view the victim unfavorably, or fear that a court-martial conviction and sentence would cause an unduly harsh punishment to be inflicted upon the accused. To illustrate, a panel may sympathize with the servicemember who assaults someone found in bed with his or her spouse, believe it would be unjust to convict a seventeen-year-old of statutory rape who falls in love with and engages in consensual intercourse with an underage female, or refuse to convict a retirement eligible noncommissioned officer who has tested positive for drug use because a conviction would jeopardize the NCO's pension.

One reported case from the Vietnam War illustrates a case of partial nullification. In *United States v. Duffy,* a panel found Lieutenant Duffy guilty of premeditated murder after ordering the execution of a prisoner, but upon learning that such an offense required a mandatory sentence of life imprisonment, the panel quickly reconsidered its findings and voted to convict Duffy of involuntary manslaughter.[72] The panel sentenced Duffy to six months' confinement rather than the original mandatory life sentence.[73]

In one court-martial of which I am aware, an NCO became increasingly frustrated with a troublesome soldier, who was pending an administrative separation from the army. Eventually, the recalcitrant soldier "mouthed-off" to the NCO in front of his platoon, causing the NCO to lose his temper and punch the soldier. The NCO refused an Article 15 and demanded a court-martial. Standing before a sympathetic enlisted panel, the NCO admitted to hitting the soldier and explained his reasons for doing so. Although the facts were beyond dispute and the accused possessed no legal defense to the charge, the panel took less than half an hour to acquit him.

However, an unbridled nullification power poses a number of significant risks to the military justice system. Nullification permits a panel to selectively enforce the law in an arbitrary or whimsical manner, undercuts Congress' authority as our nation's lawmakers, and arguably encourages a general disrespect for the law. Accordingly, military courts view jury nullification with hostility, and have dictated that an accused does not have a right to inform a panel of its power to nullify at trial.[74] Even though an accused will not be permitted to have the judge instruct a panel of its right to nullify, defense counsel will continue to argue for nullification and the occasional panel can be expected to refuse to convict even when the facts and law clearly call for such a verdict.

10

Miscellaneous Issues in Military Law

During World War II, following a series of incidents in which Lt. "Jackie" Robinson of the U.S. Army refused to succumb to racial discrimination at Camp Hood, Texas, the necessary paperwork was prepared to have Robinson court-martialed. The future baseball star's commanding officer, Lt. Col. Paul Bates, opposed taking any such disciplinary action. Military officials at Camp Hood reacted by transferring Robinson to another unit, whose commander was willing to accommodate the wishes of his superiors. Undaunted, Bates testified on Robinson's behalf at trial, contributing to a not guilty verdict on all charges.[1]

Unlawful Command Influence

Historically, commanders have exercised enormous authority in the military's criminal system. Prior to World War I, military commanders were empowered to reverse acquittals and revise sentences that they believed were inadequate.[2] Although such unbridled power has been greatly curtailed during this century, commanders continue to legitimately exercise considerable influence over the military justice system in an effort to ensure unit discipline, morale, and combat readiness.

As the court-martial of Jackie Robinson illustrates, the improper use of command authority to influence the administration of justice has been a persistent fixture in military legal history. Called the "mortal enemy of military justice,"[3] unlawful command influence refers to a superior's improper interference with a subordinate's duties or discretionary actions within the military legal system. In its most basic terms, improper command influence inhibits the accused's ability to receive a fair trial.

A superior may not discourage witnesses from testifying on behalf of an accused, force a subordinate to prefer charges, influence referral recommendations, or suggest appropriate sentences. In *United States v. Gerlich*,[4] the accused's conviction was thrown out after the court found improper command influence when the commanding general sent a letter to his subordinate commander suggesting that his proposed disposition for Gerlich's misconduct (an Article 15) was inappropriate. Further, even the creation of a command climate in which subordinates are afraid to testify on behalf of an accused may constitute unlawful command influence.[5]

The most troublesome legal land mines for well-meaning commanders in this area have come in the form of speeches, policy letters, and articles. Seemingly benign command guidance may be misinterpreted by subordinates to mean that they should not testify favorably for an accused or that certain classes of criminals should be severely punished. The most infamous example of unlawful command influence involved the commanding general of the army's Third Armored Division, who commented to his officers and senior NCOs on the inconsistency of a commander recommending a level of court-martial capable of issuing a punitive discharge and then testifying at sentencing that the accused was a good soldier and should be retained in the military.[6] Numerous subordinate commanders and senior enlisted members—including the division command sergeant major—interpreted the general's comment to discourage the division's officers and NCOs from testifying for an accused at trial.[7]

Unlawful command influence is not limited to commanders but may be committed by anyone subject to the UCMJ who improperly influences the court-martial process. Military courts have stated that improper influence may occur in action taken by military judges, noncommissioned officers, a commander's staff, the president of a court-martial panel, and the prosecutor.[8] However, not all improper interference with the court-martial process is enough to constitute unlawful command influence; the actor must at least appear to possess the "mantle of command authority."[9]

Improper interference with the court-martial process is specifically prohibited by Article 37, UCMJ, and punishable pursuant to Article 98. However, the punitive article has proved to be a paper tiger as no reported case exists holding a military superior criminally responsible for unlawful command influence, even when the misconduct appeared blatant.

The absence of a single reported case suggests that the matter is not viewed as seriously by field commanders, who usually prefer and refer criminal charges, as it is by the military's appellate judiciary. Regardless, when a case involving unlawful command influence that has prejudiced an accused does percolate to the appeals court level, the courts appear eager to correct the wrong by ordering a reduced sentence, a new sentencing hearing, or a new trial.

Sexual Harassment

As a microcosm of American society, the military brings into its ranks all the social baggage found in the civilian community, including gender stereotypes and antiquated, sexist views of what constitutes permissible conduct toward members of the opposite sex. In addition to the problems plaguing the civilian sector, the military must contend with certain qualities unique to its internal composition that create a nidus for sexual harassment.

First and foremost, the military remains a largely patriarchal society in which bravado is perceived as a necessary prerequisite for success on the battlefield. Ultimately battles are won or lost by combat forces who exert their physical dominance over the enemy under extremely dangerous and demanding conditions. Encouraging a martial attitude or warrior spirit occasionally spills over into a propensity for men to view women as inferiors, dismissing them as mere sexual objects or second-class citizens rather than treating women as coequal comrades-in-arms.

Further, military superiors exercise enormous power over their subordinates, both in terms of their ability to affect careers and the amount of raw power that they wield generally. A ship's captain, drill sergeant, or commander of a unit situated in a remote location can present an imposing and omnipotent figure to subordinates. Unfortunately less scrupulous superiors may take advantage of these positions of authority. While a system exists to report abuses of authority, many are understandably hesitant to do so. A reluctance to be seen as a troublemaker, distrust of the chain-of-command, fear of retaliation, and concerns about being believed all contribute to the problem.

Sexual harassment is a form of sexual discrimination, encompassing conduct ranging from rape to inappropriate jokes. It is neither limited to harassment of women by men nor restricted to incidents occurring at the work place. The Equal Employment Opportunity Commission (EEOC), which is charged with enforcing antidiscrimination laws within the federal civilian work force, defines "sexual harassment" as follows:

> Unwelcome sexual advances, requests for sexual favors, and other verbal or physical conduct of a sexual nature constitute sexual harassment when (1) submission to such conduct is made either explicitly or implicitly a term or condition of an individual's employment, (2) submission to or rejection of such conduct by an individual is used as the basis for employment decisions affecting such individual, or (3) such conduct has the purpose or effect of unreasonably interfering with an individual's work performance or creating an intimidating, hostile, or offensive working environment.[10]

These EEOC guidelines group sexual harassment into two distinct forms: "quid pro quo" (something for something) and the sexually offensive or hostile environment.

Military regulatory definitions of sexual harassment generally parallel the EEOC definition. For example, Army Regulation (AR) 600-20, Army Command Policy, defines sexual harassment as

> a form of sex discrimination that involves unwelcome sexual advances, requests for sexual favors, and other verbal or physical conduct of a sexual nature, when:
> a. submission to or rejection of such conduct is made either explicitly or implicitly a term or condition of a person's job, pay, or career;
> b. submission to or rejection of such conduct by a person is used as a basis for career or employment decisions affecting that person; or
> c. such conduct interferes with an individual's performance or creates an intimidating, hostile, or offensive environment.

From a disciplinary standpoint, the UCMJ provides a wide variety of punitive articles to punish conduct constituting sexual harassment. In *United States v. Athey*,[11] a marine captain who fondled the breasts of a civilian employee under his supervision was convicted of conduct unbecoming an officer and indecent acts. Similarly, in *United States v. Parini*,[12] an army colonel who attempted to make sexual favors a requirement for a positive evaluation report was convicted of conduct unbecoming. In *United States v. Hester*[13] the mere placing of the accused's hand on a junior enlisted female's thigh, under circumstances indicating that the accused was soliciting sex from her, was sufficient to convict the NCO of indecent assault.

Sexist subordinates may also be dealt with under the UCMJ. In *United States v. Dornick*,[14] an airman who said "Hi sweetheart" to a female officer was convicted of behaving with disrespect toward a superior commissioned officer.

Theoretically, military superiors who are aware of sexual harassment within their units, but do nothing to stop it, may be court-martialed for dereliction of duty. However, no reported cases reflect a superior ever being held criminally responsible under this theory of prosecution.

The sole article that specifically addresses "sexual harassment" as an offense in and of itself is Article 93, Maltreatment of Subordinate. Sexual harassment constitutes a violation of the article, which is defined as "influencing, offering to influence, or threatening the career, pay, or job of another person in exchange for sexual favors, and deliberate or repeated offensive comments or gestures of a sexual nature." MCM, ¶ 17(c)(2).

To establish a violation of Article 93, the government must prove that (1) the victim was subject to the accused's orders and (2) "the accused was cruel toward, or oppressed, or maltreated that person." MCM ¶ 17(b). Being subject to the accused's orders neither requires that the accused be in the victim's chain-of-command nor that the victim be a servicemember. MCM ¶ 17(c)(1). The article is broad enough in scope to include sexual harassment of a civilian employee under the accused's supervision or a subordinate member of another branch of the service not in the accused's unit. In *United States v. Sojfer*,[15] junior enlisted patients at a medical clinic were deemed to be subject to the orders of a navy corpsmen first class, solely because of the differences in rank.

Sexist comments or gestures need not be particularly heinous to violate Article 93, so long as they are offensive to the recipient.[16] Further, the offensiveness of the comments and gestures is measured objectively from the perspective of the victim, rather than looking at the subjective intent of the harasser. In *United States v. Hanson*,[17] for example, an air force captain was convicted of maltreating his subordinates despite his claim that his comments were made only in jest.

Article 93's requirement that the gestures and comments be "offensive" indicates that such sexist comments constitute sexual harassment only if they are unwelcome, which is a distinction drawn in civil law.[18] Accordingly, evidence that the victim was sexually provocative by words or deeds is relevant in determining whether the challenged conduct was unwelcome.[19] Further, mutually engaged in sexual banter among a group of servicemembers or in a private conversation between consenting adults should not violate Article 93 as to those participating in the conversations. However, the possibility exists that a group of servicemembers — even if composed of both sexes — may violate the article when third parties repeatedly overhear the remarks, creating a sexually hostile environment.

Fraternization

Throughout history, armies and navies have always drawn clear lines of acceptable social behavior between military superiors and subordinates, particularly regarding relations between the officer and enlisted ranks. Since the days of the Roman Empire, the military has been concerned about the adverse affects upon morale and discipline if superiors were to show preferential treatment to their subordinate/friends, or be perceived as doing so by other members of the unit.[20] In addition to a professed desire to maintain discipline, the military often drew lines to reflect the educational and social disparity between the two military castes — a distinction that has blurred in modern times.

The American military has traditionally embraced legal prohibitions against fraternization between officers and enlisted personnel. In his legal treatise, *Military Law and Precedents,* Col. William Winthrop noted that misconduct constituting conduct unbecoming an officer and a gentleman during the nineteenth century included "demeaning of himself by an officer with soldiers or military inferiors."[21] Examining court-martial convictions from the 1800s, Winthrop listed as illustrations: "drinking and carousing, or other drunken conduct, with them"; gambling; "indecently or unbecomingly familiar association or dealing with them, or indecent conduct in their presence"; "associating on familiar terms with persons of inferior social rank"; and "pusillanimously submitting to public insult or chastisement by inferiors or others without taking any measure to vindicate themselves."[22]

Albeit many of the educational and social distinctions have been blurred, all branches of the armed forces, to varying degrees, continue to prohibit undue familiarity between military superiors and subordinates. Although conduct constituting fraternization may be prosecuted as a violation of an order or regulation under Article 92, or as conduct unbecoming an officer via Article 133, the UCMJ specifically makes fraternization punishable as such pursuant to Article 134.

Military courts have expanded the parameters of the offense beyond the language found in the Manual. Although the MCM seems to limit the offense to officers and warrant officers (¶ 83(b)(1)), in *United States v. Clarke* and *United States v. Carter,*[23] the army and navy appellate courts put non-commissioned and petty officers on notice that they too could be prosecuted for fraternization with enlisted subordinates. Additionally, despite language limiting fraternization to an "enlisted member" (¶ 83(b)(2-4)), in *United States v. Callaway,*[24] the army court opined that an improper social relationship between a senior officer and a newly commissioned lieutenant under his command constituted fraternization for both Articles 133 and 134.

To prove fraternization the prosecution must also establish that the improper social relationship violated a custom of the accused's branch of the armed forces. For air force prosecutors, this has been the most difficult part of the crime to prove. The difficulty stems from the opinion of the Air Force Court of Military Review in *United States v. Johanns,*[25] that "the custom in the Air Force against fraternization has been so eroded as to make criminal prosecution against an officer for engaging in mutually, voluntary, private, non-deviate sexual intercourse with an enlisted member, neither under his command or supervision, unavailable."

Because customs vary by service, the *Johanns* decision did not affect fraternization prosecutions in the other branches of the armed forces.[26] Until 1995, however, a violation of the air force fraternization custom appeared to be limited to direct superior-subordinate, supervisory, or command relationships between servicemembers.[27] Then, in *United States v. Boyett,*[28] the pendulum began to reverse its course when the military appellate court system affirmed the fraternization conviction of an air force officer who engaged in sexual intercourse with a female airman, off post, over whom he did not enjoy a supervisory relationship. The court in *Boyett* appeared to limit *Johanns* to the specific facts of that case, suggesting that the air force had developed a new and less tolerant fraternization custom.

The military appellate courts dealt another blow to proponents of a lax air force fraternization custom in *United States v. McCreight,*[29] in which a male air force lieutenant was convicted of fraternizing with a male enlisted airman. Rejecting the argument that the air force fraternization custom was limited to sexual relations between an officer and airmen with a supervisory relationship, the court stated that fraternization was not dependent upon a sexual relationship; it was enough that the officer afforded the airman preferential treatment, that the two were on a first name basis, were drinking buddies, shared the officer's residence on a frequent basis, and generally socialized on terms of equality.[30]

The current trend of cases suggests that the military's customs against fraternization are alive, well, and gradually growing more stringent. Even more important, the air force's efforts to bring its custom back within the military mainstream is proving successful. Given the latest pronouncements by the military courts, it appears likely that the air force fraternization custom will exhibit few substantive differences from those service customs found elsewhere in the military.

Fratricide (Friendly Fire)

Historically, fratricide has been a tragic but constant by-product of what Clausewitz referred to as the "fog of war." Thrust into chaotic, stressful, life-threatening situations, American servicemen have been responsible for killing or wounding their comrades-in-arms. The likelihood of fratricide incidents is particularly pronounced when normal combat stressors are coupled with sleep deprivation, a condition regularly seen in the continuous operations that characterize modern warfare.[31]

Fratricide may have been responsible for as much as 15 percent of all American casualties during the last century.[32] America's last major military conflict, Operation Desert Storm, saw 24 percent of its dead and 15 percent of its wounded caused by friendly fire.[33] During the World War II Allied invasion of the Aleutian island of Kiska, American and Canadian forces sustained twenty-eight KIA and fifty WIA despite the fact that *all* Japanese forces had been previously evacuated from the island![34]

As abhorrent as friendly fire incidents may be, they are rarely dealt with through the military justice system.[35] The natural desire to hold responsible individuals accountable for their actions is often tempered by the recognition that individuals are more prone to make mistakes in combat situations. Oftentimes, fratricide may be caused by a series of errors making it difficult to fix responsibility on any single individual. Further, prosecution of any but the most egregious cases of negligent behavior may be viewed as second-guessing decisions made under extremely trying circumstances, undermining the morale of combatants and discouraging aggressiveness on the battlefield.[36]

One of the most infamous incidents of fratricide during World War II, which occurred during the Allied invasion of Sicily, illustrates the difficulty in dealing with such incidents through the military justice system. On 11 July 1943, Gen. George Patton ordered elements of the 82d Airborne Division to make a night jump into Sicily in support of Allied operations.

As the 145 C–47 aircraft approached the landing zone, American antiaircraft crews inexplicably opened fire, damaging thirty-seven aircraft and shooting down another twenty-three.[37] More than three hundred paratroopers and airmen were either killed, wounded, or missing.[38]

Upon learning of the disaster, Gen. Dwight Eisenhower ordered an immediate investigation, demanding that disciplinary action be taken against the responsible parties.[39] Patton feared that he would be held responsible and relieved; others tried to lay blame alternatively on the aviators, the navy, or army ground commanders.[40] Ultimately the division commander, Gen. Matthew Ridgway, recommended against taking any disciplinary action, believing that any effort to fix responsibility would be difficult, cause finger pointing among those potentially responsible, and would prove to be of questionable value.[41] Ridgway concluded that they should learn from mistakes made and accept the casualties as "the inevitable price of war in human life."[42]

More recently, the air force's efforts to hold accountable those responsible for the destruction of two army helicopters over northern Iraq highlighted the limitations of the military justice system. On 14 April 1994, two air force fighter pilots mistook two army UH-60 Black Hawk helicopters for Iraqi helicopters and shot them down, killing all twenty-six people aboard.[43] Investigations of the mishap revealed a multitude of errors at several levels of command.[44] Six air force officers were charged with negligent homicide and dereliction of duty, but the charges were dropped against everyone except Capt. Jim Wang, the senior director of the monitoring E-3 Sentry Airborne Warning and Control Systems (AWACS) plane.[45] Wang was eventually acquitted.

The air force's efforts to hold the F-15 pilot and AWACS crew criminally responsible for the deaths met severe criticism. The disciplinary efforts adversely affected the morale of other AWACS crews[46] and generated charges that the airmen were merely scapegoats to cover up larger, systemic problems.[47] When charges were dropped against the F-15 pilot but not against Wang, many questioned why Wang alone was facing charges.[48] Members of the AWACS community questioned whether the charging decision reflected an institutional bias in favor of fighter pilots.[49]

Ultimately, Wang's acquittal satisfied few and touched off a torrent of criticism that effectively branded the entire military justice effort a failure. Dissatisfied, Wang and members of the victims' families called for an outside investigation,[50] the Secretaries of the air force and army were directed to review the entire proceedings to determine if additional disciplinary action was warranted,[51] the air force chief of staff took career-ending administrative action against seven officers involved in the tragedy,[52] and Congress launched its own investigation into the air force's handling of the incident.[53]

The practical limitations of the legal system will prove a difficult pill to swallow for commanders and members of the American public who legitimately expect the military to hold accountable those servicemembers whose shortcomings result in unnecessary deaths. But as history has shown, except in cases of clear-cut, individualized gross negligence, friendly fire incidents will remain difficult to successfully prosecute and the overzealous pursuit of justice following such incidents may cause more harm than good.

11

The Law of War

No work on military criminal law would be complete without some discussion of the law of war, which refers primarily to violations of the Geneva and Hague Conventions, those practices customarily followed by the majority of nations, and that body of law created by international tribunals in the aftermath of World War II. Of note, the law of war generally is part of American law, and the policy of the United States is to prosecute American servicemembers for law of war violations under the applicable provisions of the UCMJ rather than as "war crimes."

General Principles

Three general principles overshadow any discussion of the laws of war: military necessity, unnecessary suffering, and proportionality. Military necessity justifies those actions necessary to defeat the enemy as long as they do not otherwise violate the law.[1] It does *not* mean that a combatant may do whatever he believes necessary to accomplish the mission. Legally, the ends do not justify the means. A patrol operating behind enemy lines is not permitted to kill its POWs in order to escape detection or to facilitate mission accomplishment, because the killing of the prisoners would constitute murder and would not be justified by "military necessity."

During April 1945, a German unit surrounded by, and hiding from, American ground forces wounded and captured an American army officer. Upon the orders of his battalion commander, a German lieutenant ordered a subordinate grenadier to kill the American; the order was obeyed. In *Trial of Gunther Thiele and Georg Steinert,*[2] an American military commission rejected the defense of military necessity and the German argument of *Kreigsraeson geht vor Kriegsmanier* (necessity in war overrules the manner of warfare), sentencing both soldiers to life imprisonment.

The infliction of unnecessary suffering by weaponry calculated to cause increased pain, or through unnecessary destruction of structures and property, is also prohibited.[3] That principle is discussed later in this chapter.

Finally, the anticipated death and destruction associated with a particular combat operation must not significantly outweigh the projected military benefits to be gained.[4] Destroying an entire village with artillery or air strikes in order to kill a single sniper would violate this principle. The use of such overwhelming firepower, with the attendant damage to the village and its inhabitants, would be grossly disproportionate to the slight military gain: the elimination of the sniper. The attacking force must consider less destructive options, such as suppressing the sniper with small arms fire.

The American and British aerial bombardment of the ancient German city of Dresden during World War II was of questionable legality when the resultant destruction and enormous number of civilian casualties are measured against the limited military value of the operation. Indeed, Telford Taylor, the chief American prosecutor at the Nuremberg war crimes trials, described the bombing of Dresden as a war crime, violative of the principle of proportionality and "tolerable in retrospect only because [its] malignancy pales in comparison to Dachau, Auschwitz, and Treblinka."[5]

Although it held no large concentrations of German forces, Dresden was a regional communications, administration, and industrial center, possessing some value as a military target by February 1945.[6] However, the primary object of the attack was not to strike military targets; instead, it was part of a terror bombing campaign designed to create chaos behind the German lines and undermine the morale of the German people.[7] Dresden's normal population of six hundred thousand had swollen to approximately one million with the influx of Allied POWs (including author Kurt Vonnegut, whose experiences at Dresden are reflected in his novel *Slaughterhouse Five*) and refugees fleeing from the advancing Soviet army.[8]

In a deliberate effort to create a firestorm, the initial Royal Air Force (RAF) group dropped primarily incendiary bombs.[9] Between 13 and 15 February more than eight hundred RAF and six hundred USAF aircraft reduced the city to rubble, killing over twenty-five thousand (with another thirty-five thousand unaccounted for) and destroying or severely damaging almost eighty-seven thousand homes.[10] The expected military advantage of the bombing of Dresden (creation of chaos, disruption of the German war machine, and undercutting of German morale) was far outweighed by the number of anticipated civilian casualties and damage to civilian structures.

Prohibited Weapons

The use of certain weapons during hostilities is prohibited either because they are inherently illegal or because they are used in an improper manner. Generally, weapons that are inherently illegal are those that are specifically prohibited by treaty or are intentionally designed to inflict unnecessary suffering. Dum-dum bullets, feces-covered punji stakes, and glass-filled projectiles fall into this category.[11]

To further illustrate, biological weapons have been prohibited by treaty since 1925, yet as many as a dozen nations are suspected of possessing biological weapon stockpiles, including Russia, North Korea, and Iraq.[12] In modern times, no nation has actually employed such weapons against an enemy force, with the possible exception of Japan. Ironically, the 1925 Geneva Convention outlawing the use of biological weapons encouraged the Imperial Japanese Army to develop a biological weapons program under the distorted reasoning that anything so horrible that its use had been banned by the international community just had to be a wonderful weapon.[13] Starting in the 1930s, Japan employed a biological warfare unit to China, reportedly dispatched a biological-weapon-laden submarine to Saipan to oppose its invasion by U.S. Marines (it was sunk enroute), and was prepared by 1945 to use kamikaze pilots to ferry plague-infected fleas into California.[14]

Other weapons are illegal only because of the manner in which they are used. For example, the forward observer who calls in white phosphorous artillery rounds on exposed infantrymen solely to increase their suffering has committed a crime, although white phosphorous rounds are a legitimate means of marking targets. The illegality arises when the soldier deliberately chooses to use a weapon solely because it will cause unnecessary suffering.

Contrary to popular belief, the law does not absolutely prohibit the use of large-caliber weapons against individuals. In basic training we were told that it was illegal to use a 50-caliber machine gun against soldiers, but that it could be used to target enemy equipment. Accordingly, to circumvent this legal restriction, the drill sergeants suggested we aim at equipment worn by the enemy soldiers rather than at the soldiers themselves.

There is nothing facially illegal about using any large-scale weapon, such as a 50-caliber machine gun, against individual enemy soldiers. Indeed, during the Vietnam War a marine sniper, Carlos Norman Hathcock II, set the record for the longest confirmed kill—2,500 yards—using a 50-caliber machine gun.[15] Criminality only comes into play when the servicemember intentionally uses a large-scale weapon as a means of inflicting greater, and unnecessary, suffering on the enemy. Accordingly, defenders of a base camp may direct fire artillery pieces, Vulcan antiaircraft guns, or any other available weapon system against an attacking enemy infantry force if the use of such weapons is necessary to repulse the attack.

Prohibited Targets

Certain persons and places enjoy various degrees of protection under the laws of war. Not every individual on the battlefield can be shot or every structure destroyed. Conversely, those protections can be lost through misconduct by the enemy or the local populace. Neither American nor international law precludes a servicemember from exercising the right of self-defense against the civilian who attacks our forces or against the enemy soldiers who fire on Americans from the safety of a normally protected structure, such as a church. When those special protections are not lost, however, the law of war places prohibitions on the people and places that may be brought under fire.

Protected Persons

Everyone on the battlefield falls into two basic groups: combatants and noncombatants. A combatant is anyone engaged in hostilities as a member of a military force and may be freely targeted. If recognized as a "lawful" combatant, they are afforded various protections in case of capture; "unlawful" combatants may be treated as mere criminals and prosecuted as such under domestic law. The American armed forces treat all captured combatants as being lawfully on the battlefield until a legal determination of their status is complete.

Civilians are the most obvious class of noncombatants and they may not be the primary object of an attack; but it is not illegal to attack a legitimate military target, such as a munitions factory, that may cause incidental civilian casualties. Additionally, it is not illegal to fire on an enemy who is illegally using civilians as a human shield, although every effort should be made to avoid inflicting civilian casualties. The illegal action would be committed by the enemy force hiding behind the civilian shield, not by the unit forced to return fire through that shield.

During an incident from the Vietnam War, North Vietnamese soldiers fired on American helicopters from the safety of a Montagnard village located south of Pleiku, South Vietnam. American forces attempted to warn away the villagers, but the NVA unit refused to permit their departure, resulting in several civilian casualties in the ensuring American attack. The American actions were legally justified; the NVA refusal to permit the villagers to leave and to use them as a human shield was not.[16]

Beyond civilians, other protected persons on the battlefield include detainees and enemy personnel considered hors de combat (out of combat), such as prisoners of war, sick and wounded, the shipwrecked, certain medical personnel, and chaplains. Full-time medical personnel—those exclusively engaged in medical duties, including the administration of a medical unit—and chaplains fall into a special subcategory known as "retained persons." If captured, they are not considered POWs but retained personnel who must be permitted to perform their medical/spiritual duties and be returned as soon as practicable.[17] Because of their unique status, chaplains and medical personnel normally should not assume command of a POW compound, even if they are the senior officer present. Limited protections exist for members of a force who have been trained to perform medical-related duties, such as hospital orderlies and auxiliary stretcher-bearers. If captured while performing such duties, these part-time medical personnel are treated as POWs but must be permitted to perform medical-related duties if needed.[18]

When providing medical treatment to the sick and wounded, the capturing force cannot give preferential treatment to their own forces. In what has come to be known as the "triage" concept, the priority of treatment is based on the severity of the injury, not on the nationality of the wounded person.[19]

For various reasons noncombatants may find themselves in situations in which they cross the line into the role of a combatant. Medical personnel may be detailed to guard nonmedical facilities, as the Canadian forces did recently in Somalia; medical unit commanders may be placed in charge of a base or convoy containing both medical and nonmedical units, and be responsible for the defense of such a force; or Medevac pilots may be ordered to fly ammunition resupply missions. In Vietnam, some 8 percent of U.S. Army and Marine Corps chaplains reported firing on the enemy.[20]

Generally, noncombatants who engage in combat do not become war criminals by such acts alone; they merely lose their protected status while serving in the combatant status. Nothing in the Geneva or Hague Conventions preclude prior noncombatants from later regaining their protected status. So long as medical personnel remove all protective Red Cross insignia, they commit no crime by performing combatant duties. Further, the commander who orders medical personnel to remove all Red Cross insignia from themselves and their equipment and then perform such duties acts lawfully. The Geneva Convention specifically notes that the use of the protective emblem is to be "under the direction of the competent military authority."[21]

The position of the American armed forces is that military personnel who frequently alternate between medical and combatant duties are not entitled to medical personnel status because they are not "exclusively" engaged in medical duties.[22] To enjoy full-time medical status, the servicemember must be serving in a permanent or semipermanent billet, with the performance of combatant duties being aberrational.[23]

Of particular interest to the Aviation and Airborne communities, international law has created a legal distinction between parachutists and paratroopers in terms of when they may be shot as they descend. Parachutists — members of a disabled aircraft parachuting to the ground — are considered to be out of combat and may not be fired upon unless they *clearly* continue to participate in hostilities. Conversely, paratroopers — even those from the same disabled aircraft — are considered combatants and may be fired upon as they descend, unless they are clearly attempting to surrender. Whether or not the trigger-pullers on the ground will be drawing such fine legal distinctions with a mixed group of parachutes is doubtful.

A practical distinction arises with respect to shipwrecked personnel, who are a protected class of persons under the Geneva Convention for the Amelioration of the Condition of Wounded, Sick and Shipwrecked Members. Enemy personnel floating in open water as a result of the sinking of their ship or downing of their aircraft should be presumed to be out of combat by virtue of the practical limitations on their ability to continue to fight. The same presumption cannot be applied to soldiers or marines from a landing craft destroyed during an amphibious assault, who then attempt to reach the beachhead rather than rescue craft. Such combatants are hardly out of combat and realistically should be expected to join the fight upon reaching their forces ashore.[24]

Protected Places and Things

The Hague Convention prohibits the damage or destruction of structures committed to religion, charity, education, science, and the arts; historic monuments; and objects of a similar character.[25] Included under this protective umbrella are churches, museums, civilian schools and war memorials. During the Gulf War, military lawyers persuaded Gen. Norman Schwarzkopf not to destroy a thirty-foot-high statute of Saddam Hussein located in Baghdad because it was considered a protected object.[26]

Further, medical facilities bearing the Red Cross, or equivalent symbol, are protected from attack. Captured medical supplies should not be destroyed, even if they cannot be transported to friendly control.[27] Military hospital ships may neither be attacked nor captured, but hospital ships may be searched and a warship capable of caring for wounded prisoners may demand that a hospital ship surrender those enemy personnel fit to be moved.[28] A warship may not capture a hospital ship's crew, or its religious, hospital, and medical personnel.[29]

Medical ships, units, and buildings do not lose their protected status merely because their personnel carry defensive weapons or they employ protective sentries.[30] Additionally, it is not illegal to camouflage a medical unit or structure, obscuring the Red Cross, in order to gain a tactical advantage, but the protections afforded by the protective emblem will be lost largely because the enemy will be unable to determine the medical facility's protected status.

War Booty

A reoccurring issue for American forces during the later part of this century has been the limitations on the seizure of property found on the battlefield. All public property of the enemy belongs to the government of the capturing force, *not* to the individual who finds it. Indeed, the Manual for Courts-Martial specifically states: "Immediately upon its capture from the enemy public property becomes the property of the United States." MCM ¶ 27c(1)(a).

In July 1968 an American sergeant leading a search and destroy mission in South Vietnam found over $150,000 in American money in a cave previously occupied by the enemy. After returning to the United States, Sergeant Morrison sued the United States, seeking return of the money. In *Morrison v. United States,* the U.S. Court of Claims, citing the UCMJ and Field Manual (FM) 27-10, rejected Morrison's lawsuit and ruled that the money belonged to the United States.[31]

As a general rule, combatants cannot involuntarily take private property from civilians or civilian institutions.[32] Accordingly, it would be illegal to steal art or religious objects from either a private home or the local museum. A narrow exception to this rule exists in cases where goods and services may be requisitioned to satisfy the needs of an occupying army; however, the requisitioned items may only be taken upon the orders of the local commander and the requisitioning force must reimburse the owner for the items taken.[33]

Within the ranks of the American military, Article 103, UCMJ, provides the primary mechanism by which the prohibition against looting is enforced. During Operation Just Cause an airman was convicted of taking a camera and watches from a warehouse he was guarding and during Operation Desert Storm a soldier was convicted of smuggling an Iraqi AK-47 into Germany after finding it in a bunker.[34] Federal statutes, which prohibit the possession of machine guns (18 U.S.C. § 922(o)) and the improper importation of any firearm (26 U.S.C. § 5861(k)) may be prosecuted via Article 134 or separately prosecuted in the federal system. Additionally, servicemembers who quit their place of duty to plunder or pillage may be prosecuted under Article 99. In an effort to both educate and warn its forces, the armed forces have endeavored to issue local directives providing additional guidance as to what items the individual servicemember may lawfully take home as the spoils of war.

Capturing forces may not confiscate as war booty personal items from a POW.[35] Such items include watches, wedding rings, identification cards, and individual rank insignia and military decorations. Money may be taken from a POW only upon the orders of an officer and the POW must receive a receipt for all sums taken.[36]

Tricks and Really Dirty Tricks

In war a certain amount of trickery is permitted. Ambushes, surprise attacks, psychological operations, and deceptive communications and troop movements are legal and frequently practiced. It is perfectly acceptable to place false land mine warning signs on an empty field or to drop leaflets on the enemy containing false information. The law draws the line on trickery at the point where the enemy's adherence to the law of war is taken advantage of to its detriment. For example it would be illegal to disguise an ammunition depot as a hospital displaying the Red Cross flag because a hospital is a protected structure. Bodies may not be booby-trapped because the Geneva Convention requires a military force to recover and bury the dead;[37] however, equipment may be booby-trapped because no such recovery requirement exists.

The use of American uniforms by infiltrating Nazi soldiers during the Battle of the Bulge gave rise to criminal charges after World War II. In *Trial of Otto Skorzeny and Others*,[38] several officers of the 150th Panzer Brigade were charged with improperly using American uniforms while attempting to infiltrate American lines. Acquitting all defendants, the military tribunal drew a distinction between the use of enemy uniforms during actual combat and for all other purposes. During actual combat, fighting in the enemy's uniform is prohibited because the two forces must be able to determine who they should and should not shoot, but deceptive use of the enemy's uniform when not in actual conflict is a permissible ruse of war.[39] Accordingly, it is not illegal to infiltrate enemy lines dressed in their uniform, but the infiltrators must shed their garb before engaging the enemy.

Further, the use of spies to collect information is not a war crime, but if caught the spy does not enjoy those legal protections afforded to POWs. A spy is an individual operating clandestinely or under false pretenses, oftentimes while dressed as a civilian or as a member of the friendly force.[40] Enemy soldiers in their own uniforms captured behind our lines while gathering information as part of a reconnaissance mission are not spies and should be treated as POWs. If captured, a spy may be prosecuted for espionage under the capturing force's law, which under the UCMJ is Article 106, a crime punishable by death; former spies captured after they have returned to their own lines may not be prosecuted.[41]

A white flag does not always mean the enemy wants to surrender; it is also used as a means of seeking a truce in order to talk with the opposing force. It is illegal both to fire upon those displaying the flag and to use the flag as a means of gaining a military advantage over the enemy.[42] A combatant cannot use a white flag to get closer to an enemy in order to facilitate an attack or to view enemy defenses, nor to buy time in order to shift or withdraw friendly forces.[43]

Prisoners of War

The law of war affords numerous protections to those combatants unfortunate enough to be captured. However, not every combatant captured by a military force qualifies as a POW. Generally, those individuals entitled to POW status include enemy soldiers fighting in uniform, regardless of their country of origin, and members of a resistance movement who (1) are led by an individual responsible for their conduct, (2) wear recognizable distinctive insignia, (3) carry their weapons openly, and (4) observe the laws of war.[44] Charles DeGaulle's Free French forces of World War II constituted a lawful resistance movement. Further, the Geneva Convention affords POW status to members of a regular armed force professing allegiance to a government not recognized by the capturing nation; civilians who have been permitted to accompany the captured military force, such as reporters and contractors; civil aircraft and merchant marine crews; and civilians who rise up as part of a *levée en mass* to oppose the invasion of their country.[45]

POWs must be safeguarded and humanely treated. They must be quickly transported to the safety of the rear; not used to shield military objects or areas from attack; provided with food, water, and medical services; be free from torture and medical experimentation; and be permitted to retain their personal effects, military badges and decorations, and military items necessary for personal protection, such as helmets and gas masks.[46] Articles 71 and 72 of the Geneva Convention provide that POWs may send and receive mail and packages containing food, clothing, medicine, and personal items. Significantly, POWs cannot waive — voluntarily or otherwise — their legal rights and protections under the convention.[47]

Article 13 of the 1949 Geneva Convention Relative to the Treatment of Prisoners of War mandates that "prisoners of war must at all times be protected, particularly against acts of violence or intimidation and against insults and public curiosity." During the Vietnam War, the North Vietnamese violated this provision by parading captured American pilots through the streets of Hanoi, subjecting them to public ridicule and injury. Following World War II, in *The Essen Lynching Case,*[48] a British military tribunal sentenced a German officer to death and a private under his command to prison for inciting a crowd to attack and kill three captured British airmen whom the Germans were escorting to a nearby Luftwaffe unit. Once the British POWs were in their care, the German soldiers had a duty to protect the airmen from the civilian mob.

The Geneva Convention also imposes certain obligations on POWs. Article 17 provides that once questioned, prisoners should inform their captors of their name, rank, date of birth, and serial number. Prisoners confined in a camp must render proper military courtesies to the capturing force. Enlisted personnel must salute enemy officers and officers must salute the camp commander and enemy officers of a superior rank.[49] The capturing force may require POWs to work in the administration and maintenance of the camp and in civilian enterprises having no direct military purpose; however, noncommissioned officers may only be required to perform supervisory tasks and commissioned officers are exempt from any involuntary work details.[50] POWs may not be required to perform dangerous, unhealthy, or humiliating tasks.[51]

A POW is subject to the laws, regulations, and orders of the capturing force and may be the object of either "disciplinary" or "judicial" actions for any violations.[52] Disciplinary punishment is limited to a fine, loss of privileges, work details (except for officers), and confinement, all punishments not to exceed thirty days' duration.[53] Reflecting the duty of all POWs to attempt to escape, unsuccessful attempts and related conduct, such as minor stealing, use of false papers, and wearing civilian clothing, may only be subject to disciplinary action; however, a POW may be subject to judicial proceeding for violent crimes committed during the escape attempt.[54]

The capturing force may subject a POW to judicial proceedings for more serious crimes, but international law affords the accused POW with numerous procedural rights. The POW is entitled to present a defense with the assistance of a qualified attorney and a fellow POW, may not be coerced into pleading guilty, may call witnesses, be provided with an interpreter if required, and may only be prosecuted in the same courts and in the same manner as the capturing force prosecutes its own armed forces.[55] The capturing force must notify the Protecting Power (usually the International Red Cross), and the POW of the charges and must wait at least three weeks after notification is received before starting the trial.[56] Further, the POW and the Protecting Power must be notified prior to trial if the crime is punishable by death, notified if a death sentence is in fact ordered, and the capturing force must wait at least six months before the sentence is carried out.[57]

Standards of Responsibility

International law places certain obligations on nations to enforce the laws of war against any war criminal, even a country's own citizen. Further, both international and domestic laws dictate that individuals be held accountable for their actions or omissions. As discussed earlier in this book, combatants may not rely on the defense of superior orders for the execution of obviously illegal orders. Also, commanders are held to a particularly high standard for the conduct of both themselves and their subordinates.

Obligations of Nations

The Geneva Conventions require all nations to search out and prosecute, or extradite for prosecution, any individual who either committed or ordered the commission of "grave breaches" of the conventions.[58] Grave breaches include such crimes against protected persons as the unlawful and willful killing or infliction of serious injury, torture, biological experimentation, deportation, forced conscription, hostage-taking, extensive destruction or theft of property, and depriving a person of a fair trial.[59] Nations are obligated to suppress lesser violations. Any nation may prosecute a war criminal for a grave breach of the convention, as Israel did with former Nazi Adolf Eichmann when they seized him in Argentina in 1960 and brought him back to Israel for trial.

During the Vietnam War the North Vietnamese abrogated any responsibilities it had under international law to bring its soldiers to justice. Conversely, the United States' military justice system operated throughout the war, convicting approximately two hundred soldiers, eighty marines, nine sailors, and seven airmen for serious UCMJ offenses against Vietnamese; including crimes completely unconnected with military operations such as traffic homicides and the murder of a bar girl.[60]

Although the efforts of the United States to prosecute war-related crimes were certainly more laudatory than those of our adversary, that effort left much to be desired. In his book *America in Vietnam,* historian Guenter Lewy notes that during the entire Vietnam War, the U.S. Army only produced twenty successful courts-martial, convicting a total of thirty-two soldiers — including Lt. William Calley of the My Lai massacre — for misconduct that could be labeled as a war crime.[61] These cases included murder/manslaughter (ten), rape (three), mistreatment of a detainee or POW (three) and mutilation of a corpse (five).[62]

Further, punishments against those convicted of such crimes were relatively light. Two soldiers convicted of scalping and cutting off the ears and fingers of enemy corpses were fined only one hundred dollars; sentences for murder averaged thirteen (premeditated) to three (unpremeditated) years less than army sentences for similar crimes committed in Europe and the United States; and Lieutenant Calley, who was convicted of murdering twenty-two Vietnamese civilians, was quickly pardoned, suffering no meaningful punishment other than a short period of house arrest and a few days in the Fort Benning stockade.[63]

Command Responsibility

Both international law and the UCMJ hold military commanders to high standards of accountability for war crimes committed by subordinate forces. In American military circles two conflicting standards of command responsibility currently exist — the *Yamashita* and *Medina* standards — which arose out of the trials of World War II Japanese general Tomoyuki Yamashita and Vietnam-era American captain Ernest Medina, respectively.

In 1945 an American military commission in the Philippines convicted Yamashita of failing "to discharge his duty as commander to control the operations of members of his command, permitting them to commit brutal atrocities and other high crimes against people of the United States and of its allies and dependencies, particularly the Philippines" and sentenced him to death.[64] Significantly, Yamashita was never alleged to have participated in, ordered, condoned, or even possessed actual knowledge of the atrocities committed by his forces.[65] It was enough that Yamashita *should* have known of his force's misconduct and failed to stop it. Australian military courts applied the same standard to various Japanese generals in *Trial Of Lieutenant-General Baba Masao,* and the United States Military Tribunal in Nuremberg applied this standard to high-ranking Nazi officers in *The German High Command Trial.*[66] Accordingly, a commander was held accountable for war crimes if he (1) participated in the crime, (2) ordered it, (3) was aware his forces were committing atrocities and failed to act, or (4) should have known that his forces were committing war crimes and was indifferent to their misconduct.[67]

In March 1968 a company of American infantrymen under the command of Capt. Ernest Medina attacked the Vietnamese village of My Lai as part of a battalion-sized operation into Vietcong-controlled territory, eventually killing between 175 and 200 civilians.[68] Medina was eventually charged with involuntary manslaughter for failing to control the actions of his men, including Lieutenant Calley's platoon. By the time the court-martial began in 1971, not only was the *Yamashita* standard well entrenched in the law, but the army's own authoritative Field Manual 27-10, *The Law of Land Warfare,* specifically held commanders liable for crimes committed by their soldiers about which the commander "should have knowledge."[69]

Inexplicably, the military judge instructed the panel that they could convict Medina only if he possessed *actual* knowledge of the atrocities and failed to act, eliminating the fourth prong from the *Yamashita* standard of command responsibility.[70] Although evidence was presented that Medina was in constant communication with his troops, his attorney, F. Lee Bailey, was able to achieve an acquittal on the basis that Medina had no actual knowledge of the atrocities.[71]

The *Yamashita* standard appears to be the correct statement of the law of command responsibility and *Medina* should be viewed as an erroneous application of that standard. Significantly, the army continues to use the "should have knowledge" language in FM 27-10's discussion of command responsibility despite the military judge's contrary instructions in *Medina.* Further, protocol I to the Geneva Conventions — which the United States has yet to ratify, but which may soon be binding nonetheless as customary international law — holds commanders responsible for the war crimes of a subordinate "if they knew, or had information which *should* have enabled them to conclude in the circumstances at the time, that he was committing or was going to commit such a breach and if they did not take all feasible measures within their power to prevent or repress the breach."[72]

Staff Responsibility

Although not held to the same high standard as a commander, a military staff also bears some responsibility for law of war violations. In *The German*

High Command Trial,[73] the United States Military Tribunal at Nuremberg opined that a staff officer who causes an illegal "idea" to be put into the form of an order or personally distributes such an order violates the law.[74] However, under international law the staff officer cannot be convicted of a failure to act; only "positive action" will give rise to criminal liability.[75] Accordingly the member of a military staff who is aware of an illegal order but fails to prevent its execution has committed no crime under international law, but the staff member who assists in forming or executing the illegal order by drafting it or providing expertise to create it assumes criminal responsibility for the war crime.[76]

However, domestic law may still attach criminal liability to staff members who fail to act. Within the American armed forces servicemembers have a duty to report war crimes; the failure of which theoretically could be prosecuted under Article 92, dereliction of duty, or result in some form of adverse administrative action. Additionally, the prosecution of staff members as conspirators or aiders and abettors is a distinct possibility. American staff officers do not enjoy the luxury of being deliberately indifferent to war crimes ordered by their commanders.

Notes

Preface

1. *Parker v. Levy,* 417 U.S. 733, 743 (1974).

2. Frederick Whittaker, *A Complete Life of General George A. Custer,* vol. 2 (Lincoln: University of Nebraska Press, 1993), 410; Elizabeth B. Custer, *Boots and Saddles* (Norman: University of Oklahoma Press, 1987), x.

3. Lou Potter, William Miles, and Nina Rosenblum, *Liberators: Fighting on Two Fronts in World War II* (New York: Harcourt Brace Jovanovich, 1992), 125–27.

4. Vincent Green, *Extreme Justice* (New York: Pocket Books, 1995).

5. Roger Goldman and David Gallen, *Thurgood Marshall: Justice for All* (New York: Carroll and Graf, 1992), 112–19.

6. Robert Sherrill, *Military Justice Is to Justice as Military Music Is to Music* (New York: Harper and Row, 1970); Robert S. Rivkin, *GI Rights and Army Justice: The Draftee's Guide to Military Life and Law* (New York: Grove Press, 1970).

7. *O'Callahan v. Parker,* 395 U.S. 258, 264, 265, 267 n. 7 (1969).

8. See Mary McCarthy, *Medina* (New York: Harcourt Brace Jovanovich, 1972).

9. Kathleen A. Duignan, "Military Justice: Not an Oxymoron," *Federal Lawyer* 43 (February 1996): 22.

Chapter 1. Jurisdiction

1. 483 U.S. 435 (1987).

2. *Solorio,* 483 U.S. at 436–37. The girls were daughters of fellow Coast Guardsmen. Id. at 436. Additionally, Solorio had sexually abused girls in his government quarters in New York. Id. at 437.

3. Id. at 435, 436 and 439.

4. *Miller v. United States,* 42 F.3d 297, 301 (5th Cir. 1995).

5. "That a midshipman is an officer has been understood ever since there was a navy. He is not one of the common seamen. His name indicates a middle position between that of a superior officer and that of the common seaman." *United States v. Cook,* 128 U.S. 254, 256 (1888); see also *Hartigan v. United States,* 196 U.S. 169, 173 (1905) (West Point cadet is an officer, as distinguished from an enlisted man, but a cadet is not a commissioned officer).

6. *Department of the Air Force v. Rose,* 425 U.S. 352, 384 (1976) (Burder, C.J., dissenting) (citing 7 Op. Atty. Gen. 332 (1885)).

7. Bvt. Col. W. Winthrop, Opinions of the Judge Advocate General of the Army 136, 138 (1880) (West Point cadets); see also *Weller v. United States,* 41 Ct. Cl. 324 (1906) (Naval Academy midshipmen); 7 Op. Atty Gen 323, 327 (1855) (since 1819 the law has assumed that West Point cadets are subject to trial by court-martial). Midshipmen did not become subject to military law until 1895. *United States v. Ellman,* 9 U.S.C.M.A. 549; 26 C.M.R. 329, 331 (1958).

8. Majors Allan L. Zbar and James D. Mazza, "Legal Status of Cadets," *Air Force JAG Law Review* 7 (1965): 31 (citing Act of April 1, 1954, ch. 127, § 5; 68 Stat. 47; 10 U.S.C. §§ 1851, 1854).

9. *Woodrick v. Divich,* 24 M.J. 147, 150 and n. 2 (C.M.A. 1987) (Article 2[a][2] applies to Academy cadets, but not to ROTC cadets).

10. *United States v. Gibson,* 36 M.J. 556 (N.M.C.M.R. 1992) (USNA).

11. *United States v. Ellman,* 9 U.S.C.M.A. 549, 26 C.M.R. 329 (1958) (USMA).

12. *Melvin v. United States,* 45 Ct. Cl. 213 (1910). Melvin was actually convicted of hazing fellow midshipmen.

13. 32 M.J. 687, 691 (A.F.C.M.R. 1991).

14. *Ellman,* 26 C.M.R. at 333.

15. 29 M.J. 943 (A.C.M.R. 1990).

16. *Chodara,* 29 M.J. at 944–45.

17. Lt. Col. Warren Foote, "Courts-Martial of Military Retirees," *Army Lawyer* 54 (May 1992): 55 n. 8.

18. *United States v. Sloan,* 35 M.J. 4, 8 (C.M.A. 1992).

19. 326 F.2d 982 (Ct. Cl.), *cert. denied,* 377 U.S. 977 (1964).

20. *Hooper,* 326 F.2d at 983–84.

21. *Chambers v. Russell,* 192 F. Supp. 425, 427–28 (N.D. Calif. 1961); Foote, "Courts-Martial of Military Retirees," 54.

22. U.S. Department of Army, Reg. 27-10, Legal Services: Military Justice, para. 5-2b(3) (8 August 1994) (hereafter cited as AR 27-10). Requests for recall to active duty for court-martial must be approved by the Office of the Assistant Secretary of the Army (Manpower and Reserve Affairs). Id. Violation of this policy, however, may not necessarily afford the retiree any relief. See *United States v. Sloan,* 35 M.J. 4, 9 (C.M.A. 1992) ("*policy* typically is not *law.*").

23. U.S. Department of Air Force, Air Force Instr. 51-201, ¶ 2.9 (28 July 1994).

24. Manual of the Judge Advocate General 0123a(1) (1990) (hereafter cited as JAGMAN).

25. U.S. Coast Guard Military Justice Manual, COMDTINST M5810.1c, ¶ 2-B(3)(a) (15 January 1991) (hereafter cited as MJM).

26. 35 M.J. 620 (A.C.M.R. 1992).

27. *Chambers,* 192 F. Supp. at 428.

28. *United States v. Gurganious,* 36 M.J. 1041, 1042 (N.M.C.M.R. 1993).

29. U.S. Department of Army, PAM 27-1, Treaties Governing Land Warfare 97 (7 December 1956) (hereafter cited as DA PAM 27-1).

30. Arnold Krammer, *NAZI Prisoners of War in America* (Lanham, Md.: Scarborough House, 1996), 144, 289–90 n. 73.

31. Ibid., 143, 289 n. 71.

32. Ibid., 144, 171. In 1945, five German POWs were executed after being convicted of the 1943 murder of German corporal Johann Kunze, a suspected collaborator. At least nine other German POWs were hanged for murdering suspected collaborators. Ibid., 171–73.

33. Green, *Extreme Justice.*

34. *In re Grimley,* 137 U.S. 147, 155 (1890).

35. Id. at 157 ("the oath of allegiance is the pivotal fact which changes the status from that of civilian to that of soldier.").

36. *Billings v. Truesdell,* 321 U.S. 542, 559 (1944); RCM 202a, Discussion, (2)(a)(ii).

37. *Mayborn v. Heflebower,* 145 F.2d 864, 866 (5th Cir. 1944), *cert. denied,* 325 U.S. 854 (1945); *United States v. Mellis,* 59 F. Supp. 682, 683 (M.D.N.C. 1945).

38. *Mellis,* 59 F. Supp. at 683.

39. *United States v. Davis,* 8 M.J. 575, 576 (A.C.M.R. 1979); RCM 202(a).

40. 48 C.M.R. 758, 23 U.S.C.M.A. 142 (1974).

41. *Catlow,* 48 C.M.R. at 759, 23 U.S.C.M.A. at 143.

42. Id.

43. *Catlow,* 48 C.M.R. at 758, 23 U.S.C.M.A. at 145.

44. *Catlow,* 48 C.M.R. at 762; 23 U.S.C.M.A. at 145.

45. *United States v. Poole,* 30 M.J. 149, 150 (C.M.A. 1990).

46. *United States v. King,* 42 M.J. 79, 80 (C.M.A. 1995).

47. 43 M.J. 778, 780 (A.F.Ct.Crim.App. 1995).

48. 41 M.J. 337 (A.F.Ct.Crim.App. 1994).

49. Id. at 338.

50. Id. at 339.

51. See *United States v. Reid,* 43 M.J. 906, 909 (Army Ct. Crim. App. 1996) (setting aside convictions for all offenses other than fraudulent separation where charges tried in one proceeding; a conviction for fraudulent discharge is a "predicate conviction" for jurisdiction to attach).

52. A fraudulently obtained discharge "is not a valid separation" and does "not terminate court-martial jurisdiction over the accused." *United States v. Spradley,* 41 M.J. 827, 831 (N.M.Ct.Crim.App. 1995).

53. *United States v. Clark,* 35 M.J. 730, 731 (A.F.C.M.R. 1992).

54. *Clark,* 35 M.J. at 731; RCM 202(a), Discussion, (2)(B)(iii)(b).

55. *United States v. Sonnenfeld,* 41 M.J. 765, 766 (N.M.Ct.Crim. App. 1994). In a general court-martial tried before a panel, at least five properly appointed panel members must be present. Id.

56. *United States v. Smith,* 37 M.J. 773 (A.C.M.R. 1993) (using one selection criteria, grade, was a jurisdictional defect).

57. *United States v. Moore,* 36 M.J. 795, 797 (A.C.M.R. 1993).

58. *United States v. Longmire,* 39 M.J. 536 (A.C.M.R. 1994).

59. See *United States v. Palmer,* 41 M.J. 747, 750 (N.M.Ct.Crim.App. 1994) ("The notation in the referral block to convening order '54-93' instead of convening order '51-93' was obviously only a scrivener's error.").

60. 32 M.J. 791 (N.M.C.M.R. 1990).

61. The convening authority suspended all confinement in excess of ninety days. *Sykes,* 32 M.J. at 791.

62. Id. at 792.

Chapter 2. Pretrial Confinement and Restraint

1. *United States v. Burgess,* 32 M.J. 446 (C.M.A. 1991).

2. 41 M.J. 556, 562 (N.M.Ct.Crim.App. 1994).

3. Id.

4. Id. at 562–63.

5. Id. at 564.

6. *United States v. McCarthy,* 38 M.J. 398, 400 (C.M.A. 1993).

7. *McCarthy,* 38 M.J. at 400; *United States v. Mitchell,* 12 M.J. 265 (C.M.A. 1982).

8. *McCarthy,* 38 M.J. at 403.

9. *United States v. Tilghman,* 44 M.J. 493, 495 (1996).

10. 3 M.J 14, 22 (C.M.A. 1977).

11. 29 M.J. 1052, 1053–54 (A.F.C.M.R. 1990), *reversed in part on other grounds,* 32 M.J. 93 (C.M.A. 1991).

12. 38 M.J. 292, 295–96 (C.M.A. 1993), *cert. denied,* 114 S.Ct. 1298 (1994).

13. Id. at 298.

14. 39 M.J. 278 (C.M.A. 1994).

15. *United States v. Perez,* 45 M.J. 323 (1996).

16. 17 M.J. 126 (C.M.A. 1984).

17. *United States v. Murray,* 43 M.J. 507 (A.F.Ct.Crim.App. 1995) (Yes); *United States v. McCullough,* 33 M.J. 595 (A.C.M.R. 1991) (No).

18. 19 M.J. 274 (C.M.A. 1985).

19. *United States v. DiMatteo,* 19 M.J. 903, 904 (A.C.M.R. 1985).

20. 39 M.J. 91, 94 (C.M.A. 1994).

21. *United States v. Washington,* 42 M.J. 547 (A.F.Ct.Crim.App. 1995) (menial tasks); *United States v. Latta,* 34 M.J. 596 (A.C.M.R. 1992) (public humiliation).

22. 36 M.J. 679 (A.F.C.M.R. 1992), *affirmed,* 44 M.J. 493 (1996).

23. *Mahoney,* 36 M.J. at 684.

Chapter 3. Rights Warnings

1. See *United States v. Gouveia*, 467 U.S. 180, 188 n. 5 (1984).

2. *United States v. Davis*, 114 S.Ct. 2350 (1994).

3. *United States v. Vaughters*, 44 M.J. 377 (1996).

4. *Minnick v. Mississippi*, 498 U.S. 146 (1990).

5. 47 M.J. 27 (1997).

6. *Gilbert v. California*, 388 U.S. 263, 267 (1967) (handwriting); *In re Sealed Case (Government Records)*, 950 F.2d 736 (D.C. Cir. 1991); MRE 301(a), Drafter's Analysis.

7. *Davis*, 114 S.Ct. at 2354.

8. 384 U.S. 436, 489 (1966).

9. 37 C.M.R. 249 (C.M.A. 1967).

10. Major Howard O. McGillin Jr., "Article 31(b) Triggers: Reexamining the 'Officiality Doctrine,'" *Military Law Review* 150 (1995): 28–29.

11. *United States v. Armstrong*, 9 M.J. 374, 378 (C.M.A. 1980).

12. *United States v. Duga*, 10 M.J. 206, 209 (C.M.A. 1981).

13. *Garrett v. Lehman*, 751 F.2d 997 (9th Cir. 1985).

14. *United States v. Morris*, 13 M.J. 297, 298 (C.M.A. 1982).

15. *United States v. Quillen*, 27 M.J. 312, 314 (C.M.A. 1988).

16. *United States v. Powell*, 40 M.J. 1, 3 (1994); *Quillen*, sup.

17. 31 M.J. 849, 867–68 (N.M.C.M.R. 1990), *remanded on other grounds*, 35 M.J. 396 (C.M.A. 1992), *cert. denied*, 113 S.Ct. 1813 (1993).

18. MRE 305, Drafter's Analysis (undercover); *United States v. Bowerman*, 39 M.J. 136 (C.M.A. 1994) (health care); *United States v. Payne*, 47 M.J. 37 (1997) (DIS).

19. *United States v. Price*, 44 M.J. 430, 432 (1996) (citing *United States v. Duga*, 10 M.J. 206, 210 (C.M.A. 1981)).

20. *Price*, 44 M.J. at 432; see also *Payne*, 47 M.J. at 43.

21. 10 M.J. 206, 207 (C.M.A. 1981).

22. Id. at 211.

23. *United States v. Rogers*, 47 M.J. 135, 137–38 (1997).

24. 430 U.S. 387, 399–400 (1977) (Sixth Amendment violation).

25. 26 M.J. 132 (C.M.A. 1988).

26. *United States v. Powell*, 40 M.J. 1, 3 (1994) (spontaneous); *United States v. Frazier*, 34 M.J. 135, 137 (C.M.A. 1992) (consent).

27. *United States v. Bell*, 44 M.J. 403, 406 (1996).

28. *Miranda*, 384 U.S. at 492.

29. Id. at 461.

30. Id. at 444.

31. Id.

32. 46 M.J. 80, 82 (1997).

33. Id. at 84–85.

34. *Miller*, 46 M.J. at 84.

35. See, for example, *United States v. Baird,* 851 F.2d 376 (D.C. Cir. 1988) (federal); *Commonwealth v. McGrath,* 508 Pa. 250, 495 A.2d 517 (Pa. 1985) (state).

36. 578 F.2d 827, 835 (9th Cir. 1978).

37. U.S. Department of Army, Reg. 27-26, Legal Services: Rules of Professional Conduct for Lawyers, Rule 4.4 (1 May 1992).

38. *Professional Responsibility Notes,* Army Law., January 1992, at 53.

39. Id. at 54.

Chapter 4. Search and Seizure

1. *United States v. Muniz,* 23 M.J. 201, 204 (C.M.A 1987).

2. *United States v. Brown,* 784 F.2d 1034, 1037 (10th Cir. 1986).

3. *Muniz,* 23 M.J. at 204.

4. 44 M.J. 409 (1996).

5. Id. at 413.

6. *United States v. French,* 38 M.J. 420 (C.M.A. 1993); MRE 311(c).

7. MJM, ¶ 9-A-3(d).

8. *United States v. Freeman,* 42 M.J. 239, 243 (1995).

9. *United States v. Lopez,* 35 M.J. 35, 42 (C.M.A. 1992) ("very significant"); *Freeman,* 42 M.J. at 243.

10. *United States v. Wood,* 25 M.J. 46, 48 (C.M.A. 1987).

11. *Lopez,* 35 M.J. at 38.

12. 35 M.J. 35 (C.M.A. 1992).

13. Id. at 41–42.

14. 27 M.J. 264 (C.M.A. 1988).

15. *United States v. Murphy,* 39 M.J. 486 (C.M.A. 1994).

16. 46 M.J. 733, 741 (N.M.Ct.Crim.App. 1997).

17. 34 M.J. 353 (C.M.A. 1992).

18. Id. at 357.

19. *United States v. Evans,* 35 M.J. 306, 309 (1992).

20. 46 M.J. 786, 787–88 (C.G.Ct.Crim.App. 1997).

21. Id. at 789.

22. 14 M.J. 593 (A.F.C.M.R. 1982).

23. *United States v. Gauvin,* 12 M.J. 610, 612 (N.M.C.M.R. 1981).

24. *United States v. Vargas,* 13 M.J. 713 (N.M.C.M.R. 1982).

25. *United States v. Fitten,* 42 M.J. 179 (1995) (combative patient); *Curry,* 46 M.J. at 740 (suicide).

26. *Whren v. United States,* 116 S.Ct. 1769, 1773 n. 1 (1996).

27. *United States v. Bickel,* 30 M.J. 277, 280 (C.M.A. 1990).

28. 41 M.J. 177 (C.M.A. 1994).

29. Id. at 182.

30. 41 M.J. 168 (C.M.A. 1994), *cert. denied,* 115 S.Ct. 1108 (1995).

31. Id. at 168–69.

Chapter 5. Nonjudicial Punishment

1. *A Manual for Courts-Martial, Courts of Inquiry and of Other Procedure under Military Law* (Washington, D.C.: GPO, 1916), 309.

2. War Department, *Military Laws of the United States 1915,* 5th ed. (Washington, D.C.: U.S. GPO, 1917), 614.

3. Ibid.

4. Ibid.

5. Lt. Cdr. Edward M. Byrne, *Military Law: A Handbook for the Navy and Marine Corps* (Annapolis, Md.: U.S. Naval Institute, 1970), 86.

6. Department of the Navy, *Compilation of Navy and Other Laws* (Washington, D.C.: GPO, 1875), 19.

7. A. Arthur Schiller, *Military Law* (St. Paul, Minn.: West Publishing, 1952), 298 n. 4.

8. Department of the Navy, *Compilation of Navy and Other Laws,* 19.

9. See, for example, 14 U.S.C. § 142 (1940).

10. Brig. Gen. (Ret.) James Snedeker, *Military Justice under the Uniform Code* (Boston: Little, Brown, 1953), 71.

11. *United States v. Edwards,* 46 M.J. 41, 44 (1997).

12. Thomas B. Buell, *Master of Sea Power: A Biography of Fleet Admiral Ernest J. King* (Boston: Little, Brown, 1980), 22–44. Being placed "under hatches" or "in hack" was synonymous with being restricted to quarters (24). Being placed "in hack" was a form of punishment imposed at Captain's Mast. Rear Adm. (Ret.) Harley F. Cope, *Command at Sea,* 3d ed. (Annapolis, Md.: U.S. Naval Institute, 1966), 239.

13. MJM, ¶ 1-C-5 (15 January 1991).

14. Department of the Air Force, Air Force Instr. 51-202, Nonjudicial Punishment, ¶ 4.3 (1 October 1996) (hereafter cited as AFI 51-202).

15. AR 27-10, Military Justice, ¶ 3-18(a) (24 June 1996); AFI 51-202, ¶ 3.4 ("unless privileged or restricted by law, regulation, or instruction."); Procedure Study Guide, ch. 4, Naval Justice School, at 8, ¶ D(2)(c) (hereafter cited as Procedure Study Guide).

16. AR 27-10, ¶ 3-18(f)(1); AFI 51-202, ¶ 4.7; MJM, ¶ 1-G-2; Procedure Study Guide, at 12, ¶ D(3)(e).

17. AR 27-10, ¶ 3-16(c); MJM, ¶¶ 1-C-5(d), 1-G-2(b).

18. JAGMAN ¶ 109(a) (1990).

19. *United States v. Kelly,* 45 M.J. 259 (1996) (same rule applies to summary court-martial convictions); *United States v. Godden,* 44 M.J. 716 (A.F.Ct.Crim.App. 1996).

20. AR 27-10, ¶ 3-18(h); MJM, ¶¶ 1-C-3(b) and 1-G-3; Procedure Study Guide, at 10, ¶ D(2)(f).

21. AR 27-10, ¶ 3-18h; MJM, ¶ 1-G-1 and 1-D-6(c); Procedure Study Guide, at 12, ¶ D(3)(e).

22. AR 27-10, ¶ 3-18(l).

23. JAGMAN, ¶ 110(b).

24. AFI 51-202, ¶ 3.3.

25. AR 27-10, ¶ 3-29(a); AFI 51-202, ¶ 7.4.2; MJM, ¶ 1-E-11(a).

26. AR 27-10, ¶ 3-7(a).

27. AFI 51-202, ¶ 2.1; JAGMAN, ¶ 0106.

28. MJM, ¶ 1-A-2.

29. AFI 51-202, ¶ 2.5; cf. AR 27-10, ¶ 3-8a (cadets excluded from "command").

30. AR 27-10, ¶ 3-7(d); MJM, ¶ 1-A-2(a) (and types of punishment).

31. AFI 51-202, ¶ 2.6.

32. JAGMAN, ¶ 0106e.

33. *United States v. Marshall,* 45 M.J. 268, 271 (1996).

34. AR 27-10, ¶ 3-9.

35. *United States v. Pierce,* 27 M.J. 367, 369 (C.M.A. 1989).

36. AR 27-10, ¶ 3-19(b)(2); AFI 51-202, ¶ 4.1, table 1 n. 3; MJM, ¶ 1-E-3(e).

37. AR 27-10, ¶ 3-16(a).

38. AR 27-10, ¶ 3-28(a).

39. AFI 51-202, ¶ 8.6.1.

40. AR 27-10, ¶ 3-28(a).

41. AR 27-10, ¶ 3-18d (soldiers).

42. See generally Maj. Dwight H. Sullivan, "Overhauling the Vessel Exception," *Naval Law Review* 43 (1996): 57.

43. 18 M.J. 198, 199 (C.M.A. 1984).

44. Id. at 198–99.

45. 42 M.J. 116 (C.M.A. 1995) (Sullivan, J., dissenting).

46. Id. at 116–17; Sullivan, "Overhauling the Vessel Exception," 59.

47. Sullivan, "Overhauling the Vessel Exception," 59.

48. *Fletcher,* 42 M.J. at 117.

49. 46 M.J. 41, 45 (1997).

50. Id.

51. Id.

Chapter 6. The Court-Martial Process

1. Arthur Everett, Kathryn Johnson, and Harry F. Rosenthal, *Calley* (New York: Dell Publishing, 1971), 263.

2. Federal Rule of Criminal Procedure 8(a) permits the joinder of multiple offenses in a single trial only if they "are of the same or similar character or are based on the same act or transaction or on two or more acts or transactions connected together or constituting parts of a common scheme or plan."

3. G. W. Willis, "For Article 32 Officer, It's Trial by Fire," *Army Times,* 28 July 1997, p. 10, cols. 1–2.

4. Ibid.; RCM 405(d).(1), Discussion.

5. Willis, "Trial by Fire," p. 10, col. 3.

6. Bradley Graham, "Army Pretrial Hearing Ends in Sexual Misconduct Case," *Washington Post*, 26 August 1996, p. A3, col. 1.

7. *United States v. Thompson*, 44 M.J. 598, 601 (N.M.Ct.Crim.App. 1996).

8. *United States v. Dies*, 45 M.J. 376 (1996) (unauthorized absence of the accused).

9. Compare *United States v. Thompson*, 44 M.J. 598, 602 (N.M.Ct.Crim. App. 1996) (IO does not have the inherent power to exclude delay from the speedy trial clock) with *United States v. Roberson*, 43 M.J. 732, 736 (A.F.Ct. Crim.App. 1995) (no legal error in excluding delay approved by IO) and *United States v. Longhofer*, 29 M.J. 22, 28 (C.M.A. 1989) (court notes in passing that IO has such authority under a prior version of RCM 707).

10. *United States v. Anderson*, 46 M.J. 540, 542 (N.M.Ct.Crim.App. 1997).

11. Further, if the accused is placed in pretrial confinement, Article 10, UCMJ, requires the government to proceed to trial with "reasonable diligence." *United States v. Kossman*, 38 M.J. 258, 262 (C.M.A. 1993).

12. 46 M.J. 229 (1997).

13. *United States v. Modesto*, 43 M.J. 315, 318 (1995).

14. *United States v. Moore*, 28 M.J. 366 (C.M.A. 1989) (race); *United States v. Ruiz*, 46 M.J. 503 (A.F.Ct. Crim.App. 1997) (gender); *United States v. Witham*, 44 M.J. 664 (N.M.Ct.Crim.App. 1996) (gender).

15. 45 M.J. 245, 247 (1996).

16. *United States v. Slovacek*, 24 M.J. 140 (C.M.A. 1987).

17. *United States v. Sumrall*, 45 M.J. 207, 209 (1996) (retirement eligible); see also *United States v. Becker*, 46 M.J. 141 (1996) (3 1/2 months from retirement).

18. *United States v. Sloan*, 35 M.J. 4 (C.M.A. 1992).

19. Dan Kurzman, *Fatal Voyage: The Sinking of the USS Indianapolis* (New York: Atheneum, 1990), 2, 246–47.

20. "GI Sniper Sentenced to Death in Ft. Bragg Attack," *Arizona Republic*, 13 June 1996, p. A5, col. 5; Nick Adde, "High Court Clears Way for Execution," *Army Times*, 17 June 1996, p. 20, col. 4. In 1997, the death sentences of two marines, Sergeant Joseph Thomas and Lance Corporal Ronnie Curtis, were set aside by the U.S. Court of Appeals for the Armed Forces. *United States v. Curtis*, 46 M.J. 129 (1997); Nick Adde, "Death Penalty Gets Scrutiny of Appeals Court," *Army Times*, 1 September 1997, p. 9, col. 1.

21. "GI Sniper Sentenced," p. A5, col. 5.

22. *Loving v. United States*, 116 S.Ct. 1737 (1996).

23. Burke Davis, *The Billy Mitchell Affair* (New York: Random House, 1967), 240, 247–48.

24. Ibid., 232, 241.

25. Ibid., 240–43.

26. Ibid., 251, 254, 263, 294.

27. Ibid., 326.

28. Ibid., 327; Douglas MacArthur, *Reminiscences* (New York: McGraw-Hill, 1964), 85–86.

29. *United States v. Smith,* 44 M.J.720 (Army Ct. Crim. App. 1996) (fine); *United States v. Gansemer,* 38 M.J. 340 (C.M.A. 1993) (administrative discharge board).

30. 46 M.J. 551 (N.M.Ct.Crim.App. 1997).

31. *United States v. Rivera,* 46 M.J. 52 (1997) (no pretrial motions).

32. 922 F.2d 967, 968 (9th Cir. 1993).

33. United States Sentencing Guidelines §§ 4A1.2(g), 4A1.1(c) (1997) *United States v. Locke,* 918 F.2d 841 (9th Cir. 1990) (Article 15 and summary court-martial not counted).

34. United States Sentencing Guidelines § 5H1.1.

Chapter 7. Military Crimes

1. *United States v. Austin,* 27 M.J. 227, 231–32 (C.M.A. 1988); *United States v. Stewart,* 33 M.J. 519, 520 (A.F.C.M.R. 1991).

2. *Stewart,* 33 M.J. at 520.

3. "GI Discharged for Spurning U.N. Garb: Court-Martial Jury Finds Medic Guilty of Disobeying Order," *Washington Post,* 25 January 1996, p. 21 (guilty of disobeying a lawful order).

4. *United States v. Blye,* 37 M.J. 92 (C.M.A. 1993).

5. "Military Finds Marines Guilty in DNA case," *Arizona Republic,* 17 April 1996, p. A15; "NCO Convicted in DNA Case," *Arizona Republic,* 11 May 1996, p. A28 (Air Force Sergeant).

6. *United States v. Dumford,* 30 M.J. 137 (C.M.A.), *cert. denied,* 111 S.Ct. 150 (1990).

7. *United States v. McLaughlin,* 14 M.J. 980 (N.M.C.M.R. 1982), *petition denied,* 15 M.J. 405 (C.M.A. 1983).

8. *United States v. Griffen,* 39 C.M.R. 596 (1968).

9. *United States v. Calley,* 48 C.M.R. 19, 22 U.S.C.M.A. 534 (1973).

10. *Griffen,* 39 C.M.R. at 588.

11. Id.

12. Id. at 590.

13. *McLaughlin,* 14 M.J. at 910 (emphasis in original).

14. *McLaughlin,* 14 M.J. at 911.

15. Id. at 910.

16. *United States v. Schwabauer,* 34 M.J. 709, 711 (A.C.M.R. 1992).

17. 34 M.J. 1030, 1032 (N.M.C.M.R. 1992).

18. *United States v. Ferenczi,* 27 C.M.R. 77, 80; 10 U.S.C.M.A. 3, 6 (1958).

19. "Air Force Officer Admonished in Fatal Crash," *Arizona Republic,* 23 May 1995, p. B2, col. 1; "Echoes of Air Force Crash," *Philadelphia Inquirer,* 1 May 1995, p. 1, col. 1.

20. *United States v. Rust,* 38 M.J. 726, 731 (A.F.C.M.R. 1993), *review granted in part,* 40 M.J. 36 (1994), *affirmed,* 41 M.J. 472 (1995), *cert. denied,* 116 S.Ct. 170 (1995).

21. *United States v. Wilson,* 33 M.J. 797 (A.C.M.R. 1991).

22. 36 M.J. 415, 416 (C.M.A. 1993).

23. Id. at 416–17. Significantly, the prosecution does not have to prove that the dereliction of duty had an adverse effect on the unit's mission. Id. at 422.

24. *United States v. Dellarosa,* 30 M.J. 255, 259 (C.M.A. 1990) ("the previous distinction in language need not be considered significant.").

25. *United States v. Powell,* 32 M.J. 117, 121 (C.M.A. 1991).

26. Id. at 121.

27. William Bradford Huie, *The Execution of Private Slovik* (New York: Duell, 1954), 9.

28. During World War II, more than 40,000 Americans deserted from military service, of which 2,864 were prosecuted at a general court-martial. Of this number, 49 received death sentences. Only one American deserter, Private Slovik, was actually put to death. Ibid.

29. The Comptroller General, *AWOL in the Military: A Serious and Costly Problem,* FPCD-78-52 (Washington, D.C.: General Accounting Office, 30 March 1979).

30. Ibid., 1, 3.

31. *United States v. Dukes,* 30 M.J. 793, 794 (N.M.C.M.R. 1990); MCM, ¶ 10c(6). However, they may have violated some other punitive article, such as failing to obey an order. *Dukes,* 30 M.J. at 794.

32. *Gonzalez,* 42 M.J. at 473.

33. *United States v. Huet-Vaughn,* 43 M.J. 105, 114 (1995). Captain Huet-Vaughn deserted her unit as part of a protest of the American involvement in Operation Desert Storm. The military court ruled that her motivation for protesting the military operation was not a defense and therefore irrelevant. Id.

34. *United States v. Kapple,* 36 M.J. 1119, 1122 (A.F.C.M.R. 1993).

35. Id. at 1123.

36. Col. William Winthrop, *Military Law and Precedents,* 2d ed. (1896; reprint, 2 vols. in 1, Washington, D.C.: GPO, 1920), 565.

37. Ibid., 565.

38. Ibid.

39. 17 U.S.C.M.A. 165; 37 C.M.R. 429, 432 (1967).

40. Id. at 437.

41. Kevin M. Kelly, "'You Murdered Queeg': Lawyer's Ethics, Military Justice, and the Caine Mutiny," *Wisconsin Law Review* 1991:543–44.

42. Derrick Bell, "Meanness as Racial Ideology," *Michigan Law Review* 88 (1990): 1689, 1689–90.

43. Id. at 1691–92; Robert L. Allen, *The Port Chicago Mutiny* (New York: Armistad Press, 1993), xiii–xiv.

44. *United States v. Sanchez,* 40 M.J. 508, 510–11 (A.C.M.R. 1994).

45. Id. at 509.

46. Id. at 511.

47. Id.

48. Winthrop, *Military Law and Precedents,* 578.

49. *Manual for Courts-Martial,* 225 (Article 75).

50. *United States v. Terry,* 36 C.M.R. 756, 761 (N.B.R. 1965).

51. *United States v. Sperland,* 5 C.M.R. 89, 91; 1 U.S.C.M.A. 661, 663 (1952).

52. *Terry,* 36 C.M.R. at 761 (Viet Cong).

53. Id.

54. *Manual for Courts-Martial,* 229 (Article 76).

55. *United States v. Flemming,* 19 C.M.R. 438, 448–49 (A.B.R. 1955) ("laudable motives are not a defense").

56. Don J. Snyder, *A Soldier's Disgrace* (Dublin, N.H.: Yankee Books, 1987), 52 and photo insert no. 1. Alley was released after three years and seven months' incarceration at Fort Leavenworth (53).

57. The questionnaire asked for the prisoner's "name, rank, serial number, date of birth, parents' occupation, religious affiliation, formal education, and duties in the American armed forces." Ibid., 171.

58. Ibid., 175–79, 182–83. In Alley's defense, the Chinese already had several manuals left over from WWII and other Americans engaged in similar conduct, although to a lesser degree (ibid). In a 1982 review of the court-martial, the Army Board for the Correction of Military Records upheld the conviction (ibid., 238).

59. *United States v. Garwood,* 16 M.J. 863, 866 (N.M.C.M.R. 1983), *affirmed,* 20 M.J. 148 (C.M.A. 1985).

60. *Garwood,* 16 M.J. at 867.

61. Id. at 865, 866.

62. Capt. Charles L. Nichols, "Article 105, Misconduct as a Prisoner," *Air Force JAG Law Review* 11 (Fall 1969): 393.

63. Id. at 394.

64. *United States v. Garwood,* 16 M.J. 863, 871 (N.M.C.M.R. 1983), *affirmed,* 20 M.J. 148, 153 (C.M.A. 1985). In 1973, a repatriated Army officer filed charges against five Army enlisted men who had willingly assisted the Viet Cong in various propaganda activities during their captivity. The secretary of the army, with the concurrence of the Army Chief of Staff, ordered the charges dismissed citing, in part, DoD's policy against prosecuting former POWs for making propaganda statements. Guenter Lewy, *America in Vietnam* (New York: Oxford University Press, 1978), 339.

65. *Garwood,* 16 M.J. at 866; see also Winston Groom and Duncan Spencer, *Conversations with the Enemy: The Story of PFC Robert Garwood* (New York: G.P. Putnam's Sons, 1983), 334–35 (only Vietnam POW to be tried).

66. 4 M.J. 657, 658 (A.C.M.R. 1977).

67. *United States v. Grover,* 33 M.J. 640, 642, and 643 (N.M.C.M.R. 1991).

68. *United States v. Johnson,* 26 M.J. 415, 416–17 (C.M.A. 1988).

69. *United States v. Tedder,* 24 M.J. 176, 182 (C.M.A 1987); see also *United States*

v. Moore, 38 M.J. 490, 493 (C.M.A. 1994) ("It has long been recognized that a 'higher code termed honor' holds military officers 'to stricter accountability.'"); *United States v. Court,* 24 M.J. 11, 17 n. 2 (C.M.A. 1987) (Cox, J. concurring and dissenting) ("citizens of this great Nation have a right to expect that persons who serve as commissioned officers within the armed forces will conduct themselves in accordance with the very highest standards of behavior and honor.").

70. *United States v. Hartwig,* 35 M.J. 682 (A.F.C.M.R. 1992), *affirmed,* 39 M.J. 125 (C.M.A. 1994).

71. *United States v. Jefferson,* 21 M.J. 203 (C.M.A. 1986).

72. *United States v. Graham,* 9 M.J. 556 (N.M.C.M.R. 1980).

73. *United States v. Maderia,* 38 M.J. 494 (C.M.A. 1994).

74. *United States v. Bilby,* 39 M.J. 467 (C.M.A. 1994), *cert. denied,* 115 S.Ct. 724 (1995).

75. *United States v. Jenkins,* 39 M.J. 843 (A.C.M.R. 1994), *review denied,* 42 M.J. 13 (C.M.A. 1994).

76. *Moore,* 38 M.J. at 493.

77. *Parker v. Levy,* 417 U.S. 733, 745 (1973).

78. Id.

79. *United States v. Guerrero,* 33 M.J. 295 (C.M.A. 1991). Cross-dressing in private, with the drapes closed, and with no reasonable expectation of being observed, is not a crime. Id. at 298.

80. *United States v. Choate,* 32 M.J. 423 (C.M.A. 1991). Normally, "mooning" intended as a prank is not a criminal offense even if conducted on base. Id. at 427. In *Choate,* the mooning was part of a series of lewd acts accompanied by sexually inappropriate comments to the same female. Id. at 426.

81. *United States v. Hitz,* 12 M.J. 695 (N.M.C.M.R. 1981).

82. *United States v. Sanchez,* 29 C.M.R. 32, 11 U.S.C.M.A. 216 (C.M.A. 1960).

83. *United States v. Carr,* 28 M.J. 661 (N.M.C.M.R. 1989). The intercourse occurred after midnight, during poor visibility, and behind a canvas tent, and the nearest people were more than 200 feet away. Id. at 666.

84. 33 M.J. 747 (A.C.M.R. 1991).

85. The "V" device for valor was originally limited to the Bronze Star, but the Army began authorizing its wear with the Air Medal and Commendation Medal during Vietnam. In 1963, the navy authorized wear of the device for both heroism and to indicate participation in combat operations but reversed this policy in 1976. Harry Summers, "Bits of Colored Ribbon," *Army Times,* 10 June 10 1996, p. 62, col. 1.

86. Evans E. Kerrigan, *American War Medals and Decorations* (New York: Viking Press, 1964), xiii. The Purple Heart was originally called the Badge of Military Merit (ibid.).

87. Ibid., 43.

88. Summers, "Bits of Colored Ribbon," p. 62, col. 1.

89. Kerrigan, *American War Medals,* 4.

90. Editors of the Boston Publishing Company, *Above and Beyond: A History of*

the Medal of Honor from the Civil War to Vietnam (Boston: Boston Publishing, 1985), 52.

91. Ibid., 38–39.

92. Summers, "Bits of Colored Ribbon," p. 62, col. 1; Kerrigan, *American War Medals,* 14, 16.

93. Summers, "Bits of Colored Ribbon," p. 62, col. 2; Kerrigan, *American War Medals,* 29, 35–36.

Chapter 8. Substantive Crimes

1. *Parker v. Levy,* 417 U.S. 733, 765 (1974) (Blackmun, J., concurring) (citation omitted).

2. Otis Pike, "Morality Pendulum Keeps Swinging," *Army Times,* 30 June 1997, p. 54, col. 2 ("The military simply cannot have one standard for a high-ranking man and another for a lower-ranking woman."); Jack Weible, "Double-Edged Sword," *Army Times,* 23 June 1997, p. 12, col. 4 ("Enlisteds and junior officers have been saying for years that prosecution for adultery is applied inconsistently and unfairly. Top generals . . . are allowed to retire with pensions intact while first sergeants face prison sentences and forfeiture of pay, they say."); Rowan Scarborough, "Top Brass Rarely Tarnished by Court-Martial in Sex Cases," *Washington Post,* p. A3.

3. "Officer Who Wed Enlisted Woman Faces Charges," *San Francisco Chronicle,* 4 July 1997, p. A3.

4. "McKinney Cites 23 Cases Army Didn't Prosecute," *Washington Post,* 12 December 1997, p. A13.

5. Ian Fisher, "Army's Adultery Rule Is Don't Get Caught," *New York Times,* 17 May 1997, p. 1, col. 2.

6. *United States v. Clark,* 35 M.J. 432, 436 (C.M.A. 1992).

7. "Army Judge, in Disputed Ruling, Refuses to Drop Rape Charges," *New York Times,* 19 April 1997, p. 22, col. 3; "Drill Sergeant's Power Rape Weapon, Judge Says," *Washington Post,* 19 April 1997, p. A3, col. 3.

8. *United States v. Cauley,* 45 M.J. 353, 356 (1996).

9. 40 M.J. 601 (A.C.M.R. 1994).

10. 40 M.J. 248 (C.M.A. 1994).

11. *United States v. Ambalada,* 1 M.J. 1132 (N.C.M.R. 1977) (unconscious).

12. 13 U.S.C.M.A. 278, 22 C.M.R. 278, 280 (1962).

13. Id.

14. Id. at 291.

15. *United States v. Robinson,* 37 M.J. 588 (A.F.C.M.R. 1993) (indecent assault); *United States v. Rich,* 26 M.J. 518 (A.C.M.R. 1988) (assault with intent).

16. 10 U.S.C.A. § 920 (West Supp. 1997).

17. 33 M.J. 300 (C.M.A. 1991).

18. Id. at 301.

19. Id. at 302–3.

20. *United States v. Hickman,* 22 M.J. 146, 148 (C.M.A. 1986) (previously charged under the twenty-second Article for the Government of the Navy); *United States v. Wells,* 11 B.R. 111, 118–19 (1940) (Army).

21. Rowan Scarborough, "Challenge to Adultery Ban Unlikely," *Washington Post,* 2 June 1997, p. A4, cols. 3–4.

22. *United States v. Henderson,* 22 M.J. 146, 155, and n. 12 (C.M.A. 1986) ("We have no criticism of this practice.").

23. *United States v. Perez,* 33 M.J. 1050, 1054 (A.C.M.R. 1991) (civilians must be aware).

24. *United States v. Green,* 39 M.J. 606, 609 (A.C.M.R. 1994).

25. Id.

26. *United States v. Poole,* 39 M.J. 819, 821 (A.C.M.R. 1994) (prejudicial); *United States v. Perez,* 33 M.J. 1050, 1054 (A.C.M.R. 1991) (not prejudicial).

27. 26 M.J. 764, 766 (A.C.M.R. 1988).

28. Id.

29. *United States v. Edmisten,* 37 M.J. 710 (A.C.M.R. 1993) (extended guest); *United States v. Boswell,* 35 C.M.R. 491 (A.B.R. 1964) (frequent visitor).

30. *United States v. Melville,* 8 U.S.C.M.A. 597, 25 C.M.R. 101, 106 (C.M.A. 1958) (enlisted man's wife); *United States v. McCaffree,* 33 B.R. 95, 99 (1944) (new duty station).

31. Winthrop, *Military Law and Precedents,* 718 n. 54 (conduct unbecoming an officer and gentleman).

32. *United States v. Lee,* 32 M.J. 857, 860 (N.M.C.M.R. 1991).

33. *United States v. Marcus,* 24 B.R. 189, 191 (1943).

34. *United States v. Pruitt,* 17 U.S.C.M.A. 438, 38 C.M.R. 236, 238 (C.M.A. 1968).

35. *United States v. Oglivie,* 29 M.J. 1069 (A.C.M.R. 1990).

36. Id.

37. Rollin M. Perkins and Ronald N. Boyce, *Criminal Law,* 3d ed. (Mineola, N.Y.: Foundation Press, 1982), 465.

38. Cited in Jeffrey S. Smith, "Military Policy Toward Homosexuals: Scientific, Historical, and Legal Perspectives," *Military Law Review* 131 (1991): 55, 79.

39. *Manual for Courts-Martial,* 271, 285–86.

40. *Manual for Courts-Martial,* 271; Smith, "Military Policy Toward Homosexuals," 55, 73.

41. *United States v. Henderson,* 34 M.J. 174 (C.M.A. 1992).

42. *United States v. Fagg,* 34 M.J. 179, 179–80 (C.M.A. 1992).

43. 27 C.M.R. 711, 712 (A.B.R. 1959), *affirmed,* 11 U.S.C.M.A. 216, 29 C.M.R. 32 (1960).

44. Id. at 712.

45. Id.

46. Id.

47. Id. at 712–13.

48. *Sanchez,* 29 C.M.R. at 33.

49. 22 U.S.C.M.A. 200, 46 C.M.R. 200 (C.M.A. 1973).

50. Id. at 201.

51. *United States v. Shaffer*, 46 M.J. 94 (1997).

52. 33 C.M.R. 667 (C.G.B.R. 1963).

53. *United States v. Shaffer*, 46 M.J. 94, 96 (1997).

54. 41 M.J. 446 (C.M.A. 1995).

55. *United States v. Miller*, 44 M.J. 549 (A.F.C.M.R. 1996).

56. *United States v. Gentry*, 23 C.M.R. 238, 8 U.S.C.M.A. 14 (C.M.A. 1957).

57. *United States v. Hullett*, 40 M.J. 189, 191 (C.M.A. 1994).

58. *United States v. Moore*, 38 M.J. 490, 492 (C.M.A. 1994).

59. *Hullett*, 40 M.J. at 192; *United States v. Wainwright*, 42 C.M.R. 997 (A.F.C.M.R.), *affirmed*, 43 C.M.R. 23 (1970) (offer to buy sex).

60. *Hullett*, 40 M.J. at 191 (coarse); *United States v. Collier*, 27 M.J. 806, 810 (A.C.M.R. 1988) (non-parlor-room language is typical in an army line unit).

61. *Hullett*, 40 M.J. at 192.

62. 3 M.J. 1027, 1030 (N.C.M.R. 1977).

63. *Hullett*, 40 M.J. at 191 (step-daughter); *United States v. Moore*, 38 M.J. 490, 492 n. 1 (C.M.A. 1994) (extortion); *United States v. Dudding*, 34 M.J. 975 (A.C.M.R. 1992) (bitch).

64. *United States v. King*, 34 M.J. 95, 96 (C.M.A. 1992).

65. 28 M.J. 661, 662 (N.M.C.M.R. 1989).

66. 24 B.R. 345, 346–47 (1943).

67. *United States v. Stocks*, 35 M.J. 366, 367 (C.M.A. 1992).

68. *Stocks*, 35 M.J. at 367; *United States v. Hickman*, 22 M.J. 146, 150 (C.M.A. 1986).

69. *United States v. Henderson*, 34 M.J. 174 (C.M.A. 1992).

70. *United States v. Gomez*, 15 M.J. 954, 959 (A.C.M.R. 1983).

71. *United States v. Gibson*, 17 C.M.R. 911 (A.F.B.R. 1954).

72. See *United States v. Spencer*, 839 F.2d 1341 (9th Cir. 1988) (federal feticide conviction).

73. 44 M.J. 512, 514–15 (Army Ct. Crim. App. 1996).

74. Id. at 517.

75. 11 C.M.R. 461, 463 (A.B.R. 1953).

76. Id. at 466.

77. *United States v. McMonagle*, 38 M.J. 53 (C.M.A. 1993) (sham firefight).

78. 3 U.S.C.M.A. 306, 12 C.M.R. 62 (1953).

79. *Borner*, 3 U.S.C.M.A. at 313, 316, 12 C.M.R. at 69, 72; see also *United States v. Jefferson*, 22 M.J. 315, 321 (C.M.A. 1986).

80. *United States v. Duncan*, 36 M.J. 668 (N.M.C.M.R. 1992) (no sex); *United States v. Morgan*, 33 M.J. 1055 (A.C.M.R. 1991) (racial insult); *United States v. McKay*, 18 C.M.R. 629, 644 (A.F.B.R. 1954) (domestic quarrel).

81. 43 C.M.R. 741, 744 (A.B.R. 1971).

82. *United States v. Robertson*, 33 M.J. 832, 834–35 (A.C.M.R. 1991) (parent),

reversed on other grounds, 37 M.J. 432 (C.M.A. 1993); *United States v. Mitchell,* 12 M.J. 1015, 1017 (A.C.M.R. 1982); *United States v. Perruccio,* 4 U.S.C.M.A. 28, 15 C.M.R. 28, 30 (C.M.A. 1954) (soldiers).

83. *United States v. Kick,* 7 M.J. 82, 84 (C.M.A. 1979).

84. See *United States v. Vandenak,* 15 M.J. 230 (C.M.A. 1983).

85. *United States v. Milton,* 46 M.J. 317, 319 (1997).

86. *United States v. Bonano-Torres,* 31 M.J. 175 (C.M.A. 1990) (kiss and unbutton); Perkins and Boyce, *Criminal Law,* 152–53.

87. *United States v. Outhier,* 45 M.J. 326, 328 (1996).

88. 46 M.J. 491, 492 (1997).

89. Id. at 493.

90. *United States v. Everson,* C.M.O.1, 1943, 95 at 96.

91. *United States v. Spenhoff,* 41 M.J. 772, 773 (A.F.Ct.Crim.App. 1995).

92. 42 M.J. 603 (N.M.Ct.Crim.App. 1995); 41 M.J. 772 (A.F.Ct.Crim.App. 1995).

93. *United States v. Hicks,* 6 U.S.C.M.A. 615, 20 C.M.R. 331, 339 (C.M.A. 1956).

94. *United States v. Davis,* 17 C.M.R. 473, 476 (N.B.R. 1954) (castrate, smash skull); Perkins and Boyce, *Criminal Law,* 241 (disfigurement examples).

95. Francis A. Lord, *They Fought for the Union* (New York: Bonanza Books, 1988), 14.

96. *United States v. Outin,* 42 M.J. 603, 606–7 (N.M.Ct.Crim.App. 1995); *Spenhoff,* 41 M.J. at 774.

97. *United States v. Davis,* 17 C.M.R. 473 (N.B.R. 1954) (cheekbone); *Everson,* C.M.O.1, 1943, at 97 (bite).

98. *United States v. Thompson,* 22 U.S.C.M.A. 88, 89, 46 C.M.R. 88 (C.M.A. 1972).

99. Winthrop, *Military Law and Precedents,* 913 n. 3.

100. Ibid., 914–15.

101. Charles M. Robinson III, *The Court-Martial of Lieutenant Henry Flipper* (El Paso: Texas Western Press, 1994), 20–21.

102. Ibid., 96.

103. Burke Davis, *The Civil War: Strange & Fascinating Facts* (New York: Wing Books, 1982), 64.

104. *United States v. Callaghan,* 14 U.S.C.M.A. 231, 34 C.M.R. 11 (1963); RCM 916(j).

105. *United States v. Elizondo,* 29 M.J. 798 (A.C.M.R. 1989) ("totally baffled by the mysteries of checking account management").

106. *United States v. McNeil,* 30 M.J. 648, 651 (N.M.C.M.R. 1990).

107. *United States v. Allbery,* 44 M.J. 226 (1996).

108. Karen Jowers, "Want It Moved? DITY," *Army Times,* 4 August 1997, p. 6 (80 percent, but this figure may rise to 95 percent).

109. 32 M.J. 705, 706 (A.C.M.R. 1991).

110. Kurzman, *Fatal Voyage,* 1–2.

111. 35 M.J. 579, 582 (C.G.C.M.R. 1992), *returned for a new post-trial recommendation,* 39 M.J. 223 (C.M.A. 1994).

112. *United States v. MacLane,* 32 C.M.R. 732, 735–36 (C.G.B.R. 1962).

113. Id. at 736.

114. Id. at 735.

115. 42 C.M.R. 911, 914–15 (N.C.M.R. 1970).

116. *United States v. Roach,* 26 M.J. 859 (C.G.C.M.R. 1988), *affirmed,* 29 M.J. 33 (C.M.A. 1989).

117. *United States v. Wilmoth,* 34 M.J. 739, 741–42 and n. 4 (N.M.C.M.R. 1991).

118. *United States v. Sombolay,* 37 M.J. 647 (A.C.M.R. 1993).

119. 37 M.J. 96 (1993).

120. Id. at 100–101.

121. 34 M.J. 739, 744 (N.M.C.M.R. 1991).

122. Id. at 745.

123. 11 M.J. 128 (C.M.A. 1981).

124. *United States v. Cobb,* 45 M.J. 82, 85 (1996).

125. 3 M.J. 846 (A.C.M.R. 1977).

126. *United States v. Marsh,* 13 U.S.C.M.A. 252, 32 C.M.R. 252 (C.M.A. 1962).

127. 42 M.J. 453 (1995).

128. 3 M.J. at 850.

129. *United States v. Riddle,* 44 M.J. 282 (1996) (attempt); *United States v. Garcia,* 16 M.J. 52 (C.M.A. 1983) (acquitted).

130. *United States v. LaBossiere,* 32 C.M.R. 337 (C.M.A. 1962); *United States v. Barger,* 931 F.2d 359 (6th Cir. 1991).

Chapter 9. Defenses

1. *United States v. Brown,* 26 M.J. 148, 150 (C.M.A. 1988).

2. *United States v. Robertson,* 36 M.J. 190, 191 (C.M.A. 1992).

3. *United States v. Gowadia,* 34 M.J. 714 (A.C.M.R. 1992) (uniform belt); *United States v. Scofield,* 33 M.J. 857 (A.C.M.R. 1991) (leather belt).

4. *United States v. Ray,* 44 M.J. 835, 838 (Army Ct. Crim. App. 1996) (scalding water); *Gowadia,* 34 M.J. at 717 (plastic bag over head); *United States v. Gooden,* 37 M.J. 1055 (N.M.C.M.R. 1993) (electrical cord).

5. 26 M.J. 148 (C.M.A. 1988).

6. Id. at 150.

7. 15 M.J. 124 (C.M.A. 1983).

8. Ronald Harris, "Wild Bill Didn't Retreat," *Arizona Republic,* 14 May 1995, p. E1, col. 2.

9. *United States v. Vasquez,* 42 M.J. 544 (A.F.Ct.Crim. App. 1995) (jail); *United States v. Roby,* 49 C.M.R. 544 (C.M.A. 1975) (reputation or property).

10. *United States v. Alomarestrada,* 39 M.J. 1068, 1073 (A.C.M.R. 1994).

11. 14 M.J. 671 (N.M.C.M.R. 1982).

12. 49 C.M.R. 544, 546 (C.M.A. 1975).

13. 47 C.M.R. 1 (C.M.A. 1973).

14. Id. at 3.

15. 34 M.J. 326 (C.M.A. 1992).

16. Id. at 330.

17. Id.

18. *United States v. Talty*, 17 M.J. 1127 (N.M.C.M.R. 1984) (radiation exposure in reactor compartment of a nuclear submarine).

19. "Serb Soldier Sobs While Admitting Bosnia Atrocities," *Arizona Republic*, 1 June 1996, p. A21, col. 1.

20. *United States v. Van Syoc*, 36 M.J. 461, 464 (C.M.A. 1993).

21. 47 C.M.R. 82 (A.C.M.R. 1973).

22. Id. at 83.

23. Id. at 85.

24. *United States v. Sermons*, 14 M.J. 350, 352 (C.M.A. 1982).

25. *United States v. Anzalone*, 40 M.J. 658, 661 (N.M.C.M.R. 1994).

26. 40 M.J. 178 (C.M.A. 1994).

27. *United States v. Heims*, 12 C.M.R. 174 (C.M.A. 1953) (injured hand); *United States v. Cooley*, 36 C.M.R. 180 (C.M.A. 1966) (narcolepsy); *United States v. King*, 17 C.M.R. 3 (C.M.A. 1954) (frostbite); *United States v. Mills*, 17 C.M.R. 480 (N.B.R. 1954) (mugged).

28. *United States v. Myhre*, 25 C.M.R. 294, 9 U.S.C.M.A. 32 (C.M.A. 1958) (AWOL).

29. 21 C.M.R. 22, 6 U.S.C.M.A. 700 (C.M.A. 1966).

30. *United States v. Hilton*, 39 M.J. 97 (C.M.A. 1994) (ignored debt); *United States v. Savinovich*, 25 M.J. 905, 908 (A.C.M.R. 1988).

31. Mental responsibility looks at the accused's mental status at the time of the crime as opposed to mental capacity which looks at the accused's mental status at the time of trial. RCM 909 provides that servicemembers may not be required to stand trial if they are mentally incompetent because they are either unable to understand the nature of the court-martial or unable to intelligently cooperate in their defense. A lack of mental capacity is not a defense that results in an acquittal; it merely causes the court-martial to be postponed until the accused is fit to stand trial.

32. *United States v. Lewis*, 34 M.J. 745 (N.M.C.M.R. 1991) (explosive disorder); *United States v. Baasel*, 22 M.J. 505 (A.F.C.M.R. 1986) (compulsive gambling); *United States v. Zajac*, 15 M.J. 845 (A.F.C.M.R. 1983) (compulsive gambling); *United States v. Shalter*, 85 F.3d 1251 (7th Cir. 1996) (mild personality disorder).

33. *United States v. Denny-Schaffer*, 2 F.3d 999 (10th Cir. 1993) (MPD, if dominant personality unable to appreciate); *United States v. Hensler*, 44 M.J. 184 (1996) (involuntary intoxication); *United States v. Rezaq*, 918 F. Supp. 463 (D.D.C. 1996) (PTSD); "Immigrant Is Ruled Insane in Slaying of Son, Daughter," *Washington Post*, 5 September 1991, p. D1, cols. 4–5 (postpartum psychosis; defendant unable to appreciate right from wrong); *State v. Cocuzza*, No. 1484-79 (Super. Ct. Middle-

sex Cty. N.J. 1981 (Vietnam veteran suffers PTSD flashback and attacks police believing them to be Vietcong; discussed in Ford, *In Defense of the Defenders: The Vietnam Vet Syndrome,* 19 Crim. L. Bull. 434 (1983)).

34. *United States v. Proctor,* 37 M.J. 330, 336 (C.M.A. 1993).
35. *United States v. Ellis,* 26 M.J. 90 (C.M.A. 1988).
36. *United States v. Hensler,* 44 M.J. 184, 187 (1996).
37. 24 M.J. 286 (C.M.A. 1987).
38. *United States v. Rios,* 33 M.J. 436, 440 (C.M.A. 199); *United States v. Haney,* 39 M.J. 917, 919 (N.M.C.M.R. 1994).
39. 30 M.J. 999, 1001 (N.M.C.M.R. 1990).
40. 36 M.J. 501 (A.F.C.M.R. 1992).
41. Id. at 511.
42. 42 M.J. 449, 451 (1995).
43. Id. at 451–52.
44. *United States v. Ginter,* 35 M.J. 799, 805 (N.M.C.M.R. 1992).
45. 40 M.J. 601 (A.C.M.R. 1994).
46. 40 M.J. 248 (C.M.A. 1994).
47. Id. at 250.
48. 42 M.J. 292, 293 (1995).
49. *United States v. Petrie,* 1 M.J. 332 (C.M.A. 1976) (illegal goods); *United States v. Eggleton,* 47 C.M.R. 920 (C.M.A. 1973) (values approximately the same).
50. *Sands of Iwo Jima* (Republic Pictures, 1949).
51. 20 U.S.C.M.A. 493, 43 C.M.R. 333 (1971).
52. *United States v. Johnson,* 43 C.M.R. 604 (A.C.M.R. 1970).
53. See *United States v. Sanders,* 37 M.J. 628, 631 (A.C.M.R. 1993); *United States v. Collier,* 27 M.J. 806, 810 (A.C.M.R. 1988), *reviewed in part on other grounds,* 29 M.J. 365 (C.M.A. 1990); But compare *United States v. Cheeks,* 43 C.M.R. 1013 (A.F.C.M.R. 1971) (verbal abuse may serve as defense to disrespect charge but not to disobedience).
54. *United States v. Pratcher,* 17 M.J. 388 (C.M.A. 1984) (repossession); *United States v. Lewis,* 7 M.J. 348 (C.M.A. 1978) (improper search).
55. *United States v. Middleton,* 36 M.J. 835 (A.C.M.R. 1993) (close personal relationship); *United States v. Noriega,* 21 C.M.R. 322 (C.M.A. 1956) (officer acting as bartender).
56. See, for example, *United States v. Olvera,* 4 U.S.C.M.A. 134, 15 C.M.R. 134 (1954).
57. *United States v. Lee,* 22 M.J. 767 (A.F.C.M.R. 1986), *petition denied,* 23 M.J. 406 (C.M.A. 1987); *Olvera,* sup. (disadvantage).
58. 30 C.M.R. 724 (N.B.R. 1961).
59. Id. at 726.
60. 33 M.J. 337 (C.M.A. 1991).
61. *Fain v. Commonwealth,* 78 Ky. 183 (1879).
62. C.M.O. 3-1944, 511 (26 October 1944).
63. Id. at 512.

64. Id. at 513–14.

65. *United States v. Bush,* 44 M.J. 646 (A.F. Ct. Crim. App. 1996), *affirmed,* 47 M.J. 305 (1997) (cocaine).

66. *United States v. Pabon,* 42 M.J. 404 (1995), *cert. denied,* 116 S.Ct. 780 (1996); *United States v. Mance,* 26 M.J. 244 (C.M.A. 1988).

67. 26 M.J. 244 (C.M.A. 1988).

68. *United States v. Vandelinder,* 20 M.J. 41 (C.M.A. 1985) (good military character); *United States v. Price,* 24 M.J. 643 (A.F.C.M.R. 1987) (innocent use of cocaine).

69. 37 M.J. 972, 975 (A.C.M.R. 1993).

70. 118 S.Ct. 1261 (1998).

71. *United States v. Manuel,* 43 M.J. 282 (C.M.A. 1995) (sample destroyed in violation of regulation, precluding retest; conviction for cocaine use set aside).

72. 47 C.M.R. 658, 663 (A.C.M.R. 1973).

73. Id. at 658.

74. *United States v. Hardy,* 46 M.J. 67 (1997).

Chapter 10. Miscellaneous Issues in Military Law

1. Summarized from Potter, Miles, and Rosenblum, *Liberators,* 125–28.

2. Luther C. West, *They Call It Justice* (New York: Viking Press, 1977), 26.

3. *United States v. Thomas,* 22 M.J. 388, 393 (C.M.A. 1986), *cert. denied,* 479 U.S. 1085 (1987).

4. 45 M.J. 309 (1996).

5. See, for example, *United States v. Gleason,* 43 M.J. 69, 73 (1995) ("the command climate, atmosphere, attitude, and actions had such a chilling effect on members of the command that there was a feeling that if you testified for the [accused] your career was in jeopardy.").

6. *United States v. Thomas,* 22 M.J. 388, 392 (C.M.A. 1986); *Treakle,* 18 M.J. at 649.

7. *Thomas,* 22 M.J. at 392; *Treakle,* 18 M.J. at 652.

8. *United States v. Mabe,* 33 M.J. 200, 206 (C.M.A. 1991) (judge); *United States v. Carlson,* 21 M.J. 847, 849 n. 1 (A.C.M.R. 1986) (NCO); *United States v. Accordino,* 20 M.J. 102 (C.M.A. 1985) (senior panel member); *United States v. Grady,* 15 M.J. 275 (C.M.A. 1983) (trial counsel argued command policy to panel).

9. *United States v. Strombaugh,* 40 M.J. 208 (C.M.A. 1994) (junior officers pressuring fellow officer not to testify insufficient).

10. 29 C.F.R. Section 1604.11(a) (1997).

11. 34 M.J. 44 (C.M.A. 1992).

12. 12 M.J. 679 (A.C.M.R. 1981).

13. 44 M.J. 546 (Army Ct.Crim.App. 1996).

14. 16 M.J. 642 (A.F.C.M.R. 1983).

15. 44 M.J. 603 (N.M.Ct.Crim.App. 1996).

16. See, for example, *United States v. Dear,* 40 M.J. 196, 197 (C.M.A. 1994).

17. 32 M.J. 301 (C.M.A. 1991).

18. *Meritor Savings Bank v. Vinson*, 477 U.S. 57, 68 (1985) ("The gravamen of any sexual harassment claim is that the alleged sexual advances were 'unwelcome.'"); *Burns v. McGregor Electronic Industries, Inc.*, 989 F.2d 959, 962 (8th Cir. 1993) (behavior must be unwelcome, which is determined by examining whether it was uninvited and offensive.).

19. *Meritor Savings Bank*, 477 U.S. at 69.

20. *United States v. Boyett*, 42 M.J. 150, 154–55 (1995). It is unrealistic to expect a commander to unhesitantly assign a friend to hazardous or unpopular duty. Id. at 155.

21. Winthrop, *Military Law and Precedents*, 716.

22. Ibid., 716 n. 44.

23. 25 M.J. 631, 635 (A.C.M.R. 1987), *affirmed*, 27 M.J. 361 (C.M.A. 1989); 23 M.J. 683, 685 (N.M.C.M.R. 1986).

24. 21 M.J. 770 (A.C.M.R. 1986).

25. 17 M.J. 862, 869 (A.F.C.M.R. 1983), *affirmed*, 20 M.J. 155 (C.M.A. 1985).

26. *United States v. Van Steenwyk*, 21 M.J. 795, 811 (N.M.C.M.R. 1985) ("The Naval Service has manifestly neither abandoned its custom against fraternization, nor has it condoned fraternization nor has it institutionally mixed socially the officer and enlisted grades."); *Callaway*, 21 M.J. at 777 ("the custom has not been so eroded in the Army.").

27. *United States v. Fox*, 34 M.J. 99, 103 (C.M.A. 1992).

28. 42 M.J. 150 (1995).

29. 43 M.J. 483 (1996).

30. Id. at 484–85.

31. Col. Kenneth K. Steinweg, "Dealing Realistically with Fratricide," *Parameters* (Spring 1995): 16–17; see also Sean D. Naylor, "No Snooze . . . You Lose," *Army Times*, 18 September 1995, p. 12 (sleep deprivation increases the likelihood of fratricide in combat).

32. Rick Atkinson, "Fratricide Problem Defies Decades of Efforts," *Washington Post*, 15 April 1994, p. A19; Steinweg, "Dealing Realistically with Fratricide," 26 (10–15 percent).

33. Atkinson, "Fratricide Problem," p. A19.

34. Steinweg, "Dealing Realistically with Fratricide," 11.

35. Harry Summers, "Court-Martial Charges Set Dangerous Precedent," *Army Times*, 10 October 1994, p. 70 ("In the past, such legal action was almost unheard of in friendly fire incidents."); Larry Walker, "Blaming Pilot Just More Scapegoat Justice," *Arizona Republic*, 21 September 1994, p. B5 ("a sharp departure from the military's long unspoken 'non-legal' response to fratricide."); "Charges Mount in Iraq Shootdown," *Army Times*, 19 September 1994, p. 2 ("Negligent homicide charges are rarely placed against a pilot in a fatal accident, officials said.").

36. Bradley Graham, "Commendations Revoked in Friendly Fire Case," *Washington Post*, 19 April 1995, p. 1 ("The armed forces have been reluctant to punish anyone for the gulf war cases, contending generally that second-guessing life-or-death combat decisions is unfair and risks breeding timidity on future battlefields.").

37. Clay Blair, *Ridgway's Paratroopers* (New York: Dial Press, 1985), 100–101.

38. Ibid., 102.

39. Ibid.

40. Ibid., 102–3.

41. Ibid., 103.

42. Ibid.

43. Steven Watkins, "The Verdict Is in, but the Case Goes On," *Army Times,* 3 July 1995, p. 14.

44. "Black Hawk Downing: What Failed, How to Fix It," *Army Times,* 25 July 1994, p. 4 ("a myriad of command failures and errors in procedure that lead to the tragedy."); "Air Force Drops Charges in Downing of Copters," *Arizona Republic,* 21 December 1994, p. A6 (Pentagon "investigation revealed command failures at several critical levels and a dangerous pattern of lax communications between the Army and Air Force.").

45. Vago Muradian, "Key Players in the Iraqi Shootdown," *Army Times,* 3 July 1995, p. 14.

46. Steven Watkins, "Beyond the Verdict," *Air Force Times,* 3 July 1995, p. 12 (Wang's court-martial worsened poor morale among AWAC crews).

47. Walker, "Blaming Pilot Just More Scapegoat Justice," p. B5; Watkins, "Beyond the Verdict," p. 12 (retired Air Force General Andrew Iouse characterized Wang's trial as a railroad job); "Court-Martial to Begin in 'Friendly Fire' Deaths," *Arizona Republic,* 29 May 1995 (Wang argued that he was a scapegoat); "Discipline for AWACS Duo," *Army Times,* 28 November 1994, p. 2 (AWACS officer complained that it was unfair that AWACS members being punished but higher commanders were not).

48. Steven Watkins, "Perry Refuses to Intervene in Trial," *Air Force Times,* 9 January 1995, p. 3.

49. Watkins, "Beyond the Verdict," p. 12 ("Several AWACS crew members said the Air Force's response after the shootdown — blaming the AWACS crews and not the fighter pilots — reflects a strong institutional bias favoring pilots.").

50. George C. Wilson, "Military Leaves Justice Undone," *Army Times,* 10 July 1995, p. 54 ("The families of the shootdown victims, and even Capt. Wang are so unsatisfied with how the military justice system worked that they are asking for an outside inquiry by Congress or, failing that, the General Accounting Office.").

51. "Pentagon Orders Review of '94 Shootdown," *Arizona Republic,* 2 August 1995, p. A9.

52. Steven Watkins, "Getting Tough," *Air Force Times,* 28 August 1995, p. 12.

53. Steven Watkins, "Panel Orders Testimony in Shootdown," *Army Times,* 25 November 1996, p. 21.

Chapter 11. The Law of War

1. U.S. Department of Army, Field Manual (FM) 27-10, The Law of Land Warfare, ¶ 3a (1956) (hereafter cited as FM 27-10).

2. 3 Law Reports of Trials of War Criminals, Case No. 14, at 56–59 (1948).

3. Hague Convention No. IV Respecting the Laws and Customs of War on Land, 18 October 1907, Annex, Article 23(e) and (g). All cited Hague and Geneva Conventions are contained in U.S. Department of Army Pamphlet No. 27-1, Treaties Governing Land Warfare (1956).

4. FM 27-10, ¶ 41.

5. Telford Taylor, *Nuremberg and Vietnam: An American Tragedy* (New York: Bantam Books, 1971), 143.

6. Denis Richards, *The Hardest Victory: RAF Bomber Command in the Second World War* (New York: W. W. Norton, 1994), 269.

7. John Terraine, *A Time for Courage: The Royal Air Force in the European War, 1939–1945* (New York: Macmillan, 1985), 677; Hans Rumpf, *The Bombing of Germany* (New York: Holt, Rinehart and Winston, 1963), 152.

8. "Germans Still Dodge Issue of Dresden Raid," *Arizona Republic,* 11 February 1995, p. A28, col. 1.

9. Richards, *Hardest Victory,* 271 (75 percent of the bomb load).

10. Terraine, *Time for Courage,* 677–78; Richards, *Hardest Victory,* 273.

11. Hague Convention, Annex, Article 23; FM 27-10, ¶ 34.

12. Barbara Opall, "Study: Chemical, Biological Weapons Could Boost N. Korea," *Army Times,* 18 November 1996, p. 21, col. 1; B. Denise Hawkins, "Plan OK'd to Give Troops Anthrax Shots," *Army Times,* 21 October 1996, p. 8, col. 3.

13. Nicholas D. Kristof, "Japan Confronting Gruesome War Atrocity," *New York Times,* 20 March 1995, p. 1, col. 4.

14. Ibid., p. 15, cols. 1–4.

15. James P. Sterba, "Big Bang Theory: How the .50 Caliber Became a 'Fun' Gun," *Wall Street Journal,* 24 March 1997, p. A1, col. 4.

16. Discussed in Capt. Jordan J. Paust, "My Lai and Vietnam: Norms, Myths and Leader Responsibility," *Military Law Review* 57 (1972): 99, 150.

17. Article 33, Geneva Convention Relative to the Treatment of Prisoners of War (GPW), 12 August 1949; Articles 24 and 28, Geneva Convention for the Amelioration of the Condition of the Wounded and Sick in Armed Forces in the Field, 12 August 1949 (GWS).

18. Articles 25 and 29, GWS.

19. Article 12, GWS ("Only urgent medical reasons will authorize priority in the order of treatment to be administered.").

20. Grant Willis, "Chaplains Fired Weapons, Researchers Report," *Army Times,* 25 April 1988, p. 17, col. 1.

21. Article 39, GWS.

22. W. Hays Parks, "Memorandum of Law: Status of Certain Medical Corps and Medical Service Corps Officers under the Geneva Conventions," *Army Lawyer* (April 1989), 5, 6, ¶ 12 (The Judge Advocates General of the Navy and Air Force concurred with the Army memorandum).

23. Ibid.

24. Selected Problems in the Law of War, Training Circular (TC) 27-10-1, p. 15 (1979).

25. Hague Convention, Annex, Article 56.

26. "He Blew It," *Dallas Morning News,* 18 April 1994, p. 2A, col. 3.

27. Article 33, GWS.

28. Articles 14, 22, and 31, Geneva Convention for the Amelioration of the Condition of Wounded, Sick and Shipwrecked Members of Armed Forces at Sea (GWS Sea), 12 August 1949.

29. Article 36, GWS (Sea).

30. Article 22, GWS; Article 35, GWS (Sea).

31. 492 F.2d 1219 (Ct. Cl. 1974).

32. Hague Convention, Annex, Articles 46–47 and 56.

33. Hague Convention, Annex, Article 52; FM 27-10, ¶ 412 (almost anything the military force needs may be requisitioned).

34. *United States v. Mello,* 36 M.J. 1067 (A.C.M.R. 1993) (AK-47); *United States v. Manginell,* 32 M.J. 891 (A.F.C.M.R. 1991) (camera and watches).

35. Article 18, GPW.

36. Id.

37. Article 17, GWS.

38. 9 General Military Government Court of the U.S. Zone of Germany 90, Case No. 546 (1947).

39. Ibid., 92–93. This standard may change with the adoption of Protocol I to the Geneva Conventions, which would make it illegal to use the uniform of an enemy to "shield, favour, protect or impede military operations." Article 39(2), Protocol I, Protocols to the Geneva Conventions of 12 August 1949, DA PAM 27-1-1 (1979).

40. Hague Convention, Annex, Article 29; FM 27-10, ¶ 75.

41. Hague Convention, Annex, Articles 30–31; FM 27-10, ¶¶ 74–78.

42. Hague Convention, Annex, Article 23; FM 27-10, ¶ 467.

43. FM 27-10, ¶ 53.

44. Article 4, GPW.

45. Id.

46. Articles 13, 15, 18–19, 23, and 26, GPW.

47. Article 7, GPW.

48. 1 Law Reports of Trials of War Criminals, Case No. 8, p. 88 (1947).

49. Article 39, GPW.

50. Articles 49–50, GPW.

51. Article 52, GPW.

52. Article 82, GPW.

53. Articles 89–90, GPW.

54. Articles 92–93, GPW.

55. Articles 99, 102, and 105, GPW.

56. Article 104, GPW.

57. Articles 100, 101, and 107, GPW.

58. Article 146, Geneva Convention Relative to the Protection of Civilian Persons in Time of War (GC), 12 August 1949.

59. Article 147, GC.

60. Lewy, *America in Vietnam,* 324, 350.

61. Ibid., 348 and 350.

62. Ibid.

63. Ibid. at 352–53; Everett, Johnson, and Rosenthal, *Calley,* 281; *United States v. Calley,* 48 C.M.R. 19, 22 U.S.C.M.A. 534 (1973).

64. *In re Yamashita,* 327 U.S. 1, 13-14 (1946).

65. Id. at 28 (Murphy, J., dissenting). Most of the atrocities occurred while the Japanese forces were in retreat, under constant attack by Allied air, ground, and naval forces. Id. at 32–33.

66. *Trial of Lieutenant-General Baba Masao,* 11 Law Reports of Trials of War Criminals 56, Case No. 60, at 57–60 (1947); *The German High Command Trial,* 12 Law Reports of Trials of War Criminals 1, Case No. 72, at 105–12 (1948).

67. *Trial of Lieutenant-General Baba Masao,* 60.

68. Lewy, *America in Vietnam,* 325–26.

69. FM 27-10, ¶ 501. Significantly, the publication states: "The purpose of the Manual is to provide *authoritative* guidance to military personnel on the customary and treaty law applicable to the conduct of warfare on land" (emphasis added).

70. Lewy, *America in Vietnam,* 359.

71. Ibid., 359–60.

72. Article 86(1), Protocol I, Protocols to the Geneva Conventions of 12 August 1949 (contained in DA PAM 27-1-1 [1979]).

73. 12 Law Reports of Trials of War Criminals 1, Case No. 72, at 105–12 (1948).

74. Id. at 113 n. 1.

75. Id. at 113.

76. Id. at 117–18.

Bibliography

Books

Allen, Robert L. *The Port Chicago Mutiny.* New York: Amistad Press, 1993.

Blair, Clay. *Ridgway's Paratroopers.* New York: Dial Press, 1985.

Buell, Thomas B. *Master of Sea Power: A Biography of Fleet Admiral Ernest J. King.* Boston: Little, Brown, 1980.

Byrne, Edward M. *Military Law: A Handbook for the Navy and Marine Corps.* Annapolis, Md.: U.S. Naval Institute, 1970.

Cope, Harley F. *Command at Sea.* 3d ed. Annapolis, Md.: U.S. Naval Institute, 1966.

Custer, Elizabeth B. *Boots and Saddles.* Norman: University of Oklahoma Press, 1987.

Davis, Burke. *The Billy Mitchell Affair.* New York: Random House, 1967.

———. *The Civil War: Strange and Fascinating Facts.* New York: Wing Books, 1982.

Editors of the Boston Publishing Company. *Above and Beyond: A History of the Medal of Honor from the Civil War to Vietnam.* Boston: Boston Publishing, 1985.

Everett, Arthur, Kathryn Johnson, and Harry F. Rosenthal. *Calley.* New York: Dell Publishing, 1971.

Goldman, Roger, and David Gallen. *Thurgood Marshall: Justice for All.* New York: Carroll and Graf Publishers, 1992.

Green, Vincent. *Extreme Justice.* New York: Pocket Books, 1995.

Groom, Winston, and Duncan Spencer. *Conversations with the Enemy: The Story of PFC Robert Garwood.* New York: G. P. Putnam's Sons, 1983.

Huie, William Bradford. *The Execution of Private Slovik.* New York: Duell, 1954.

Kerrigan, Evans E. *American War Medals and Decorations.* New York: Viking Press, 1964.

Krammer, Arnold. *Nazi Prisoners of War in America.* Lanham, Md.: Scarborough House, 1996.

Kurzman, Dan. *Fatal Voyage: The Sinking of the USS Indianapolis.* New York: Atheneum, 1990.

Lewy, Guenter. *America in Vietnam.* New York: Oxford University Press, 1978.

Lord, Francis A. *They Fought for the Union.* New York: Bonanza Books, 1988.

MacArthur, Douglas. *Reminiscences.* New York: McGraw-Hill, 1964.

McCarthy, Mary. *Medina.* New York: Harcourt Brace Javonovich, 1972.

Perkins, Rollin M., and Ronald N. Boyce. *Criminal Law.* 3d ed. Mineola, N.Y.: Foundation Press, 1982.

Potter, Lou, William Miles, and Nina Rosenblum. *Liberators: Fighting on Two Fronts in World War II.* New York: Harcourt Brace Jovanovich, 1992.

Richards, Denis. *The Hardest Victory: RAF Bomber Command in the Second World War.* New York: W. W. Norton, 1994.

Rivkin, Robert S. *GI Rights and Army Justice: The Draftee's Guide to Military Life and Law.* New York: Grove Press, 1970.

Robinson, Charles M. III. *The Court-Martial of Lieutenant Henry Flipper.* El Paso: Texas Western Press, 1994.

Rumpf, Hans. *The Bombing of Germany.* New York: Holt, Reinhart and Winston, 1963.

Schiller, A. Arthur. *Military Law.* St. Paul, Minn.: West Publishing, 1952.

Sherrill, Robert. *Military Justice Is to Justice as Military Music Is to Music.* New York: Harper and Row, 1970.

Snedeker, James. *Military Justice under the Uniform Code.* Boston: Little, Brown, 1953.

Snyder, Don J. *A Soldier's Disgrace.* Dublin, N.H.: Yankee Books, 1987.

Taylor, Telford. *Nuremberg and Vietnam: An American Tragedy.* New York: Bantam Books, 1971.

Terraine, John. *A Time for Courage: The Royal Air Force in the European War, 1939–1945.* New York: Macmillan, 1985.

West, Luther C. *They Call It Justice.* New York: Viking Press, 1977.

Whittaker, Frederick. *A Complete Life of General George A. Custer,* vol. 2. Lincoln: University of Nebraska Press, 1993.

Winthrop, William. *Military Law and Precedents,* vol. 2. 2d ed. Boston: Little, Brown, 1896.

Periodicals

Bell, Derrick. "Meanness as Racial Ideology." *Michigan Law Review* 88 (1990): 1689.

Duignan, Kathleen A. "Military Justice: Not an Oxymoron." *Federal Lawyer* 43 (February 1996): 22.

Foote, Warren, Lt. Col. "Courts-Martial of Military Retirees." *Army Lawyer* 54 (May 1992).

Kelley, Kevin M. "'You Murdered Queeg': Lawyer's Ethics, Military Justice, and the Caine Mutiny." *Wisconsin Law Review* 1991:543.

McGillin, Howard O., Jr.. "Article 31(b) Triggers: Reexamining the 'Officiality Doctrine.'" 150 *Military Law Review* (1995): 1.

Nichols, Charles L., Capt. "Article 105, Misconduct as a Prisoner." *Air Force JAG Law Review* 11 (Fall 1969): 393.

Parks, W. Hays. "Memorandum of Law: Status of Certain Medical Corps and Medical Service Corps Officers under the Geneva Conventions." *Army Lawyer* (April 1989).

Paust, Jordan J., Capt. "My Lai and Vietnam: Norms, Myths and Leader Responsibility." *Military Law Review* 57 (1972): 99.

Smith, Jeffrey S. "Military Policy Toward Homosexuals: Scientific, Historical, and Legal Perspectives." *Military Law Review* 131 (1991): 55.

Steinweg, Kenneth K. "Dealing Realistically With Fratricide." *Parameters* (Spring 1995).

Sullivan, Dwight H. "Overhauling the Vessel Exception." *Naval Law Review* 43 (1996): 57.

Zbar, Alan L., and James D. Mazza. "Legal Status of Cadets." *Air Force JAG Law Review* 7 (1965): 31.

Newspapers

Air Force Times
Arizona Republic
Army Times
Dallas Morning News
New York Times
Philadelphia Inquirer
San Francisco Chronicle
Wall Street Journal
Washington Post

Government Publications

A Manual for Courts-Martial, Courts of Inquiry and of Other Procedure under Military Law. Washington, D.C.: GPO, 1916.

Comptroller General. AWOL in the Military: A Serious and Costly Problem. FPCD-78-52. Washington, D.C.: General Accounting Office, 30 March 1979.

Department of the Navy. Compilation of Navy and Other Laws. Washington, D.C.: GPO, 1875.

Manual for Courts-Martial, United States. Washington, D.C.: GPO, 1995.

Military Laws of the United States 1915. 5th ed. Washington, D.C.: U.S. GPO, 1917.

Secretary of the Navy. Manual of the Judge Advocate General (1990).

United States Naval Justice School, Newport, Rhode Island. *Procedure Study Guide.*

United States Sentencing Commission, Guidelines Manual. Washington, D.C.: U.S. GPO, 1997.

U.S. Coast Guard Military Justice Manual, COMDTINST M5810.1c. (15 January 1991).

U.S. Department of the Air Force. Air Force Instr. 51-201 (28 July 1994).

———. Air Force Instr. 51-202. Nonjudicial Punishment (1 October 1996).

U.S. Department of the Army. Field Manual 27-10, The Law of Land Warfare (1956).

———. PAM 27-1. Treaties Governing Land Warfare (7 December 1956).

———. PAM 27-1-1. Protocols to the Geneva Conventions of 12 August 1949 (1979).

———. Reg. 27-10. Legal Services: Military Justice. (8 August 1994).

———. Reg. 27-26. Legal Services: Rules of Professional Conduct for Lawyers. (1 May 1992).

———. Selected Problems in the Law of War. Training Circular (TC) 27-10-1 (1979).

Winthrop, Bvt. Col. W. *Opinions of the Judge Advocate General of the Army.* Washington, D.C.: GPO, 1880.

Winthrop, William. *Military Law and Precedents.* 2d ed. Washington, D.C.: GPO, 1920.

Index

183

About the Author

Michael J. Davidson enlisted in the U.S. Army in 1977 and graduated from West Point in 1982. He served as a field artillery officer in Korea and the United States before attending law school at the College of William and Mary. He also holds master's degrees in military law from the army's Judge Advocate Generals School and in federal procurement law from George Washington University.

As a member of the army's Judge Advocate Generals Corps, Mr. Davidson has served as a military prosecutor, a federal prosecutor, a civil litigation attorney in discrimination cases, and a contract and administrative law attorney. He lives in Peachtree City, Georgia, with his wife, Nancy, and their three daughters.